An **Official** History of Scouting

hamlyn

An Official History of Scouting

Foreword by
Lord Baden-Powell

To every adult volunteer over the last
100 years who has made Scouting possible.

First published in Great Britain in 2006 by
Hamlyn, a division of Octopus Publishing Group Ltd
2–4 Heron Quays, London E14 4JP

Copyright © Octopus Publishing Group Ltd 2006

The Scout 'Be prepared' logo is a registered trademark of
The Scout Association. Charity no. 306101.

Distributed in the United States and Canada by
Sterling Publishing Co., Inc.
387 Park Avenue South, New York, NY 10016–8810

The Scout Association asserts the moral right to be identified
as the author of this work.

ISBN-13: 978-0-600-61398-5
ISBN-10: 0-600-61398-4

A CIP catalogue record for this book is available from the
British Library.

Printed and bound in China

10 9 8 7 6 5 4 3 2 1

Contents

Foreword

I am delighted that the theme of Scouting's centenary year is peace; my grandfather spent much of his life dedicated to creating what he called 'an international desire for peace on the part of the people themselves'. What's more, he knew that young people were the key. How could Scouts who have shared a meal at a jamboree, enjoyed activities together and exchanged neckerchiefs take up arms against each other? Of course, he was an optimist; he knew that the world was a complicated place – but he also knew that friendship among young people and a common set of values formed a solid basis for mutual understanding.

As I leaf through the pages of this book, I am still incredibly proud of his achievement and not a little astonished. When I hear the numbers again – 28 million Scouts in 216 countries – I still find it hard to believe that he really was behind it all – and this not to talk of the parallel success of the Guide Movement, which he also conceived. He was a man with a particularly broad sort of vision, who himself liked to remind people to 'kick the "im" out impossible'. He was not afraid to be different and encouraged young people to be just as brave. He was a great advocate of the power of believing in yourself and that's a message I would commend to all those who are reading this.

It sounds odd, but what encourages me most about this story of Scouting is that it is incomplete. In many parts of the world, Scouting is still growing at the same phenomenal rate as it did in its earliest days. More young people than ever are getting their first taste of adventure, leadership and responsibility through the Movement. As a non-political organization, it is bringing together diverse communities and providing opportunities for those from the poorest backgrounds

Our members get involved in environmental and community projects and provide activities for those with special needs, as well as taking part in major international projects. In India, Scouts and Guides have been working together on health projects to screen more than a million children for leprosy. In Africa, Scouts have taken responsibility for the peer-education programme on HIV and AIDS.

This is something that has to be encouraged – Scouts playing a full and active part in their communities, tackling real issues and showing strong leadership, initiative and citizenship. Here in the UK, Scouting is helping to bridge divided communities – whether it is in crossing sectarian divides or bringing together inner-city communities with large ethnic minorities. Because membership is open to all, regardless of age, colour, economic background or religion, Scouting has a genuinely healing effect. Scouts see themselves as Scouts first and foremost.

When my grandfather set about creating a programme for young people, he didn't lock himself away in a room. He knew that if he was going to inspire and motivate the youth of his day, he would need to spend time with them, get to know them – and this is exactly what he did. Those who met him speak of his unique ability to connect with people, put them at their ease and make them feel valued. Most tellingly, they speak of his ability to listen. Those who have read any of his inimitable writings will already be familiar with his humorous, surprising and slightly conspiring tone of voice – never patronizing and always full of fun.

On Brownsea Island in August 1907, he gathered together a small band of boys, devised a demanding timetable of activities – and of course, he made sure it happened entirely outdoors. He was a great lover of nature and shared with young people his delight in the world around him. He had learned a thousand wonderful things as a soldier – tracking, knotting, the study of animals, the identification of birds, plants and stars – and he wanted to pass all of this on. Get to know and respect the natural world, he seemed to be saying, and you'll get more out of life.

Enjoy the stories in this volume – the triumphant jamborees, the dark years of the two world wars and the great projects going on today. You'll get to know my grandfather and learn about the key people and moments that brought the Scouting phenomenon into being. But let me leave you with this: my grandfather would be the first to say that Scouting was not his Movement. It belongs to everyone who has ever played a part in it and who has cared enough about young people to give them the chance to shine.

Across the world, and in all walks of life, there are people who owe their values and positive outlook on life to Scouting. If you're not one of them already, all I ask is that you find out more – it's never too late to be a Scout.

Robert Baden-Powell
3rd Baron Baden-Powell of Gilwell
Vice-President of The Scout Association

Left: Robert Baden-Powell on Brownsea Island, August 1907.

Right: Lord Baden-Powell reviewing Queen's Scouts, Windsor Castle, April 2006.

Introduction

With some 28 million members and counting, Scouting is a worldwide phenomenon. In all but a handful of countries, young people, men and women (because Scouting is for girls too of course), continue to enjoy the adventure, opportunities and friendship it offers. Founded on a set of values that is still respected today, in its Promise and Law, Scouting has been compared to a religion, a cult and an army. But it is none of those things. It is a Movement that continues to change and evolve to meet the needs of today's society.

It provides informal education and the chance for young people to realize their potential, to experience the freedom of the outdoors, to grow in independence and, in an age of conflict, to learn how to become true world citizens. Scouts are tolerant, understanding of different cultures; they care for the world around them and each other. For the millions of adult volunteers who give up their time to make it all possible, it is one of the most rewarding experiences of their lives.

The history of Scouting

This book is one of the first attempts to document the world history of Scouting. With over 100 million members since those first 20 boys on Brownsea Island, in Poole Harbour on the south coast of England, in 1907, this would be an ambitious project at any time. But at the time of Scouting's centenary, it is a vital one. This book is a snapshot of the Movement today. It is also a time machine that will transport you back to some of the Movement's defining moments. It spans over a century, from Baden-Powell's first writings to the preparations for the world centenary in 2007. It is also just one account of the events.

The story of Scouting is, in many ways, also the story of the 20th century. Young people in Scouting have played their part in almost all of its most significant events. Its inception in 1907 heralded the optimism of a new era – a nation of healthy young people who wanted to take to the outdoors and prevail against the 'seen and not heard' attitude of the 19th century. 'The open-air is the real objective of Scouting,' Baden-Powell once said, 'and the key to its success.'

Duty and honour

But this Movement wasn't just about young people playing in the woods and messing around on the river. Inspired by their Founder, Scouts were encouraged to live their lives by a code of honour. In doing their duty to God, to themselves and, in particular, to other people, the first Scouts set themselves apart from their peers. They prided themselves on their skills and woodcraft, but took their duty just as seriously.

This had its first test during the First World War. Besides those former Scouts who served in the forces – many of whom did not return – young people rose to the

Left: Dutch Scouts at EuroJam 2005 in Hylands Park, Essex, England.

occasion in many capacities. Baden-Powell's first-hand experience of the Western Front confirmed his resolve to direct the Movement as a force for peace.

By the time of the first World Scout Jamboree in 1920, peace was still at the forefront of his mind. The jamboree itself was a way to bring young people from every nation together to build trust and promote cultural understanding and international friendship. This jamboree 'is to mark the restoration of peace,' he declared, 'to pay homage to the Scouts who have fallen and to inaugurate an era of better world relations'. The jamboree is a tradition that survives to this day, with 40,000 Scouts attending the 2007 21st World Scout Jamboree in the UK and almost as many expected for 2011 in Sweden.

But Scouting alone could not preserve the peace, and when war broke out in 1939, its members again took up their duties. This was a new kind of war and Scouts took on different sorts of roles. In the UK, they were involved in civil defence, building air-raid shelters and even guiding fire engines to the places they were needed during the Blitz. In the United States Scouts led food-growing programmes and distributed war bonds.

An international role

Scouts have always held firm in moments of national crisis and emergency. When, on 26 December 2004, a massive tsunami devastated parts of the Asia-Pacific Region, Scouts took a leading role in the rebuilding and reconstruction that followed. 'As well as clearing rubbish from the streets, we are running information camps and reuniting young people with their families,' reported Rasheed, an Indonesian Scout. 'We are also providing games and lessons for those children whose schools have been destroyed.' This work still goes on. Today Scouting is at the heart of local, national and international communities. In many countries it takes the lead in healthcare education and literacy programmes, providing clean water and sanitation. Scouts help tackle homelessness, support local environmental issues and get involved in the leadership of other young people.

The future of Scouting

Scouting has entered its second century, and it is in better shape now than ever. With so much achievement, so many stories and so many examples of leadership to learn from, it is now for the next generation to take up the challenge. And the challenges in this new century are even greater, with the health of the planet in the balance from human conflict, the protection of the earth's species and its environment and the need to achieve a sustainable world. The ethos of Scouting and the young people who follow its course have a big part to play.

Peter Duncan, Chief Scout of the United Kingdom

Baden-Powell: His life before Scouting

The period between 1860 and 1950 saw the greatest social change in Britain in any century, and it coincided with Baden-Powell's lifetime. During this time the Industrial Revolution was at its height and the British Empire stretched across the globe.

In the 1850s and onwards into the 20th century men wore hats – silk top hats, bowlers or boaters – in public, and gentlemen carried canes (walking-sticks) to replace the swords of previous eras. Their dress was formal, their collars stiff. Horse-drawn carriages, cabs and omnibuses were gradually disturbed by bicycles and new motorcars in the course of the following decades. It was a world of lamplighters and ragged crossing sweepers, a world where straw was strewn in the road in front of a house where someone was ill to deaden the noise of the traffic. Most houses were still lit by gas or oil lamps, and so much of what we take for granted today did not yet exist.

A rigid class system

Although there were peace and prosperity, there was also great poverty. In the East End of London one-third of the population lived in a state of chronic destitution. There was widespread drunkenness, and ragged, hungry, dirty, barefoot children were commonplace. Thousands of Londoners, many under 16 years of age, lived on the streets.

At the other end of the social scale were the very wealthy, who lived in comparative ease and luxury,

The early years

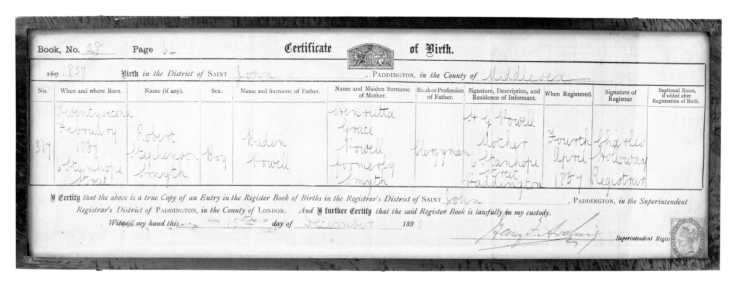

effectively insulated from the poverty around them. In between were the middle classes, respectable citizens driven by both the work ethic and social conscience, with a dire warning on one side of them and inspiring wealth on the other. Self-betterment was the aim for many, by either merit or marriage – or both.

At the turn of the century the school-leaving age was nominally ten, but many boys were out working and earning before that. They played games in the street and collected pictures of their heroes. It was a country of sharp social division, and Scouting, the vision of Robert Baden-Powell, was designed to bridge the gap.

A child of his time

Robert Stephenson Smyth Powell was born on 22 February 1857 at 6 Stanhope Street (now 11 Stanhope Terrace), near Paddington, London. He was christened a few days later in St James's Church nearby. His father, Professor Baden Powell, was an Oxford clergyman and academic. He was the first cleric to declare openly his support for Darwinian evolutionary theory. The author of *The Order of Nature*, Powell did considerable harm to his own career by holding such scientific views about Creation.

Powell had already been married and widowed twice, with four children by his first wife surviving, when he married Henrietta Grace Smyth. She was one of the six daughters and three sons of Captain William Henry Smyth, a naval captain (later an admiral) and a senior member of the Royal Astronomical Society. It was through science that Professor Powell met Captain Smyth and his daughter in Oxford. Powell and Henrietta Grace married in 1846, when she was 21 and he was 48.

They had ten children together before Professor Powell died in 1860. Four of the children died in childhood, as was common in those days, even in wealthy families, and the young Robert was bereft of his favourite older brother, Augustus.

'Laws for me when I am old'

I will have the poor people to be as rich as we are, and they ought by rights to be as happy as we are, and all who go across the crossings shall give the poor crossing sweeper some money and you ought to thank God for what he has given us and he made the poor people to be poor and the rich people to be rich and I can tell you how to be good. Now I will tell you. You must pray to God whenever you can but you cannot be good with only praying but you must try very hard to be good.

By R.S.S. Powell
26 February 1865

Above left: Baden-Powell aged five; his early education was at home and already he was showing his talent as an artist.

Right: A watercolour painting by Baden-Powell at the age of 18 of Charterhouse, his school at Godalming, Surrey.

Left: The birth certificate records the name Robert Stephenson Smyth Powell. Baden was added to the surname some years after his father's death in 1860.

Social climbing

As a tribute to her late husband, but principally as a means of social advancement, Henrietta had her husband's first name, Baden, added to the family's surname to create the double-barrelled surname of Baden-Powell. This had some slightly ludicrous consequences for her stepson, Baden Henry Powell, who never used it, and her youngest son, Baden, who became Baden Baden-Powell.

Henrietta kept her children close throughout her life, well into their adulthood, and they supported her financially. It was desperately important to her that they did well in every way. 'Remember to help others,' she told them. 'We cannot be good ourselves unless we are always helping others.' Her son would remember this message in later life when he introduced the 'daily good turn' to Scouting.

Laws for me

When he was eight Robert, or Stephe (pronounced 'Stevie'), as he was known in the family, wrote a statement of his beliefs for his maternal grandfather. He gave it the title 'Laws for me when I am old' (see page 13), and it was the basis for a code of values by which he would lead the rest of his life and that would find later echoes in the Scout Law and Promise.

Baden-Powell at school

After early education at home and at a preparatory school in Kensington, west London, when he was 11 he progressed to his father's old school, Rose Hill, near Tunbridge Wells in Kent. His reports noted his progress, saying that his conduct was 'very good'. From here, having turned down a place at Fettes College, Edinburgh,

he won a scholarship to one of Britain's leading public schools. At this time, 1868, Charterhouse School was based near St Paul's Cathedral in London, but after two years there B-P moved with his school to new premises in Godalming, Surrey. This new environment allowed him to develop his skills in tracking and his love of the outdoors, but he did not do so well in his studies. Baden-Powell 'has to all intents given up the study of mathematics,' wrote one teacher in his report. 'Often sleeps in class,' wrote another.

Baden-Powell did, however, do well at sport, especially football. He also joined the school's newly formed Band and Rifle Corps. He played the piano, fiddle, bugle and flugelhorn, sang in the choir and was a member of the school's shooting team. Inheriting his mother's artistic talent, he excelled as an artist, producing sketches and watercolours. His other great talent was for acting, and he performed in over 20 school productions. He wrote frequently for the school magazine, joined the debating and literary societies and became a member of a secret school social club of 12 senior students called the Druids, where he was nicknamed 'Lord Bathing-Towel', an ironically prescient title!

During the school holidays he and his brothers enjoyed themselves fishing, racing, hunting wild birds and sailing. The naval base at Portsmouth in the south of England was a favourite haunt, but they also sailed further, to the harbours of Southampton, Bournemouth and Poole, passing by Brownsea Island, and inland to trace the source of the River Thames.

Above: Pages from an album of material relating to Baden-Powell's childhood, including early examples of his talents as an artist.

Left: Baden-Powell's mother, Henrietta, the third wife of Professor Powell, was a socially ambitious lady and keen for her children to do well.

Studies in the Horticultural Garden 1864

aged 12.

Horticultural Gardens Kensington

What now?

Any thoughts of becoming a professional actor were quashed by his mother, and in 1876 he sat the entrance exams for Oxford University, hoping to follow in the footsteps of his father and brothers. He was rejected by both Balliol and Christ Church colleges but with his mother's encouragement he entered an open competitive examination for commissions in the army in both infantry and cavalry regiments.

At the age of 19 he was only just young enough to sit the preliminary exams in London – arithmetic and geometry, French, geography and written English. He progressed to the next stage, picking four subjects from a choice of mathematics, English composition, Latin, Greek, French, German, science, geography and free-hand drawing. Out of 718 candidates, Baden-Powell was placed fifth for the infantry and second for the cavalry, gaining 5,350 marks out of a possible 11,300.

Flying colours

On 11 September 1876 Baden-Powell received his army commission. Successful candidates were usually sent for two years of further study at the Royal Military College at Sandhurst. In this instance, however, the first six candidates were immediately assigned to regiments to be posted overseas. Baden-Powell joined the crack 13th Hussars and was ordered to northern India, where the regiment was stationed. He sailed from Britain on 30 October 1876, on the eve of Queen Victoria's proclamation as Empress of India.

Right: Portrait of Baden-Powell aged 18. His years at Charterhouse school taught him the importance of resourcefulness, teamwork and courage.

Now aged 20, Baden-Powell arrived in India to join his regiment at Lucknow, and he soon became immersed in army life as a sublieutenant. His commanding officer, Sir Baker Russell, was a somewhat unorthodox soldier who encouraged the development of initiative in his young officers, even if it meant diverging from accepted practice and the rule book.

Early army career

Baden-Powell was in his element in India and soon earned the respect of his soldiers. He took up horse riding and was successful in breaking and training raw horses bought cheaply, learning to play polo in the process. His theatrical and artistic skills were also put to good use in many army plays and entertainments as his gifts for impersonation and mimicry became well known.

He supplemented a low salary by selling articles and sketches to newspapers and magazines. After two years, during which he was promoted to lieutenant, he returned home on sick leave. After a year spent visiting family and friends, he returned to India and met for the first time Kenneth McLaren (known as 'The Boy' because of his youthful looks), who would become a close friend. He would later be taken prisoner during the Boer War while attempting to relieve Mafeking and in 1907 would assist B-P on Brownsea Island.

Mapmaking and B-P's first books

When the regiment moved to Afghanistan in 1880 Baden-Powell was able to demonstrate his skill in making and updating maps of the battlefield of Maiwand and reconnoitring. 'I enjoy this business awfully, there is

always something to do,' he wrote home. Following the example of his brothers who had published books, he turned to writing about what he was good at – army instruction and the training of soldiers. His first book, *Reconnaissance and Scouting*, which was published in 1884, was based on some of his military lectures. This was followed a year later by *Cavalry Instructions*, another army manual, and in 1889 by *Pig-Sticking*, about boar hunting with spears, a sport popular in India at which he had become an expert.

South Africa

The regiment returned to India, where Baden-Powell served for a time on the staff of the Duke of Connaught, working in his private office. From here in 1885 the 13th Hussars were sent, not home as had been expected, but to South Africa, where the Dutch Boers were causing trouble. This gave Baden-Powell his first experience of this great continent that was to play such an important part in his life. In 1886, when the regiment was stationed in Norwich, England, Baden-Powell was able to visit Germany and France, and also Russia, where he was briefly arrested as a spy.

Above left: Having achieved success in the army entrance exam, Baden-Powell was commissioned as an army officer in the 13th Hussars.

Right: Baden-Powell (left) and his friend Kenneth McLaren with their servants in India during 1882, on his second period of service in that country.

Chief Dinizulu and the wood beads

Baden-Powell returned to South Africa in 1887 to take part in the campaign against the Zulus, who were led by their chief, Dinizulu. He found an ornate necklace of beads worn by Dinizulu in a tribal camp that the chief had abandoned in escaping capture by British troops. B-P kept this as a souvenir and later used it to create the Wood Badge award that was given to trained Scout leaders (see page 63). He was also impressed by the Zulu soldiers, and their exuberant spirit inspired him when he was later devising choruses and campfire rituals for the Scouts.

Promotion

His reputation growing, Baden-Powell acted as military secretary and intelligence officer and was promoted to brevet major, becoming military secretary to the acting governor of South Africa. He was then appointed

secretary to Sir Francis de Winton's Anglo-Boer mission to Swaziland. He left South Africa in 1890 and went to Malta as military secretary to his uncle, General Smyth. While there he attended Italian manoeuvres and reported to the British War Office on the defences of the Straits of Messina. He carried out other missions in Albania, Greece, Turkey, Algeria, Bosnia and Herzegovina, and Austria.

The Ashanti campaign

After three years and with the end of his uncle's appointment, Baden-Powell rejoined the 13th Hussars and his old friend Kenneth McLaren at Cork, Ireland, and was soon back in the swing of things, taking part in army manoeuvres at the Curragh and staging entertainments. It was as though he had never been away. He left Ireland in 1895, assigned to take command of an expedition to the Ashanti in the Gold Coast (now Ghana) in West Africa

and to fight their king, Dua III, better known as Prempeh. He relished at long last the opportunity for some field service and the chance to use his wits. It was a successful campaign, which led to the surrender of Prempeh and another book, *The Downfall of Prempeh*, published in 1896. For his services he was awarded the campaign medal and promoted to brevet lieutenant colonel. The campaign had also proved to B-P the value of wearing a broad-brimmed hat for protection and of carrying a wooden staff to test the depths of swamps. Both items would feature in later plans for the Scout uniform.

Adventures in Matabeleland

Baden-Powell returned home, but not for long. In May 1896 he was appointed chief of staff to Sir Frederick Carrington in his operations against the rebelling tribes in Rhodesia's Matabeleland. B-P personally led scouting expeditions into the Matopo Hills, spying on the enemy and mapping the land. He wore a broad-brimmed hat with a grey handkerchief around his neck to protect him from sunburn. He also encouraged his men to be wide awake and alert at all times, ready for anything, concepts that he would sum up in later years with the Scout motto, 'Be prepared.' Despite ill health, he commanded a column of soldiers on the Shangani River and helped re-establish law and order in the country. His work done and now a colonel, Baden-Powell rejoined his regiment, stationed in Dublin, where he found himself a higher rank than those in command.

India and the first 'Scouts'

The War Office solved this problem by appointing him to command the 5th Dragoon Guards, then stationed at Meerut in India. He took his new role seriously, introducing ideas and practices to improve the soldiers' health and welfare. Because he was convinced that many soldiers became ill because of the food and drink they bought in the local town, he opened a regimental bakery, dairy and drink factory, ideas that other regiments then copied. With his long-held views on the value of the

army practice of scouting and reconnaissance, he developed a new syllabus of instruction centred on these subjects but with special emphasis on scouting, and he started to give lectures to groups of volunteers. When the lectures were completed, the men were given practical work in various scouting exercises, working in pairs and individually. Those who passed the tests were awarded the honorary title 'scout' and a special badge in the shape of a fleur-de-lys or the north point of a compass.

Baden-Powell not only set an example of hard work himself but also deliberately aimed at encouraging initiative and enterprise in all ranks. He later summarized his methods used at the time as '1. The giving of responsibility to the N.C.O.s (down to Lance-Corporals); 2. Making the training enjoyable to the men. I went possibly rather further … in this direction – but it paid off handsomely. Keeping the men in permanent small units and these units in competition with one another … roused their keenness and raised the level of efficiency all round.' These concepts were used again by him when creating the Scout training scheme.

Return from India

While he was on leave, B-P visited Kashmir and began to sketch his ideas for another book, which he planned to call *Cavalry Aids to Scouting*. It would be based on the lectures and tests he had given his soldiers as well as including personal anecdotes. He was convinced that this form of scouting encouraged self-reliance by making soldiers use their own intelligence and act on their own judgement without waiting for advice from an officer, ideas that would find themselves expressed again in 1907 through the pages of *Scouting for Boys*.

After receiving news of the death of his brother George, who had been a Member of Parliament, Baden-Powell travelled home in 1899 on four months' leave, planning to return to India as soon as he could. But it was not to be. The Boer War had started in South Africa, and, although he did not know it, Baden-Powell's career in India and as a regimental officer had ended for good.

Above: In 1891, and with the rank of captain, Baden-Powell (second from left in the back row) was stationed in Malta as military secretary to his uncle.

Right: Some of the military honours awarded to Baden-Powell prior to 1901, mainly for service in South Africa.

In July 1899, while he was on leave in London, Baden-Powell was summoned to the War Office and given new instructions. He was to return to South Africa to raise two regiments of mounted infantry and to organize the defence of the frontiers of the Rhodesia and Bechuanaland Protectorate with the Transvaal in preparation for a possible war. In the event of war, he was to keep the enemy's troops occupied in this direction, well away from their main forces. Baden-Powell left at once, elated at this, the greatest challenge that had so far been given to him.

Under siege

War did come, and in October 1899 B-P found himself besieged in the small township of Mafeking, a name that means 'place of stones', attacked by six thousand Boers with a 18-kilometre-range (11-mile-range) gun that fired 94-pound shells. All Baden-Powell had to defend the town's inhabitants were one thousand men, a few guns and some cannons that fired 7-pound shells. They found a further long-range weapon in the town which they called 'Lord Nelson' and made another, 'The Wolf', in the railway workshops. His commanding officer informed him that the deployment of his troops at Mafeking was not in accordance with what had been planned but, as there was no other force available to defend the town, its

The siege of Mafeking was a defining moment not only in Baden-Powell's military career but also of the late Victorian era. The courage, ingenuity and resilience shown by B-P and his small garrison were an inspiration to a country desperately in need of good news.

The siege of Mafeking

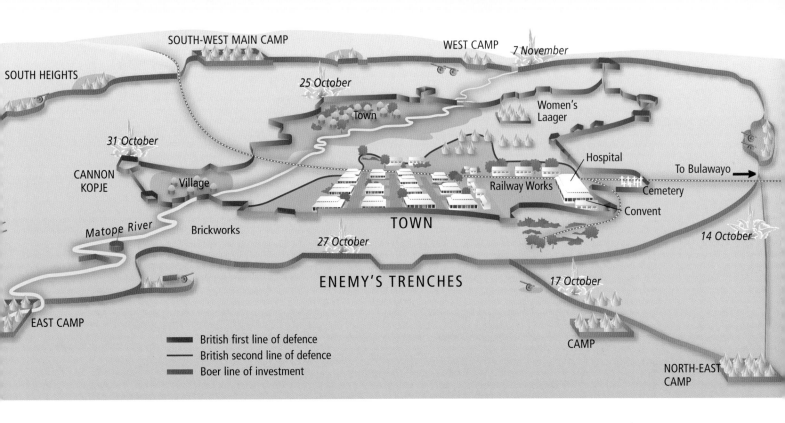

SOUTH-WEST MAIN CAMP
WEST CAMP
7 November
SOUTH HEIGHTS
25 October
Town
Women's Laager
31 October
Hospital
CANNON KOPJE
Village
To Bulawayo →
Railway Works
Cemetery
Convent
Matope River
Brickworks
TOWN
14 October
27 October
17 October
ENEMY'S TRENCHES
EAST CAMP
CAMP
■■■ British first line of defence
— British second line of defence
■■■ Boer line of investment
NORTH-EAST CAMP

people and its supplies, he would have to make the best of the situation. It did not look at all promising.

Baden-Powell's strategy

The Boers, led by General Piet Cronje, held back at first, giving the resourceful and imaginative Baden-Powell time to prepare his defences and motivate his men. This he did by pure bluff and cunning, employing a mixture of bizarre tricks and strict discipline. He proclaimed martial law in the town and encircled the place with earthworks and bogus minefields. The mines were, in fact, simple wooden boxes with protruding wires. Most were filled with sand, but one contained dynamite and was detonated to give the impression of live mines and to mislead the watching spies.

There was also 'invisible' barbed-wired surrounding the town (an impression given by men pretending to climb over the wire) and lots of 'searchlights' (there was actually only one with a cowl made from biscuit tins on top of a pole that stood on the ground and was turned slowly before being moved to another location). A ring of 60 small forts manned by trained troops was created around a 10-kilometre (6-mile) perimeter, with an inner line of defences manned by the town guard. It was Baden-Powell's belief that the further away he could keep the Boers' modern, long-range guns, the worse would be their aim.

Life in Mafeking

Shelters were constructed to protect the women and children inside the town. Trenches were also dug and barricades erected as the townsfolk prepared for a long

Above: The British lines of defence and the position of the Boers during the siege of Mafeking, October 1899–May 1900.

Left: The British troops at Mafeking, while heavily outnumbered by the attacking Boers, fought valiantly with what few weapons they had to withstand the 217-day siege.

Right and below: As the siege of Mafeking began Baden-Powell was correcting the proofs of *Aids to Scouting for NCOs and Men*, which were smuggled out through Boer lines.

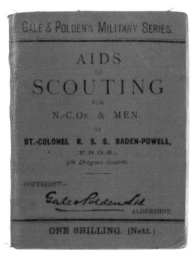

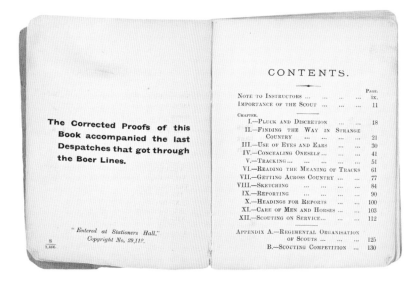

siege. While all this was going on, Baden-Powell incredibly found the time to check the printers' proofs of the book that he had begun writing while he was in Kashmir. Now called *Aids to Scouting for NCOs and Men*, the proofs were smuggled out of the town and back to Britain, where the book was published in 1899. It sold well, not just to soldiers but also to boys, who used it for 'scouting'.

The boys inside Mafeking played an important part in its defence, and a cadet corps was formed for those aged nine and over. Led by 13-year-old Boy Cadet Sergeant Major Warner Goodyear, the boys had their own khaki uniform, and they were trained to carry messages, deliver mail, act as orderlies and take turns in the lookout posts. This experience showed Baden-Powell that, given training and responsibility, young people could rise to any occasion and that they responded and worked well in small teams. This idea would later be developed in *Scouting for Boys* as the Patrol System.

B-P captures a nation's heart

The shelling of the town by the Boers began in earnest but to little effect. Baden-Powell was able to scribble a note and send it by a native runner, who evaded the Boer lines, to his commander, Lieutenant Colonel Herbert Plumer. It read: 'All well. Four hours' bombardment. One dog killed.' Plumer sent the note back to Britain, where it was picked up by the press. Up to this point the war had been going badly, so the fact that there were British troops in Mafeking holding out against the odds caught the public imagination. The eyes of Britain watched the unfolding drama in Mafeking with interest.

Keeping up spirits

Messages, light-hearted but derisory, passed regularly between the Boers and the British. There were some serious attacks on the town by the Boers and attacks on the Boer lines by the British. Casualties began to rise, more on the Boer side than on the British. Because of their strict religious beliefs, the Boers did not fight on Sundays, so Baden-Powell used the opportunity to encourage games and amusements among the soldiers and townsfolk as a means of keeping up people's spirits. He took a full part himself, serving tea, acting as a circus ringmaster or whatever the occasion demanded.

One determined attack by Cronje was driven off, after which the Boer general withdrew with a large number of his men, leaving General Snyder in charge. By night Baden-Powell slipped out of Mafeking on lone scouting expeditions to see if guns had been moved or the enemy trenches had been pushed nearer. He was also able to check that his own men were on the alert.

The situation deteriorates

As the months went by, conditions inside the town worsened. With food supplies running low, horses and other animals were eaten and bread was made from oat husks as a substitute for flour. Various emergency arrangements were made, including the production of their own banknotes and postage stamps, one of which featured B-P and another the boy cadet Warner Goodyear on a bicycle. The last serious attack came on 12 May 1900, when the Boers were repelled and the cadets helped to escort prisoners inside.

Mafeking is relieved

A few days later a relief column, which included Baden-Powell's young brother Baden, arrived at the town, and on 17 May the siege was over. Mafeking had held out for 217 days, during which some twenty thousand shells had been fired into it and there had been nearly a thousand casualties, including half the officers.

When the news that Mafeking had been relieved reached Britain the country erupted in joy, and crowds took to the streets, particularly in London near the home of Baden-Powell's mother. Within days manufacturers had started to produce a wide range of souvenirs, all bearing B-P's image: china, glass, pin badges, tobacco pipes, tins, boxes of cigars and alarm clocks. Even cast-iron pub tables and washing mangles were made and boats, streets and newborn children were named after the new national hero. For his services, Baden-Powell was promoted to the rank of Major-General and honoured by Queen Victoria.

B-P's next assignment

It was some time before Baden-Powell could return home, for the war was far from over. After a few months spent campaigning to the east of Mafeking, Baden-Powell was asked to undertake a new role, that of recruiting and training a corps of men to police the country when peace eventually came. He drew up his plans for the South African Constabulary with his usual enthusiasm.

When he did return home he was surprised to find that his little military handbook, *Aids to Scouting for NCOs and Men*, was being used to train boys in schools and clubs. He was invited to inspect a Boys' Brigade parade by its founder, Sir William Smith, and although he was impressed he suggested that more boys would join if there was a more adventurous and exciting programme. Smith asked for a practical scheme, and this set Baden-Powell thinking about his book *Aids to Scouting* and his recent experiences in Mafeking.

Baden-Powell was always interested in people, listening to their stories and ideas. The following people all had an influence on Baden-Powell and his thinking and in their own way played a part in the development of Scouting.

B-P's people and the genesis of an idea

Professor Baden Powell (1796–1860)

Baden-Powell's father, Reverend Professor Baden Powell, Savilian Professor of Geometry at Oxford, died when B-P was three years old. A courageous cleric with an unusually scientific mind, he was among those academics who believed that geological discoveries and fossil remains proved that the Old Testament stories of the Creation could not be taken literally. An excellent artist and an original thinker, Professor Powell died in June 1860, having just published *The Order of Nature*. Charles Darwin expressed his admiration of Powell's work in later editions of *The Origin of Species*. B-P read *The Order of Nature* as an adult and took to heart the arguments relating to evolution and 'improvement' being dependent on fitness and adaptation to surroundings. B-P's focus on physical well-being and alert intelligence, rather than on bookish pursuits, matched well with the 'social Darwinism' that became popular in the wake of such writing.

Baden Henry Powell (1841–1901)

Baden Henry Powell, the eldest son of Professor Powell and B-P's step-brother, was a legal scholar of note. He went to India as a civil servant and became a judge in the High Court and an authority on Indian land ownership. Like his father and his younger half-brother, B-P, Baden was a natural draughtsman and enthusiastic amateur artist. He submitted paintings to the Simla Academy exhibition, as did B-P later. The author of *The Manufactures and Arts of the Punjab*, Powell became connected with the Kipling family through his fascination with arts and crafts. Lockwood Kipling, Rudyard's father, was principal of the Mayo School of Industrial Art and curator of the Central Museum in Lahore. Baden Henry Powell was an enthusiastic supporter of the Central Museum, which Rudyard Kipling was later to make famous as the 'Wonder House' in *Kim* (1901). Although Baden and B-P were 16 years apart in age and had only

Above left: Baden-Powell's father, Reverend Professor Baden Powell, in gown and hood as Savilian Professor of Geometry at Oxford University.

Right: Baden Henry Powell, Indian High Court judge and arts and crafts enthusiast.

Far right: Field Marshal Lord Roberts of Kandahar in dress uniform replete with decorations.

their father and a love of drawing in common, B-P later depended on Baden to support him socially and financially when he went out to India in 1876 to join the 13th Hussars.

Lord Roberts (1832–1914)

Frederick Sleigh Roberts, Field Marshal Lord Roberts of Kandahar, VC, KG, KP, GCB, OM, GCSI, GCIE, was affectionately known to soldiers and the British public as 'Bobs'. Commander of British forces in India for more than 40 years, he was the commanding officer when B-P returned to service in India in 1880 and when Kipling arrived as a cub reporter, aged 17, in 1882. Roberts had won great acclaim for his leadership of the campaigns in Afghanistan, notably at Kandahar, and B-P arrived in Afghanistan in the aftermath of those battles.

Until his death, 'Bobs of Kandahar' was influential, even instrumental, in the lives of both B-P and Kipling. He was B-P's commander-in-chief again in South Africa, making B-P responsible for the South African Constabulary following his successful defence of Mafeking. Despite having some misgivings about B-P as a soldier, Roberts was supportive of Scouting. He was a founding father of the National Service League and was involved in the creation of Britain's first official secret service. B-P sent him the earliest draft of *Scouting for Boys* for his comments, and Roberts put Ernest Thompson Seton (see page 26) in touch with B-P about starting up groups of Woodcraft Indians in Britain. Roberts, Kipling and Baden-Powell had a triangular relationship that affected many aspects of their lives and careers, and more than one British institution.

Ernest Thompson Seton (1860–1946)

Ernest Thompson Seton was a reclusive and eccentric character, but he was another 'original mind' whose ideas would contribute to Scouting. Born in South Shields, County Durham, but growing up in Toronto, Canada, he became fascinated by the culture and lifestyle of Native Americans and used to escape to the wilderness whenever he could to build camps and observe wildlife. The official naturalist to the government of Manitoba, he became a wildlife illustrator, anatomist and champion of the natural world.

In 1902, Seton was asked by the *Ladies' Home Journal* to write a series of articles on the new organization he was creating, the Woodcraft Indians. He showed his pieces to Rudyard Kipling (who was then living in Vermont), and Kipling encouraged Seton to expand his work into fiction to illustrate his methods. Following the publication of *Two Little Savages; being the adventure of two boys who lived as Indians and what they learned* (1903) and *The Birch-bark Roll of the Woodcraft Indians* (1906), Seton became interested in expanding his fledgling organization in Britain. He contacted Lord Roberts, who suggested that he should meet Baden-Powell, and the two men met in London in 1906.

At the time B-P had been working on the earliest stages of a handbook for boys, but reading *The Birch-bark Roll* sharpened his focus. He certainly adapted aspects of Seton's ideas (including totem poles and non-competitive skills badges), but his approach was very different from Seton's and he drew from many different sources in addition to Seton's Native American model. Seton later became the first Chief Scout of the Boy Scouts of America.

Rudyard Kipling (1865–1936)

It is probable that the 26-year-old B-P and the 18-year-old Rudyard Kipling met for the first time at the Central Museum, Lahore, in 1883, when B-P was on leave visiting his half-brother. Both Kipling and B-P were involved with the Simla Amateur Dramatic Club at different times, but it was Kipling's friendship with and admiration for Lord Roberts that kept him in touch with Baden-Powell throughout B-P's career. Both Kipling and B-P later supported Lord Roberts's creation of the National Service League.

B-P met Kipling again in South Africa in 1900 and 1906. Kipling was writing the *Just So Stories*, including the separately published 'The Tabu Tale' about a little girl whose father teaches her to scout. B-P discussed with Kipling his idea for turning *Aids to Scouting for NCOs and Men* into a book for 'civilian use'. Kipling supported B-P's new movement and was happy to allow B-P to quote from his poetry, his books and his journalistic reports on military matters. Kipling's *Kim* is quoted more than once in *Scouting for Boys*, and many excerpts from his work appear in *The Scout* magazine. Kipling was invited to attend various Scout events in Britain, and he wrote the 'Boy Scouts' Patrol Song' for the 1909 Crystal Palace Rally. B-P had invited Kipling's

son, John, to join one of the earliest Scout camps (Buckler's Hard), and when John went 'missing, believed killed' at the Battle of Loos in September 1915, B-P sent a letter of condolence.

The extent to which B-P used Kipling's *The Jungle Books* for the Wolf Cubs is discussed more fully on pages 57–9, but each 'Bite' of the *Wolf Cub's Handbook* revolves around a Mowgli story. Kipling's tolerance of B-P's treatment of his work shows the extent of his approval of the cause. Writing to B-P to congratulate him on his barony, Kipling applauded the way in which B-P had 'changed the outlook of Young England in the last 12 years'.

Kipling was later made honorary Commissioner of Wolf Cubs. In turn, he created the *Land and Sea Tales for Scouts and Guides* (1923), compiled from previously published short stories and poems and some specially written pieces. 'His Gift' is a story about an overweight and unmotivated boy who discovers a new and important talent at Scout camp. It showed, with uncanny perception, that Scouting was valuable for even the most unlikely and unathletic people.

Above: Ernest Thompson Seton at home in the study where the Woodcraft Indians were born.

Right: Rudyard Kipling as a very young man, new to Anglo-Indian society. He had a moustache from his early teens and it became a hallmark beloved of cartoonists.

Scouting
for Boys

Brownsea Island: The adventure begins

On 1 August 1907 20 boys gathered on Brownsea Island for what was to be the first ever Scout camp. The events of the subsequent eight days would make it the most momentous camp ever held.

Baden-Powell certainly did not set out to start a new movement. He originally intended simply to provide a programme of activities suitable for use by the Boys' Brigade and the other youth organizations that already existed. However, he took care that all activities could be enjoyed by young people from the most privileged to the poorest of backgrounds. He had chosen the 20 boys from a cross-section of society, something that was quite revolutionary at a time when Britain was more rigidly divided by class than it is today.

The site

Brownsea Island was to be the location of the camp. The island, in Poole Harbour on the south coast of England,

was ideally positioned, and it was a place with which Baden-Powell was already familiar – he had sailed in the harbour as a boy. However, it was a chance encounter in May 1907 with the island's owner, Charles van Raalte, that secured an offer to use the site for B-P's camp.

The camp

By the time the boys arrived on the island, tents had been pitched in preparation and a flag erected in the middle of the camp. On arrival, the boys were divided into four Scout Patrols – Wolves, Bulls, Curlews and Ravens. The nearest thing to a 'uniform' was a long coloured 'shoulder knot', given to the boys to indicate which Patrol they belonged to: yellow for Curlews, red for Ravens, blue for

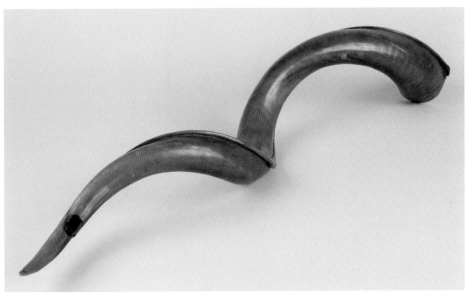

Above left: The Union flag used at Mafeking flew over the experimental camp run by Baden-Powell on Brownsea Island in August 1907.

Above right: Baden-Powell with the kudu horn that he acquired during his army career in Africa and used as a 'whistle'.

Right: The original kudu horn was subsequently used at the first World Scout Jamboree and other major events.

Programme

Day 1 – Preliminary
Settling into camp
Formation of Patrols
Distribution of duties, orders, etc.
Each subject of the course explained with demonstrations
Patrol Leaders received a special course of instruction in the field for them to impart subsequently to their Patrols.

Day 2 – Campaigning
Camp resourcefulness
Hut- and mat-making
Knots, fire lighting, cooking, health and sanitation, endurance
Finding way in strange country
Boat management

Day 3 – Observation
Noticing and memorising details far and near landmarks, etc.
Tracking
Deducing meaning from tracks and signs
Training eyesight, etc.

Day 4 – Woodcraft
Study of animals and birds, plants, stars, etc.
Stalking animals
Noticing details of people, reading their character and condition, thereby gaining sympathy

Day 5 – Chivalry
Honour-code of the Knights
Unselfishness
Courage
Charity and thrift
Loyalty to king and to employers or officers
Practical chivalry to women
Obligation to do a 'good turn' daily, and how to do it, etc.

Day 6 – Saving Life
From fire, drowning, sewer gas, runaway horses, panic, street accidents, etc.
Improvised apparatus
First aid
Albert Medal, etc.

Day 7 – Patriotism
Colonial Geography
History and deeds that won the empire
Our navy and army
Flags
Medals
Duties as citizens
Marksmanship
Helping Police, etc.

Day 8 – Games
Sports comprising games or competitive practices in all subjects of the course

Above: Fun and games then, but six of the boys would be dead by the end of the First World War.

Above left: Sports and games based on all the subjects of the course formed a key part of the programme on the final day of the camp.

Wolves and green for Bulls. Each Patrol Leader sported a short staff with a white flag bearing a picture of their Patrol animal (painted by Baden-Powell). They also had the distinction of wearing a fleur-de-lys badge – the same symbol that B-P had used as an award when training his army scouts and that, slightly modified, would soon become better known as the Scout badge.

The programme

The eight-day programme, which began on 1 August 1907, was designed to teach key skills, ranging from fun games to noble values, such as chivalry and discipline.

The first day began with Baden-Powell rousing the camp by blowing on a kudu horn, a souvenir of his expedition to the Somabula Forest during the Matabeleland campaign in 1896. After a quick wash, some cocoa, a short demonstration and a brief session of physical drill, the flag was hoisted, prayers were said and breakfast was eaten. Then it was on to whatever Scouting exercises were to feature that day.

The second day was concerned with teaching practical skills for outdoor living, including many things that the modern-day Scout is expected to know, such as how to:
• put up tents;
• lay and light a fire;
• kill, cut up and cook their food;
• tie logs together to make bridges and rafts;
• find their way by night and day in a strange country.
Most of the techniques taught over the eight days were taken from army training and had been employed by Baden-Powell's men during the Boer War. He taught the Scouts by allowing them to experiment first:

Make each boy lay a fire in his own way and light it. After failures, show them the right way (i.e. delicate use of dry chips and shavings, and sticks in a pyramid) and make them do it again.

The last full day was a sports day, prepared and run by the boys. The van Raaltes were invited to watch, after

which the whole camp went to the van Raaltes' home for tea. They returned to their campsite and a final campfire.

A movement is born
On 9 August the boys returned home, exhausted and exhilarated – the great adventure had come to an end. Despite their cultural and social differences, the groups of boys had lived, worked and played together in a way that would not have been thought possible on the mainland. The success of the camp had exceeded Baden-Powell's expectations in every way, and he was now ready to take his idea to a wider audience.

Present at Brownsea
To the best knowledge available today, these are the 20 boys who took part in the camp and their Patrols:

Wolves
Musgrave C. (Bob) Wroughton – Patrol Leader
Cedric Curteis
John Evans-Lombe
Reginald Giles
Percy Medway

Bulls
Thomas Brian Evans-Lombe – Patrol Leader
Bertie Blandford
Marc Noble
Arthur Primmer
James Rodney

Curlews
George Rodney – Patrol Leader
Terry Bonfield
Richard Grant
Alan Vivian
Herbert Watts

Ravens
Herbert Emley – Patrol Leader
Herbert Collingbourne
Humphrey Noble
William Rodney
Bertie Tarrant

The adults
In addition to Baden-Powell himself, also present were:

Donald Baden-Powell
Percy W. Everett
George Walter Green
Kenneth McLaren
Henry Robson
William Stevens
An unknown army chef.

Left: Of the 20 boys at the camp, ten came from the Poole and Bournemouth Boys' Brigade, the others were the sons of B-P's friends attending public schools.

⚜ Camp kit
Each boy was requested to bring a camp kit, rolled up in a waterproof sheet or valise with straps
Knife, fork and spoon
2 enamelled plates and 1 mug
Waterproof sheet
2 Blankets (no sheets)
1 Pillow and p. case
2 Rough Towels
1 smooth Towel
Tin cooking 'Billy' *
Canvas haversack *
2 coat straps 8" long *
Jack knife and lanyard *
Soap & sponge
Toothbrush
Brush & comb.
Small looking glass

* Optional. Can be bought in camp at low
   price if desired

The boys also had to bring clothing packed in a handbag or canvas 'dirty clothes' bag

1 Pr Flannel Trousers
1 Pr flannel 'shorts' or knickerbockers
2 Pr stockings & garters
   (if possible with green tabs showing
   below the roll of stockings)
2 Flannel shirts
Neckerchief (preferably dark green)
1 suit pyjamas
1 pr bathing drawers
Sweater or old jacket
Cap
Hat; preferably grey wideawake,
   for sun
2 Pr strong boots or shoes
1 Pr slippers or canvas shoes
Warm great coat and warm gloves
Leather waistbelt
Waterproof coat or cape (Optional)
Wrist watch (Optional)
Compass (Optional)
Housewife (a sewing kit) with needles,
   thread and buttons

Even before Baden-Powell ran his experimental camp on Brownsea Island he had started work on the manuscript that would become his most famous book, *Scouting for Boys*.

Scouting for Boys

B aden-Powell began his historic work by sketching out some of his initial thinking in two pamphlets, *Boys Scouts: A Suggestion* and *Boy Scouts: Summary of Scheme*, which he had published and circulated to a few friends. In these he summarized the skills that he saw as essential in a Scout, the training required and the organization of the Scouts into Patrols, and Patrols into a Troop under a Scoutmaster. But, he noted, expenses would be very small, 'no apparatus or uniform is absolutely necessary beyond badges', and, he continued, 'an inexpensive handbook called *Scouting for Boys* is being prepared'.

Time to write

From 1907, with his term of office as Inspector-General of Calvary over after a tour of Egypt and the Sudan, Baden-Powell was free to concentrate on writing. In June 1907 he spent some time writing at the Izaak Walton Hotel in Dovedale, Derbyshire, and met with Arthur Pearson, his publisher, to discuss the best means of bringing the Boy Scout scheme to the attention of a wider public and especially those interested in the training of boys.

Pearson declared his interest, and together they worked out a programme for the next 12 months. If the experimental camp that Baden-Powell planned was a success, he would tour the country during the winter of 1907–8, explaining his scheme. In the meantime, *Scouting for Boys* would be finished and Pearson would arrange for its publication. Pearson also offered £1,000 to cover initial expenses and provided office space in Henrietta Street, London. They also made plans to produce a new boys' magazine, which would appear in 1908 and be called *The Scout*. This magazine, with its mixture of fiction and factual articles, was published every week until 1966.

Above: Baden-Powell wrote part of *Scouting for Boys*, before and after Brownsea Island camp, in Mill House Cottage alongside the windmill on Wimbledon Common.

SCOUT LAW (34)

Scouts all the world over have unwritten laws which bind them just as much as if they had them printed in black and white.

They come down to us from old times.

The Japanese have their Bushido or laws of the old Samurai warriors, just as we have the chivalry or rules of the Knights of the Middle Ages. The Red Indians in America have their laws of Honour, the Zulus, the natives of India, the European nations all have their ancient codes.

The following are the rules which apply to Boy Scouts and which you swear to obey when you take your oath as a Scout, so it is as well that you should know all about them.

The Scouts motto is founded on my initials, it is:

BE PREPARED

Which means you are always to be in state of readiness in mind and body to do your DUTY:

Be Prepared in Mind by having disciplined yourself to be obedient to every order, and also by having thought out beforehand any accident or situation that might occur, so that you know the right thing to do at the right moment and are willing to do it.

Be Prepared in Body by making yourself strong and active and able to do the right thing at the right moment, and do it.

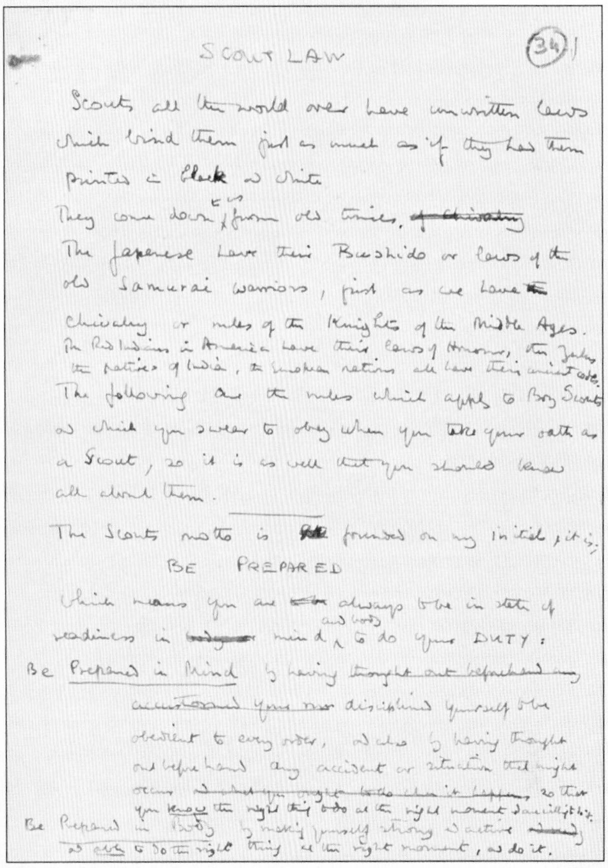

Scout law

Scouts all over the world have unwritten laws which bind them just as much as if they had them printed in black and white.

They come down to us from old times.

The Japanese have their Bushido or laws of the old Samurai warriors, just as we have chivalry or rules of the Knights of the Middle Ages. The Red Indians in America have their laws of Honour, the Zulus, the natives of India, the European nations all have their ancient codes.

The following are the rules which apply to Boy Scouts and which you swear to obey when you take your oath as a Scout, so it is as well that you should know all about them.

The Scout's motto is founded on my initials, it is:

BE PREPARED

which means you are always to be in a state of readiness in mind and body to do your DUTY:

Be Prepared in Mind by having disciplined yourself to be obedient to every order, and also by having thought out beforehand any accident or situation that might occur, so that you know the right thing to do at the right moment and are willing to do it.

Be Prepared in Body by making yourself strong and active and able to do the right thing at the right moment, and do it.

The cottage next to the windmill

Baden-Powell returned to his writing, borrowing a cottage sited next to the windmill on Wimbledon Common in south-west London, and he stayed there for ten days. The cottage was owned by a Mrs Fetherstonhaugh, whom he had met while he was with his uncle in Malta, and it had its own menagerie of penguins, owls and lemurs. During his time there, by writing in his own hand and dictating to a succession of shorthand writers, he completed a first draft of the book. The first third of the original manuscript survives in The Scout Association's archives, handwritten on a variety of scraps of papers (see page 37).

There was a break for a couple of weeks while the experimental camp took place on Brownsea Island, and then he resumed work with even greater confidence in his scheme. Having seen the effect of his nightly campfire yarns on those who had taken part, he felt he had a sounder notion of what appealed to boys.

A lecture tour – the idea develops

Much of Baden-Powell's time during November and December was taken up with the lecture tour that had been agreed with Pearson. At the first meeting on 8 November 1907 he told his audience that this was the beginning of his 'crusade' and that it had a twofold purpose: first, to arouse public opinion to the urgent need to provide some kind of character training for boys, and, second, to expound the idea of Scouting as a meanings of attracting boys to existing organizations or to a new body, the Boy Scouts. His own fame was, of course, an attraction, but he was an excellent speaker with good humour and wit, with many stories of real adventures. He used the latest technology – lantern slides – to illustrate his points, but later, when the scheme was more developed, he would have a Boy Scout on the platform and explain the details of the uniform and badges.

These two months saw Baden-Powell give eight lectures throughout Britain, and this left him little time for writing, but he was able to send off some additions to the manuscript to his typist. In order to be free of distractions, he returned to Mill House Cottage on 26 December 1907 and stayed until 6 January to get the book into shape and ready for the printers. By February he had given 50 such lectures to great acclaim.

The work appears

Scouting for Boys was published as a part work, in six consecutive fortnightly parts. The first part appeared on 15 January 1908. Its cover picture showed a Scout with hat and stave, lying low behind a rock, observing a smugglers' ship in the distance – promising the young reader not just tales of adventure but the chance to experience them too. The text was a ragbag of short, pithy chapters and articles, culled from a wide range of sources and illustrated with sketches by the author. There were games to be played and stories to be read, but there were details of the Scout oath or Promise, the Scout Law and the Scout uniform. It offered adventure and gave the opportunity for it, with the result that this sort of patchwork-style book appealed to boys with even the shortest attention span.

Interspersing 'yarns' drawn from the works of Rudyard Kipling, Sir Arthur Conan Doyle and Native American lore with practical advice and woodcraft, *Scouting for Boys* was the original 'adventure handbook'. Scouts could find out how to stop a runaway horse, track and catch a thief, make a straw mattress, identify trees and even how to drag an insensible man to safety.

As well as addressing young people themselves, B-P included 'tips for instructors' and thereby succeeded in creating a one-size-fits-all manual – pulling off that rare trick of appealing to several different audiences at the same time. He had an uncanny knack for knowing exactly what young boys wanted – plenty of practical skills together with lots of blood and gore – which perhaps accounts for the stories of a man tumbling to his death over Niagara Falls, a double fatality on a railway line and a murderer hanged. It was a unique approach, but it was his tone above all – funny, companionable, but never patronizing – that endeared him to his young readership.

Below: Believed to be one of the world's bestselling titles ever, Baden-Powell's book has also been translated into many different languages.

A runaway bestseller

The fortnightly parts sold well, so well, in fact, that shortly after the sixth and final part had been published a complete edition containing a slightly revised text appeared in May 1908, in both hardback and paperback editions. It was reprinted a further five times that same year. The sales were phenomenal and, as Scouting spread, the book was translated into many foreign languages – not only French, Italian and German, but also Chinese, Japanese and Hebrew, to name but a few. It continues in print to this day, making it now one of the world's bestselling books ever, after the Bible, the Qu'ran and Mao Zedong's *Little Red Book*.

Repercussions

It should be remembered that Baden-Powell did not have a great masterplan for the development of Scouting. All he was trying to do was to provide a scheme for existing organizations to use. The fact that Scouting established itself as a movement was just as much a surprise to him as to everyone else. In the months following, having accepted command of the Northumbria Division of the Territorial Army, he was once again too occupied with military matters to devote much time to his new movement. But boys read the book, formed Patrols and Troops and persuaded adults to become Scoutmasters. The true answer to the question 'Who started the Scouts?' is most probably 'The boys,' rather than Baden-Powell himself.

Humshaugh:
A 'proper' Scout camp

If Baden-Powell wanted Brownsea to be an experiment and not attract any publicity, his next camping venture was to be the opposite. This time he wanted publicity, both before and after, and for the event to be seen as a 'model' of good practice, showing his new band of leaders and boys – and the wider world – what could be done with a little imagination and enterprise.

The boys who attended the 1907 camp on Brownsea Island were not Scouts. They did not belong to Scout Troops, there were no Law and Promise for them to accept, and there was no Scout uniform. But in the early months of 1908 a number of 'proper' Scout camps – the first – did take place.

The opportunity of a lifetime

The publisher of *Scouting for Boys*, Arthur Pearson, also published the first issue of *The Scout* magazine on 18 April 1908, and it, too, enjoyed immediate and considerable success. Of its 20 or so pages, six were related to Scouting and there was always a page written by Baden-Powell himself (something he continued to do until his death in 1941). The content may have been like that of many other comics of the period, but it was a link between the Scouts themselves – it was their newssheet, textbook and inspiration, all on a weekly basis. Most importantly, it provided news of where troops were being formed and what they were up to. A magazine for adults followed the following year with the publication of the first edition of *Headquarters Gazette* (later called *The Scouter* and, later still, *Scouting*).The announcement of the Humshaugh camp – a 'proper' Scout camp – came in the first issue of *The Scout*: 'Who of you would want to spend a fortnight

Left: The 30 boys who won places at the Humshaugh camp, plus six others specially invited by Baden-Powell, gather around the flagpole.

Below left: Published every week from April 1908 onwards, *The Scout* magazine was instrumental in helping the Scout Movement's considerable early growth.

Below right: *The Scout* magazine carried advertisements such as this, promoting the chance to win a place at the camp in Humshaugh in August 1908.

under canvas with a troop of other boys, and under the care of General Baden-Powell?' For the magazine's thousands of readers, many of whom would have loved the chance to camp with their hero, it seemed too good to be true. And it was – like all things 'too good' – because there was a catch. What the magazine was announcing was a competition, with an invitation to the camp as a prize. The winners would be the top 30 names listed in *The Scout* of those who had collected the most 'votes' in the issue published immediately before the camp.

A controversial ballot

The 'votes' had little to do with democracy. Readers could vote for themselves, but only by using the special coupon in the magazine each week. Baden-Powell may not have liked the concept of this competition, but he did not own *The Scout* so there was little he could do about it.

The idea of the competition was Pearson's, an arch-publicist. Scouts were to encourage friends to buy the magazine so that they could use the coupon. At least that is how it was intended, and each week there were exhortations and lists of the top 50. By the end of the competition, Scout F. D. Watson, who had accumulated the most 'votes', appeared to have over 29,000 friends, while the 50th boy in the league table had 5,350. The scheme must have attracted tens of thousands of sales by the time the camp was held at the end of August 1908.

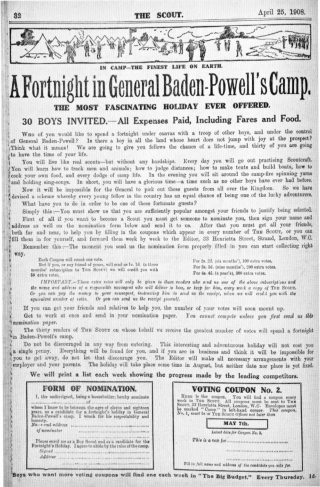

Daily programme

6.30 a.m. Turn out, air bedding; coffee and biscuit.

7.00 a.m. Physical exercises or instruction parade

7.30 a.m. Stow tents and wash.

8.00 a.m. Prayers and flagbreak

8.30 a.m. Breakfast

9.00 a.m. Scouting practice

11.00 a.m. Biscuit and milk

11.30 a.m. Scouting games

1.30 p.m. Dinner

2.00 p.m. Rest (compulsory)

3.00 p.m. Scouting games

5.30 p.m. Tea

6.00 p.m. Recreation, camp games

7.30 p.m. Camp fire

9.00 p.m. Biscuits and milk; turn in

9.30 p.m. Lights out

Baden-Powell's reservations

Baden-Powell was not impressed. In a letter to Pearson's agent, Peter Keary, he wrote: 'There is something in it which I fear will put off some readers of the better sort.' Possibly to compensate for Pearson's moneymaking scheme, Baden-Powell arranged for the first 20 unsuccessful boys to receive a special Scout camera that the winners had also been given and the next 50 to receive a personally signed copy of *Scouting for Boys*.

A late deal

At the last minute Baden-Powell and Pearson agreed that an additional six boys – the sons of some friends and his nephew Donald – could attend in addition to the 'voted' 30. This Patrol was called the Wolves. The other five Patrols of six boys were Kangaroos, Curlews, Ravens, Bulls and Owls. They came from Ireland, Scotland, Wales and all parts of England. Perhaps regretting the way the selection had been handled, B-P wrote during the camp: 'I wish every Boy Scout in Britain could be with us here today.'

The camp location

The location of the camp was not revealed until the end of the competition for a good reason – it had not been found. On 9 August that Baden-Powell was able to write:

> I have arranged camping grounds thus: Camp at Walewick Grange five miles from Hexham … for a week, then Tramps to neighbouring spots and bivouacs for the nights

The actual site was just south of Hadrian's Wall, on a gently sloping hillside, adjacent to Carr Edge Plantations.

B-P misses the opening

Army inspection duties of three weekend encampments of Territorials prevented Baden-Powell from being

Left: The Scouts at Humshaugh learned how to make a bivouac out of natural materials for use as a night shelter.

Below: A demonstration of the Eegongyama chorus, as described in *Scouting for Boys*, was photographed and used afterwards for promotional purposes.

presented at the camp's opening on 22 August 1908, but he arrived in time for that Saturday night's campfire.

Much of the food had to come from local farms. Tents were also hired locally, and Baden-Powell flew the same Union flag that he had used at Mafeking and Brownsea.

The end of the camp

In his final campfire address, Baden-Powell invoked the spirit of King Arthur and his Knights of the Round Table, who were associated with the area. 'You must never forget,' he said, 'that the distinguishing mark of a Scout should be his unselfishness. He should always think of others and try to help them before thinking of himself.'

A model for the future

The Humshaugh camp had been planned as a model, not just for those who had already joined the Scouts but for the world at large, to show what Scouting was all about. Pictures of the camp were produced as postcards and lantern slides to 'spread the message'. There was also press coverage in the national papers, bringing the Scout Movement to wider attention. But the best publicity came from the boys themselves. It was 'the very best holiday of my life,' said John Coats. 'I am sure every boy in the camp must wish to go there again next year.' But they didn't. By next summer there was another idea and another type of a camp at Beaulieu, involving boats and water.

Extracts from camp diaries

Monday, 24 August – overcast and raining
Physical exercises led by W. Wakefield
Setting up of a loom in the woods and building a hut
Bivouac and straw mattress making
Making ration bags with needle and thread
Short game of football
How to make bread without yeast or chemicals
Campfire
Talk 'hints on tracking' by Pearse

Thursday, 27 August – showers
P.E.
Changed position of tent
Played 'Scout meets Scout'
Patrol activities
First aid instruction
Visit to Mr Chapman's home at Houxty; as it was wet the boys stayed over in the stables

Friday, 28 August – cold and rain all day
Physical drill in saddle room
Stretcher drill
Tracking, whistles and hand signals
Chapman shows off his collection of 'Big Game' mounted trophies
Signalling practice

Tea, campfire, heard phonograph
At night Patrol Leaders went out rabbit shooting

Tuesday, 1 September – heavy showers
Patrol Drill raising section tents as practice for sports day
Straw rope making
Badgework and 1st class tests
Debate in Bulls tent: 'Should rabbits be kept in tents?'
Evening lecture on kindness to animals

Thursday, 3 September – overcast but dry
P.E.
Assist farmer with fence mending
Self-measurement as in 'Scouting for Boys'
First aid
Campfire for 1st class badge
March to Fourstones to take train to Newcastle upon Tyne to visit the Armstrong Whitworth Armoury Works at Elswick
Visited sail training ship 'Calliope' and a large crane
Campfire with Baden-Powell's yarns about Mafeking

Registrations and requests for information started coming in after the first part of *Scouting for Boys* was published. In a small office space provided by Arthur Pearson, Baden-Powell installed his old friend Kenneth ('The Boy') McLaren and a secretary to try and cope with the numerous requests for hats, flags, badges and advice while he was away on military business. They were quickly overwhelmed by the work.

The first Troops

It has never been possible to state with any degree of certainty which was the first Scout Troop to be formed – it was all happening too quickly. Most registration details were kept locally, and in many cases Troops were active long before anyone got around to filling in forms. While there are some good claimants for this honour, there are at least 25 Scout Troops in Britain today that have been in continuous existence since 1908.

Scouting spreads abroad

Within two years there were over 100,000 Scouts in Britain alone, and the Movement had already spread abroad; first to other parts of the British Empire – Australia, Canada, New Zealand, India and South Africa – and then to other countries, Chile being the first in 1909.

During the first months of 1908 Patrols and Troops started by the Boys' Brigade and the YMCA began to spring up across Britain. However, these were soon heavily outnumbered by those starting up independently.

Getting going

Manufacturers were also quick to cash in on the growing phenomenon, producing toys and games with a Scouting theme and range of Scout books. Some handbooks were published, but most of the books were fiction. Gamages, a famous department store in London, soon had a whole floor and shopping catalogue devoted to Scout equipment of varying kinds.

Getting organized

The chaos and lack of organization at the grassroots could not continue because it was damaging to the reputation of both Scouting and its founder. In September 1908 Baden-Powell sent a letter to interested adults whose names were on file. After admitting that there were shortcomings in some of the adults who had taken up the role of Scoutmasters, he proposed to establish a proper system. He asked local advisory committees to get in touch with all Patrols and Troops in a District, to register them, to appoint as Scoutmasters only adults who were considered 'fit and proper', to award badges and generally to help the growing Movement as best they could. Two travelling inspectors were appointed – W. Wakefield for the north of England and Eric Walker for the south – and they were available to help, advise and encourage.

A headquarters in London

Baden-Powell himself made no money from *Scouting for Boys*, even though it was a runaway bestseller. All the royalties were ploughed back into funding the Movement, its office and its growing staff. By 1909 the Scouts had acquired their first national headquarters at 116–118 Victoria Street, London, where the paid staff worked hand-in-hand with senior volunteers. The same year saw the first party of British Scouts travel abroad – they undertook a tour of Germany.

Royal approval

Towards the end of the year Baden-Powell was invited by Edward VII to stay at Balmoral Castle in Scotland. During his visit the king knighted B-P for his services to his country and for creating Scouting. The king, a keen supporter, agreed to review a rally of Scouts the following year, and he approved the introduction of the King's Scout badge. So convinced was he of the value of the work that Baden-Powell was doing, the king also persuaded him to retire from the army and devote himself to Scouting on a full-time basis. It was what was needed. As a souvenir, the king later sent Baden-Powell a small piece of venison bone mounted with a silver edge and bearing an inscription of a royal crown – the bone was all that remained of the joint of meat they had eaten together.

The king died the following year and it was left to his son, George V, to review a large Scout rally at Windsor in 1911. George V continued the royal patronage of Scouting and approved the grant of a Royal Charter in 1912 to give legal protection and standing to the Movement.

Sea Scouting

Scouting was spreading across Britain, but Baden-Powell saw no reason why it should stop at its shores. Sea Scouting became an instantly popular branch of the Scout Movement and remains so to this day.

Water activities were part of Scouting right from the start. As a boy Baden-Powell had enjoyed boating holidays with his brothers and had once sailed a canvas boat up the River Thames and over to the rivers Severn and Wye in the west of England, camping out overnight. Their leader was his brother Warrington, who achieved fame as a canoeist and later, after a career at sea, became a lawyer and an expert in maritime law. B-P also loved to visit his maternal grandfather, Admiral William Smyth, who would tell him sea stories as they paced an imaginary 'quarterdeck'.

Sea Scouting gets under way

Baden-Powell had written in *Scouting for Boys* that 'a Scout should be able to manage a boat, to bring it properly alongside a ship or pier' and had included other advice on boat handling. In February 1909 *The Scout* reported:

A new branch of Boy Scouts is springing up in Glasgow under the title of Sea Scouts. These Scouts will be just the same as Land Scouts, in that they will be trained in the power of observation, the value of discipline, patriotism and chivalry. The only difference is that they will be trained on a naval basis, learning naval drills and visiting His Majesty's ships whenever possible.

Activity badges

Among eight new special activity badges that were introduced in June 1909 was one for Seaman, and after he had performed the specified tasks, the Scout who gained it 'may be recognized by the rank of his badge. For instance, one who gets the Seamanship badge would be called Sea Scout Jones, or, for the Fireman's badge … Fire Scout Atkins.' With many troops formed in the towns around Britain's extensive coastline and rivers, it is not surprising that some of them developed an affinity with water activities and were called Sea Scouts.

Above left: Some of the lucky winners who took part in the first Sea Scout camp in 1909.

Above right: Washing the deck of the TS *Mercury*, used as a base for the two-week camp.

Right: The popularity of the camp – both on land and on the water – caused the creation of Sea Scouting as a permanent part of the Scout Movement.

The first 'sea camps'

Following the success of the camp at Humshaugh, another competition was run in *The Scout*, this time for a fortnight's camp that would last from 7 to 21 August 1909 and have a hundred places on two sites. A troop of 50 would sleep in hammocks on the training ship *Mercury*, moored on the River Hamble, Hampshire, while the other 50 would camp on dry ground nearby. Both troops – called wet bobs and dry bobs – spent one week at each site, swapping over at the mid-weekend.

Of the participants, 92 were the competition winners, the remaining eight being 'guests'. These included Baden-Powell's nephew, Donald, George Rodney and Humphrey Noble, all of whom had been at the previous camps at Brownsea and Humshaugh, and the son of the author Rudyard Kipling. Again, the camp was judged to have been a great success, even though Baden-Powell could not spend as much time there himself as he had wished – two days at the start and part of the final week – because of his army duties. But he was very much at the centre of its planning and arranged for the boys to be provided with sailors' caps bearing Sea Scout name bands. Soon Sea Scouts were to have their own distinctive uniform, which has remained to this day relatively unchanged.

A handbook for Sea Scouts

Baden-Powell saw Sea Scouting as another form of training that could be as useful as mainstream Scouting. He wrote a booklet, *Sea Scouting for Boys*, which was published in 1911, but realized that there was a need for a proper handbook. Knowing his own brother Warrington's expertise, he persuaded him to write it, and it was published in 1912 under the title *Sea Scouting and Seamanship for Boys*. This laid out a complete and coherent philosophy and training plan, and set the pace for the development of Sea Scouting. At the Birmingham Scout Exhibition in 1913 more than 50 Sea Scout boats were displayed.

Right: At his brother's request, Warrington Baden-Powell wrote a proper handbook based on his own sea expertise.

Below: Souvenirs from the Leysdown tragedy include an issue of the *Daily Mirror* which devoted a whole issue to the Scouts' funeral.

The Leysdown disaster

There were, however, some early setbacks. On 4 August 1912 eight Scouts and one other boy drowned in a freak accident off Leysdown-on-Sea on the Isle of Sheppey, Kent, when there was a sudden squall and an ex-naval boat taking 23 Scouts from Walworth, south London, to their summer camp capsized. Their deaths were the first serious loss of life suffered by Scouting since its start, and Scouts from many countries were among the thousands who attended the mass funeral service on 10 August. The newspapers gave extensive coverage to the tragedy, and memorial cards and souvenirs of it were produced.

Another accident occurred the following year when *The Mirror*, a 50-ton ketch presented to Sea Scouts by the *Daily Mirror* newspaper, was hit by another vessel while at sea and four people lost their lives. Today Sea Scouting retains its international popularity and thousands of its members have gone on to make careers in the world's navies.

Scouting for girls?

From the outset of Scouting girls as well as boys were attracted to the idea. Sisters did not want to be left out when their brothers were enjoying the Scouts' special activities and going off to camp.

Troops in which girls were involved in Scouting were listed in *The Scout* and *Headquarters Gazette* in 1909 – after all, there were no rules to forbid it. The most public appearance of these girls occurred at a rally on 4 September 1909, when some 10,000 Scouts gathered at Crystal Palace in south London. As Baden-Powell inspected the Scouts, he was introduced to the Wolf Patrol of Girl Scouts. This public appearance, much photographed and commented on at the time, hastened the creation of the Girl Guides, a sister Movement similar to the Scouts but especially for girls.

Girl Scouts at Crystal Palace

From early 1907, when his first pamphlet outlining his scheme for Scouting had been published, Baden-Powell had described his proposals as suitable for both

boys and girls. In the early columns of *The Scout* he had encouraged girls to join, believing they could benefit as much as boys. But the attitudes of society at the time, when it was believed that involving girls in 'boys' activities' was absurd, were against him. In January 1909, therefore, he wrote in *The Scout* that he hoped to find time soon to 'devise a scheme of Scouting better adapted' for girls.

By the time of the Crystal Palace rally much work had been done to prepare for this new venture. In *Headquarters Gazette* the previous month it had been announced that, since over 6,000 Girl Scouts were already registered at Headquarters, 'a scheme [was] being prepared for them'. In anticipation of the new Movement's launch in 1910 a booklet had already been drafted to outline the Girl Guides and their programme. It was to have the same aims of character development and citizenship training as Scouting, but the activities would include 'home-making and mother-craft'. However, Baden-Powell insisted that they would become equal partners to boys and not just 'dolls'. He also wanted the girls' Movement to exist in its own right and not be seen as a pale image of Scouting.

Above: Girls were involved in Scouting from its beginning and by 1909 over 6,000 girls had registered at Headquarters.

The Girl Guides are formed

Baden-Powell picked the name Girl Guides from a corps of Indian guides who were 'distinguished for their general handiness and resourcefulness under difficulties … their keenness and courage … a force trained to take up any duties required on them, and to turn their hand to anything'. Symbolically, guides also knew the way and could lead others.

The pressure of his existing army commitments and leadership of the Boy Scouts meant that Baden-Powell would not have the time to run a second Movement. He was delighted when his sister Agnes took a keen interest in this phase of his work. She wrote a handbook, *How Girls Can Help to Build the Empire*, and this was followed by the more elaborate *Handbook for Girl Guides*, which was published in 1912 and gave the Guides their own version of *Scouting for Boys* and formed its foundation stone. As had happened with the Scouts, girls joined in their thousands both in Britain and overseas as the new Movement spread around the world. By 1922 the UK Movement would be larger than the Scouts and has been so ever since.

A match for B-P

In January 1912, while he was sailing on the SS *Arcadian* to America to give a lecture tour, Baden-Powell met 23-year-old Olave St Clair Soames, whom he recognized as someone he had seen in Hyde Park walking her dog some two years before. Born in 1889 in Derbyshire, Olave had been educated at home by a series of governesses, and from her earliest days she had been a great enthusiast for sports and outdoor living. By a remarkable coincidence, she and Baden-Powell shared

the same birthday – 22 February – but despite their age difference of 32 years they were ideally matched and had much in common.

By the time the ship reached Jamaica they were secretly engaged. They married on 30 October that same year at St Peter's Church near Poole, not far from Brownsea Island, in a simple ceremony without any music and attended by only a few close relatives and friends. This was to avoid undue attention and to prevent the arrangements from getting out of hand. They held a reception some weeks later at the Mercers' Hall, London, at which they received wedding presents. They were later given a Triumph Standard car by the Scouts, for which 100,000 Scouts had each given a penny.

An active role for Olave

Olave took a great interest in the Scouts, accompanying her husband on his visits as Chief Scout as well as running her own Scout troop. In 1915 she joined the Guides and quickly became County Commissioner for Sussex and Chief Commissioner for England. However, her relations with Agnes Baden-Powell, who was then in charge of the Guides, were never good and the two clashed. Baden-Powell was concerned about Agnes's level of commitment and grasp of Girl Guiding and particularly about the time it had taken her to prepare the Guide handbook. Olave – young, totally committed and enthusiastic – replaced Agnes as Chief Guide in 1918. As husband and wife they could together devote themselves to travelling the world to promote the two great Movements.

Their first child, Arthur Robert Peter, was born on their first wedding anniversary. Two more children were to follow: Heather, born in 1915, and Betty, born in 1917.

Above: Baden-Powell and Olave deep in conversation on the SS *Arcadian* during its voyage to America in January 1912.

Below: Baden-Powell and Olave's son Peter, seen with them here as a Wolf Cub. He was born in 1913 and died in 1962.

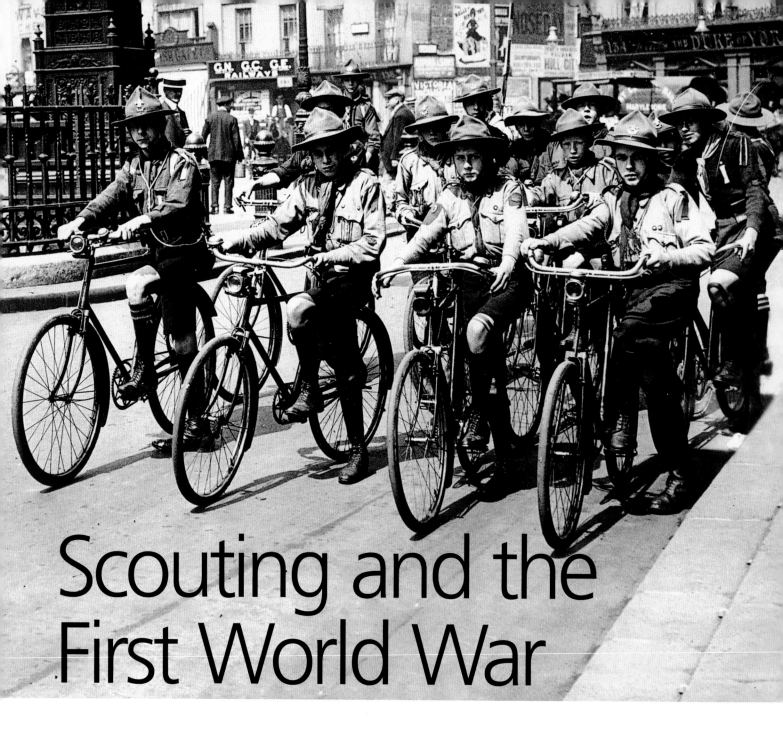

Scouting and the First World War

As a former soldier, Baden-Powell took a huge personal interest in the Great War, but as the situation on the Western Front deteriorated, he was faced with a dilemma: how could his new Movement make the most effective contribution while remaining committed to peace?

David Lloyd George, prime minister of Britain, praised the Scouts when, in 1917, he wrote:

I do not think that I am exaggerating when I say that the young boyhood of our country, represented by The Boy Scouts Association, shares the laurels for having been prepared with the old and trusted and tried British Army and Navy. It is no small matter to be proud of that the Association was able within a month of the outbreak of war to give the most energetic and intelligent help in all kinds of service.

However, at the outset of the war it is doubtful if the Movement was anything but prepared. In fact, the war threatened the Movement's existence and long-term future, for large numbers of adult leaders would be called on to serve their country, never to return.

Above: A Scout Messenger Corps with their cycles at Victoria, London. They performed valuable work for the War Office in the First World War.

The outbreak of war

On 28 June 1914, the day Archduke Franz Ferdinand was shot dead in Sarajevo, Baden-Powell was inspecting Scouts in Liverpool. He did not welcome the war, and when it was suggested that he should seek War Office recognition for the Movement in response to the plan put forward by Lord Haldane, the Secretary of State for War, to militarize all youth organizations, he refused to do so. Nevertheless, despite his reservations about the war and its impact on Scouting, just before the declaration of war on 4 August, he offered the services of the Movement to the government. And the government accepted them.

How Scouting could help

The Scouts' duties were to be non-military and to come under the scope of the police. They were to be carried out through their own Scout Commissioners under the general direction of the chief constable in each county. The duties included:

- guarding and patrolling bridges, culverts and telegraph lines against damage by spies;
- collecting information about supplies and transport available;
- handing out notices to inhabitants and other duties connected with billeting, commandeering and warning;
- carrying out organized relief measures among inhabitants;
- carrying out communications by means of dispatch riders, signallers and wireless;
- helping families of men employed in defence duties, or the sick or wounded;
- establishing first aid, dressing or nursing stations, refuges, dispensaries and soup-kitchens in their club rooms;
- acting as guides and orderlies.

Some of this was perhaps a little optimistic and was probably meant for only the first few months as the country turned its mind to the practicalities of war, but the Scouts did all this and more. For instance, as early as

Right: Among the many civil defence tasks undertaken, Scouts guarded railway lines, bridges and telephone lines to protect them from damage by spies.

Below: Scouts practising first aid and ambulance work in readiness for any wartime emergency that required their services.

7 August 1914 the Admiralty had requested the immediate service of 1,000 Scouts to assist coastguards on the east coast. Eventually, more than 23,000 Scouts would be involved in this line of work alone. Scouts also helped for some days to embark the British Expeditionary Force to France.

A versatile force

Throughout the war Scouts turned their hands to all manner of tasks and acquitted themselves well. They acted as messengers at railway stations, police stations, post offices and even the War Office itself. They formed first aid detachments and were hospital orderlies. They worked day and night and even came under fire in the north of England, where they were guarding telegraph wires and doing coastguard duty. Some, it would seem, were also involved behind the front line in France, helping to move ammunitions.

A military role for B-P?

Baden-Powell wanted a more active, front-line role for himself, but he was rebuffed by Lord Kitchener, who had replaced Lord Haldane at the War Office. After all, he was 57 years old, most of his experience was with cavalry regiments, and he had retired some years before. Kitchener did admit that he could have found any number of retired generals but that only one of them could mobilize the nation's youth. Although volunteer battalions from other youth organizations, such as the Church Lads' Brigade, were engaged in front-line service, there was no Scout battalion – in fact, Kitchener seemed against the formation of any irregular Scout corps.

The Scout Defence Corps

This did not deter Baden-Powell. In the November 1914 edition of *Headquarters Gazette* he announced his plans for a new scheme for Scouts who were 16 and 17 years old called the Scout Defence Corps. Fearing invasion, he wrote: 'A boy of 16 trained in discipline and marksmanship will be worth a dozen trained to nothing in particular.' Membership was voluntary, and the corps was not to be thought of as a permanent feature of Scouting. In order to pre-empt the inevitable criticism, he added: 'It is not militarism but a struggle against militarism.'

Although Baden-Powell wrote a small book, *Marksmanship for Boys*, to support the scheme, it was not universally popular, and when the corps failed to secure Home Office recognition it was the beginning of the end. Normal troop activities suffered as Scouts in the corps could not devote time to their customary practices in addition to corps training, but the demise of the Defence Corps caused a problem with retention.

Baden-Powell in France

As an honorary colonel, Baden-Powell was invited in 1915 to visit his two old regiments, which were on duty in France. He enjoyed being back in army uniform and among fellow soldiers for ten days, but he was shocked by the carnage that was unfolding. 'Someone ought to be hung for this,' he said. But the trip did give him an opportunity to visit some of the hospitals and YMCA

recreation huts that had been established. More were needed, Baden-Powell believed, to improve the welfare and morale of the soldiers.

He came away determined: here was a way in which Scouting could make a direct and valuable contribution to the war effort. As well as issuing a fundraising appeal to the Movement as a whole, he approached the Mercers' Company, one of the ancient trade guilds of the City of London. The Baden-Powell family had links with this guild going back centuries and prior to the war he had held the post of Master of the Guild. With their typical generosity,

Left: The Red Feather Badge and book published to support the Scout Defence Corp scheme, plus *Quick Training for War*, Baden-Powell's handbook for soldiers.

Below: In the course of this war the Victoria Cross for outstanding bravery and valour was awarded to 15 members of the Scout Movement, including Jack Cornwell.

Left: The Scout recreation hut at Étaples, France, opened in December 1915, where Baden-Powell and Olave worked for some weeks.

Below: Scouts provided much needed labour during harvest each year in the absence of adult farm staff who had been called up for war service.

the Mercers funded the first and largest of six Scout huts and, later, another hut and a marquee.

The 'Mercers Arms' hut opened near Calais on 21 July 1915 with a troop of French Scouts forming a guard of honour. It was staffed by Scouters in their uniforms who had responded to appeals in *Headquarters Gazette* for volunteers who were unfit or over the age for military service. Another hut, this time funded entirely by the Scouts, was opened by Olave Baden-Powell at Étaples in December the same year. It could accommodate up to one thousand men. Both Baden-Powell and Olave worked here for some weeks, serving tea and attending to the men themselves. Scouts also raised funds to buy and equip ambulances for the Western Front.

Baden-Powell spent so much time in France that the Germans suspected that he was spying again, and although it was not true, British intelligence did nothing to deny the rumours. In fact, Baden-Powell added to the confusion by publishing *Quick Training for War* in 1914 (which sold 65,000 copies in the first month) and *My Adventures as a Spy* in 1915.

Scouting's loss

It is estimated that 250,000 members of the Movement in Britain went to fight in the First World War. It is also estimated that 10,000 did not return and now lie in war graves across western Europe. Fifteen members were decorated with the Victoria Cross for their great courage and acts of bravery. Below is one example.

John Travers Cornwell, VC

Known throughout his short life as Jack, John Cornwell was born in Leyton, east London, on 8 January 1900. Like many boys of his age, Jack became a keen Scout, joining

the St Mary's Mission, Little Ilford Troop. 'Nothing was too hard for him,' his Scoutmaster, J. F. Avery, later recalled. Cornwell left school at the end of 1913, and when he was 15 he enlisted at a local Navy recruiting office. With his training complete, Cornwell passed out on 27 July 1915 as Boy Seaman, First Class, J. T. Cornwell J/42563, proudly drawing his pay of one shilling (5p) a week.

In 1916 Cornwell was ordered to Rosyth to join HMS *Chester*, a new light cruiser which was about to embark on its maiden voyage as part of the 3rd Cruiser Squadron. But by 31 May the *Chester* was on station ahead of the fleet in the North Sea, and the Battle of Jutland was about to begin. This battle, fought off the Danish coast, changed the face of sea warfare forever.

The lookouts heard distant gunfire and the ship was put on action stations. Jack's job was to stand by his gun and take orders, relayed through his headphones, from the gunnery officer on the bridge. He was responsible for setting the gun's sights, so that the gun could be brought to bear on its target. Four enemy cruisers appeared out of the mist and concentrated their fire on the *Chester*, hitting her 17 times with large-calibre shells and leaving only one gun operational. Jack's forward gun was one of the first to be knocked out before it could be brought into action, leaving Cornwell surrounded by devastation, the dying and the dead. Although he had been mortally wounded, he remained standing by his weapon, even though it could not be fired, until the ship was eventually relieved by the rest of the fleet.

In this first and only full-scale engagement of the British and German fleets in the First World War, the British lost 14 ships and 6,784 lives, while the Germans lost 11 mainly smaller ships and 3,058 men. HMS *Chester*, hopelessly outclassed, lost 35 lives, six of them listed as 'boys'.

As the scale of the losses began to be known, a heavy toll was also being exacted in the trenches of the Somme. The nation's morale sank. What was needed was a hero.

Unable to continue fighting, *Chester* returned to Immingham on the east coast, where she was met by tugs, and the wounded, including Jack, were taken off. Cornwell was taken to Grimsby hospital, where he died on 2 June 1916, aged 16 years and 6 months. As his family were poor, he was quietly buried in a common grave in Manor Park cemetery, east London. But the national papers took up the story of Jack's heroism, expressed outrage at his burial and demanded public recognition. It did not take long. Jack's body was exhumed and given a funeral procession and reburial with state and naval honours before reburial in Manor Park on 29 July 1916 in a more dignified grave.

On 15 September 1916 the *London Gazette* announced:

The King has been graciously pleased to approve the grant of the Victoria Cross to Boy, First Class, John Travers Cornwell ONJ 42563 (died 2 June 1916), for the conspicuous act of bravery specified below: 'Mortally wounded

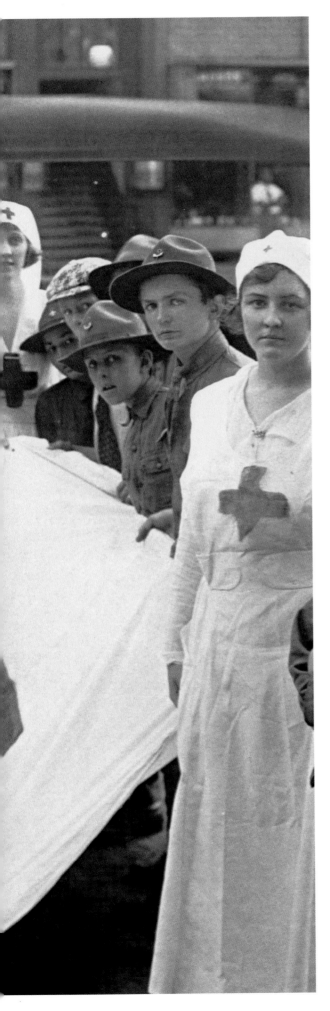

Left: Red Cross workers and Scouts display the donations received during an American Red Cross parade in Birmingham, Alabama, in May 1918.

early in the action, Boy, First Class, John Travers Cornwell remained standing alone at the most exposed post, quietly awaiting orders, until the end of the action, with the gun's crew dead and wounded all around him. His age was under sixteen and a half years.'

Baden-Powell also wished to pay tribute to the boy's heroism and in the September 1916 edition of *Headquarters Gazette* announced the introduction of the Cornwell Scout Badge for bravery by young people, which continues to be awarded to this day.

'Every Scout to Feed a Soldier'

Elsewhere Scouts also rallied behind the war effort. In 1917, when the USA entered the war, Scouts were encouraged to plant vegetable gardens under the slogan 'Every Scout to Feed a Soldier'. As in Britain, Scout farms sprang up, soon numbering some 12,000.

Working with the US Navy, Scout coastal patrols began guarding the nation's shores, and the organization also pledged aid to the American Red Cross. Other duties involved distributing literature (over 300 million items were delivered by Scouts), and they also helped to conserve the USA's supplies of food and fuel. American Scouts also made a significant financial contribution, selling 2,350,977 Liberty Loan bonds, totalling $147,876,902. They also sold war savings stamps, to a value of $53,043,698.

By the end of the war Scouts had proved themselves a loyal and efficient force for good. Working under the slogan 'The War Is Over, But Our Work Is Not', Scouts continued to serve their communities, notably during the influenza epidemic that followed the war.

Scouts defend their freedom

The first Scout troops were formed in western Ukraine in 1911, and by 1913 they had begun to establish themselves. The war led to the collapse of the two powers occupying Ukrainian territory, the Austro-Hungarian monarchy and tsarist Russia, which inevitably threw the fledgling Movement into turmoil. Hundreds of boys who were involved with Scouting volunteered to join the armed forces to defend their country's freedom. Although forgoing any hope of normal Scouting, they did help bring about the formation of the Ukrainian National Republic in 1918.

Sacrifice and propaganda

In Ottawa, Canada, Boy Scouts responded by forming the Headquarters Patriotic Relief. In 1914 they took to the streets in support of the war, wearing their uniforms and accompanied by bagpipes, flags, drums and bugles – literally drumming up public support for the war. It was still hoped that the conflict would end quickly and decisively, but as the war progressed it became clear that the human cost would be much greater than anticipated, and the country suffered heavy casualties. Thousands of former Scouts lost their lives.

Wolf Cubs

The rapid growth of Scouting soon led to demand from boys – and girls –
outside its age range. The Wolf Cubs were Baden-Powell's answer for those
who couldn't wait to grow up.

Baden-Powell had specifically designed Scouting for boys of 11 and over, but, of course, their younger brothers wanted to join in the fun. They turned up at Troop meetings and would not be sent away, but Scouting could not be 'watered down' to suit them. Junior Troops therefore came into being as early as 1909 in order to keep Scouting 'proper' as it had originally been intended.

From 1913, during the experimental stages of the junior Movement, the unofficial uniform mimicked that of Scouts, with a broad-brimmed hat, scarf, rucksack and broomstick-handle staff. The younger boys were taught the simplest of knots, the Scout tracking signs, basic semaphore and rudimentary first aid. There was general agreement among Scout leaders that more advanced activities, such as learning the Morse code, stretcher drill and camping, should be the preserve of Scouts. But camping was, of course, the one thing the youngsters craved. The outbreak of the First World War in 1914 changed things. Former

Scouts and many Scoutmasters joined up and were posted overseas, and women were moving into positions formerly held by men. Small boys were desperate to join Scouting and prove themselves 'soldierly', just like their fathers and older brothers. A properly organized junior Scout section would meet a great number of needs. However, it had to be done on a proper footing, so, with the assistance of his aide, Vera Barclay, Baden-Powell threw himself into developing the structure and philosophy of the new section. Several experimental Cub Scout Packs, affiliated to existing Scout Troops and churches, were registered before the official launch of the section in December 1916, so that information could be fed back to Headquarters.

The wolf – a good Scout

Baden-Powell recognized the importance of imaginative games for younger boys, and he wanted a back-story that would give them all the fun and activity they needed

Above: Early Cub Scouts testing each other's skill at semaphore. Many former Scouts were to enter the Royal Navy and the Merchant Navy, where such a skill was essential.

Right: Before the official launch of Cub Scouting, experimental Cub Packs were registered to give their meetings proper authority and support.

and would also whet their appetite for Scouting. He chose the title Wolf Cubs because he had already likened a good Scout to a wolf, the Native American accolade for a good scout. He also believed that his own title among Native African military scouts, Impeesa, meant 'the wolf that never sleeps'.

The *Jungle Book* theme

This wolf theme of the Cub Scouts inspired him to persuade Rudyard Kipling to allow *The Jungle Books* to be used as the imaginative setting for his new section. *The Jungle Books*, published in 1894 and 1895, had been extremely popular and were already known to many younger boys.

Cub Scouting had to be entirely different and distinct from Scouting, yet it would start the youngsters on the trail of Scoutcraft and Pack cooperation, with all the controlled fun that Mowgli experienced in Kipling's jungle story. It was exactly right for boys at that time and captured the imagination of all concerned. *The Wolf Cub's Handbook* ran to 16 editions between 1916 and 1966, with each edition slightly updating the previous one.

The Law and Promise

Requirements for the first Tenderpad tests included a knowledge of the Grand Howl, the Wolf Cub salute and the Wolf Cub Promise and Law. The salute and the Law both bore the hallmark of the jungle, the salute being symbolic of the two ears of the wolf and the two parts of the Law:

'The Cub gives in to the Old Wolf,

'The Cub does not give in to himself.'

The Promise was a simplified version of the Scout Promise, only omitting the phrase 'On my honour', which was thought to demand too much of an eight-year-old and to dilute the power of the Scout Promise. 'Do Your Best' became the Cub motto, accounting for the peculiar 'dyb dyb dyb' (Do Your Best) and 'dob dob dob' (Do Our Best) shouts that originally accompanied the Grand Howl at the formal opening and closing of every Pack meeting.

The Cub uniform

The new uniform, with its green jersey, green and yellow piped cap and yellow scarf, was joyfully received. Initially, there was no handbook or specific training for leaders, other than the 'Hints for Cubmasters' appended to *The Wolf Cub's Handbook*. However, the principle suggested by B-P would be equally applicable now: 'We teach them small things in play which will eventually fit them for doing big things in earnest.'

Today there are millions of Cub Scouts in almost every country of the world, most of whom still bear more than a passing resemblance to the very first.

Below: This Six of early Cub Scouts is getting dinner under way for their Pack with cheerful resignation.

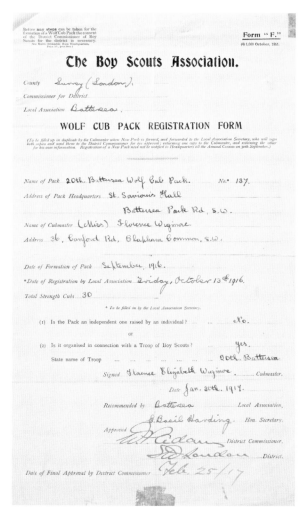

'The Law of the Jungle – Mr Kipling's excellent idea.' B-P was an astute man, outstanding at spotting 'going concerns' and exploiting them to the full. Faced with the questions of what to give the younger boys to do and how to make their programme different from 'real Scouting', he and Percy Everett turned to Kipling's popular *Jungle Books*.

The Wolf Cub's Handbook

28 July 1916

Dear Kipling,

You were kind enough to give me leave (some eight years ago already) to quote your story of Kim in giving the boys a lead in becoming Boy Scouts. We are now encouraging a junior branch of the Movement under the name of Wolf Cubs for youngsters between 8 and 11, and I want to enthuse them through your Mowgli and his animal friends of the Jungle Book. Would you have any objection to my introducing it to them on the lines of the enclosed proof? It would be a very great help to me if I may and I hope that it might also help in a small way to add to the demand for your book.

Believe me,
Yours truly,
RBP

Bateman's
29 July 1916
Private
Dear Baden-Powell,

I am in receipt of your letter of July 28th, and am forwarding to my publishers the article that you have made for the Scout's Magazine from The Jungle Books. If they agree to your using it, I will let you hear. My permission is gladly given, only it will be necessary for you to say that the extracts are from The Jungle Books and that they are quoted by the kind permission of the author and publishers, Messrs. Macmillan & Co.

Believe me,
Yours truly
Rudyard Kipling

B aden-Powell's article appeared a fortnight later, on 12 August 1916, in the next edition of *The Scout*. The same article appeared again as the fourth 'Bite' of *The Wolf Cub's Handbook* in December 1916.

Piracy or partnership?

There has been considerable debate about whether Kipling's permission was actually asked about the use of *The Jungle Books* in *The Wolf Cub's Handbook*, and, if so, whether Kipling realized that Baden-Powell would rewrite his work in his own way for this new audience.

Kipling's writing was already quoted extensively in Scout publications. Large sections of his stories, articles and poems, especially those involving up-to-date reporting on new weaponry and machinery (from rifles to cars and submarines), appeared frequently in *The Scout*. His novel *Kim* (1901) had been quoted with permission in *Scouting for Boys*, and Kim's Game had been based on the story.

There is no longer any record of exactly the point at which Baden-Powell and Percy Everett decided to use *The Jungle Books* as comprehensively as they did. The idea for the Wolf Cubs may originally have come from Ernest Thompson Seton's work for youngsters in the *The Birch-bark Roll of the Woodcraft Indians*, which incorporated the Native American title of 'wolf' for the best scouts. The relevance of *The Jungle Books* to this wolf theme may been realized relatively late in the planning process, but it was instrumental to the published programme of the new section.

Quoting from Kipling

Kipling's permission had already been asked for an article by B-P in *The Scout* magazine that used stories from *The Jungle Books* only five months before the publication of *The Wolf Cub's Handbook*. By then, there were already 10,000 Cubs in experimental Packs attached to existing Scout Troops.

Baden-Powell must have been very sure of Kipling's support, but he was taking a huge risk by gambling that Kipling would grant him permission to take the original text, rewrite large sections of it and draw his own moral from the stories. Kipling had already fought legal battles over publication rights for his work.

What Baden-Powell did with Kipling's text is a fascinating subject, and it reveals a great deal about both men's characters. B-P wanted the boys to be inspired to adventure and to act as a pack to develop teamwork; Kipling, on the other hand, focused on Mowgli, the individual who would come to lead the pack.

Reinterpreting the stories

Baden-Powell reinterpreted the stories for the Cubs in his own language, with a Scouting moral attached. *The Wolf Cub's Handbook* was divided into wolfish Bites, each Bite being a combination of a jungle story, new games and jungle 'dances'. The dances were group re-enactments of themes from *The Jungle Books*, and Kipling saw the dances and the Grand Howl for himself at the rally at Alexandra Palace in north London in 1922.

Bateman's
Burwash
Sussex
December 1916
Dear Baden Powell,
I'm afraid I can't be up on Saturday much as I should like to see your Wolf Cubs. The more I see what the whole Scout movement has done and is doing in this world, and the more I realize what the great mass of youth might not have done if it had been left undirected, the more impressed I am with the immense value of your work. The only thing I can compare it to is what the Salvation Army did years back. You ought to be a happy man these days.

Yours sincerely
Rudyard Kipling

Above: From 1922 until 1925 Wolf Cub Leaders who completed training were awarded a Wolf's Fang or an Akela Badge instead of the traditional Wood Badge beads.

Left: Two 'Lady Cubmasters' overseeing a Grand Howl at an early Pack meeting, in a public park.

Until recently, no researcher has known whether Kipling approved of the treatment his books had been given. However, a letter from Kipling to Baden-Powell has come to light, donated to The (British) Scout Association archive by Baden-Powell's family. It shows that Kipling had been invited to the formal celebrations to launch the Wolf Cub section in December 1916, at which *The Wolf Cub's Handbook* was to be launched. His response reveals the degree of his affection, admiration and enthusiasm for Baden-Powell and Scouting, and it is the best possible conclusion to the subject.

The Wolf Cub's Handbook

The following introduction appeared in every edition of *The Wolf Cub's Handbook*, from 1916 to 1968.

Every boy, like every young Wolf, has a hearty appetite. This book is a meal offered by an old Wolf to the young Cubs. There is juicy meat in it to be eaten, and there are tough bones to be gnawed. But if every Cub who devours it will tackle the bone as well as the meat, and will eat up the fat with the lean, I hope that he will get good strength, as well as some enjoyment, out of every bite. B-P

To Rudyard Kipling, who has done so much to put the right spirit into our rising manhood, I am very grateful for the permission to quote as my text his inimitable 'Jungle Book'. My thanks are also due to his publishers, Messrs. Macmillan and Co., Ltd., for their courtesy in allowing these extracts to be made.

Gilwell Park:
The home of Scouting

Known throughout the world as the home of Scouting, Gilwell Park on the Essex London border is a country estate that has been owned by The Scout Association since 1919. Over the years, thousands of people of every nationality have camped here and received their leadership training.

The training methods developed at Gilwell Park are today emulated in every part of the world and have attracted the most senior Scout leaders from different countries, from early times to the present day. The site itself is now enhanced by many structures and buildings of significance to the Scouting world, including signposts giving directions to every World Scout Jamboree. Many former Scouts have deposited their memoirs and log books at Gilwell Park for safe-keeping

and future use, and Gilwell Park now houses the entire archives of The British Scout Association.

The White House

Gilwell's central feature is a country manor house whose origins go back to Tudor times. Before the Reformation the land had belonged to Waltham Abbey, but on the dissolution of the monasteries it was given to Sir Anthony Denny, a member of Henry VIII's circle of friends and advisers. Denny built a hunting lodge, from which vantage point guests could participate in hunting parties in Epping Forest. In 1771 the property was bought by Leonard Tresilian, who built a fine country manor house, which was passed to his daughter, Margaret, on her marriage to William Bassett Chinnery. They and their three children made the house their family home.

The White House, timber-framed with external slate cladding, is a listed building. It was extensively restored in 1994–5 to become a hotel and conference centre, and a

Above: Gilwell Hall, now known as the White House, shortly after its purchase for Scouting in 1919. It had been empty for many years previously.

modern office block was added in 2000 to accommodate the staff of the UK Scout Association. Today, the whole estate covers some 44 hectares (108 acres), most of which are used as a campsite and activity centre. Work is under way to raise money to improve and extend the campsite's facilities.

Among many artefacts inside the White House are nine Scout-related paintings by Ernest Carlos, done between 1910 and 1914. These often-reproduced pictures were almost as important in promoting the concept behind Scouting in the early days as was B-P's book *Scouting for Boys*.

Left: Percy Nevill, Commissioner for east London and Warden of the Scout hostel at Roland House, Stepney, is credited with the discovery of Gilwell Park.

Below: The 'Pigsty', where the first Scouts at Gilwell Park spent their first night. It has been preserved as a memorial to those 'pioneers' ever since.

B-P's vision for a training school

In 1918, as the First World War was coming to a close, Baden-Powell expressed his wish to establish a training school for leaders and to provide a campsite for Scouts from east London. William de Bois Maclaren, a wealthy Scottish businessman and District Commissioner for Roseneath, had offered to pay for such a site if one could be found.

P. B. Nevill, Commissioner for east London and the Warden of Roland House, was charged by B-P with finding such a site. He later wrote:

> The entries in my diary show that Maclaren dined with me at Roland House on 29 November 1918. This was at the request of B-P who sent him to me as he wanted to give a camping ground for the boys of East London. He said 'you find what you want and I will buy it'. I told him that what I wanted was a site adjoining Epping or Hainault Forest and I spent every available weekend on my motorbike touring the area trying to find somewhere. The small committee that had been set up viewed one or two sites suggested by agents.

Gilwell rediscovered

Thanks to a tip from John Gayfer, a local assistant Scout Leader and a birdwatching enthusiast, Gilwell Park was discovered. At the time it was an overgrown and derelict estate of some 22 hectares (55 acres), and no one had lived there for over 15 years. Its last owner, William Gibbs, a Victorian scientist (who created Gibbs toothpaste), had died in 1900, but some of his family had continued to live in other properties on the estate for some years afterwards. Nevill continued: 'I went to Gilwell on Saturday, 8 March 1919. I did not know the extent of the estate at the time but I found the old notice board advertising its sale on the ground behind a hedge and from this I managed to get the agent's name.'

A delighted B-P

B-P was on a lecture tour in the USA and he was sent a telegram advising him of the discovery. He cabled back to tell Nevill to go ahead with the purchase if he thought the place was right, and as soon as he returned, B-P

went to see it for himself. His secretary, Eileen Wade, accompanied him and recalled in her autobiography how, despite the pouring rain, his face lit up when he realized that his dream of a home for Scouting, where his vision could be lived out, was to become a reality at last.

The first Scouts at Gilwell Park

Negotiations to purchase the estate began, and by Easter weekend 1919 things had gone far enough for work to commence on clearing up the place. On the Thursday before Easter a small group of Nevill's East London Rovers became the first Scout campers at Gilwell. Arriving in the pouring rain, they spent their first night sleeping inside an old wooden gardener's shed, now known as the Pigsty and preserved as a monument to these 'pioneers'.

The opening ceremony

The eventual purchase price was £7,000, and Maclaren made an additional donation to help restore the White House. The official opening, delayed by a week because there was a large peace rally in London, was held on 26 July 1919 and included a rally of 700 Scouts. Maclaren's wife cut ribbons in the Scout colours of green and yellow, and Baden-Powell presented Maclaren with the Movement's highest award for good service, the Silver Wolf.

Although Gilwell was never Baden-Powell's home, the place meant a great deal to him, and he visited there frequently, camping or sleeping in a caravan. It was where his great vision of Scouting was lived daily, and it became the 'home of Scouting'. When he was offered a barony in 1929, B-P chose as his title Lord Baden-Powell of Gilwell.

Right: Baden-Powell's own Wood Badge beads, made from six original beads, alongside a necklace replica.

Right: Baden-Powell's own Wood Badge beads, made from six original beads, alongside a necklace replica.

Below: The participants in the first Wood Badge course held at Gilwell in September 1919. Seated on B-P's right is Captain Frank Gidney, the first Camp Chief.

⚜ Gilwell training – the Wood Badge

When Baden-Powell was working on the first leader training programme, he needed a badge or insignia of some kind to indicate to others the highest level of training achievement. He referred, in the end, to a necklace in his own possession, dating from his time in the Ashanti in 1888 (see page 18). The Zulu necklace, over 3 metres (3 yards) long and made from beads of acacia yellow wood, was a badge awarded to great chieftains and the bravest warriors, and there might be thousands of beads in the necklaces given to the highest-ranking officials. Baden-Powell's necklace had once belonged to Chief Dinizulu, and now he had a further use for it.

He took two of the original beads and strung them on a leather thong given to him at Mafeking to create the Wood Badge. These original wooden beads were then used as a template for beads made in beech wood, often by hand at Gilwell in the early days. The two beads represented the individual's achievement of the required standards in both practical and theoretical aspects of training.

There have been some variations in the manner in which these beads were worn – in a buttonhole or on the hat brim – and in the number of beads awarded, but nowadays two are normally worn proudly on a thong necklace placed over the head and twisted round the tails of the neckerchief.

All those who have been awarded their Wood Badge become honorary members of the 1st Gilwell Park Scout Group and are entitled to attend an annual meeting at Gilwell Park to be reunited with their fellow leaders and course attendees.

The first World Scout Jamboree

The event that took place at Olympia, London, in 1920 is referred to as the first World Scout Jamboree, but it bore little similarity to those that were to follow. Instead, it was a great indoor exhibition, intended to give the general public the opportunity of seeing for themselves the meaning and fun of Scouting.

Scout rallies were already being held in Britain, but Baden-Powell wanted to hold an international event in June 1918 to mark the Movement's tenth anniversary, as long as the war was over. The objective, he wrote, was:

To make our ideals and methods more widely known abroad; to promote the spirit of brotherhood among the rising generation throughout the world, thereby giving the spirit that is necessary to make the League of Nations a living force; to inculcate in a practical way the fundamentals of good and happy citizenship.

He also discussed the proposed programme: 'exhibition of articles made by Scouts; exhibition of equipment, literature, etc.; displays and demonstrations of Scouting activities to educate the general public; competitions in Scoutcraft'.

Although it was intended to be an international event, inviting Scouts from overseas was an afterthought. In his monthly column in *Headquarters Gazette* in July 1920 he added:

It is to mark the restoration of Peace, to render homage to the Scouts who have fallen [during the First World War], and to inaugurate the era of reconstruction and better world relations all round. The occasion would be incomplete if we did not invite our brother Scouts from overseas, not only those who are our close allies but those who remained neutral and even those who were for the time being our enemies, where they exist.

Planning and preparation

The biggest problem was accommodation. Those Scouts taking part in performances would sleep at Olympia, but finding a suitable campsite for the rest within reach of the exhibition hall was not easy for the London Scout Council, which was given this responsibility. More than 15 sites were visited, but there were insurmountable difficulties in every case. Eventually, permission was obtained to use the Old Deer Park at Richmond, and a camp was set up to take 3,000 Scouts.

Olympia was an ideal venue – it had a large arena for displays and side halls for small exhibitions – but hiring it for three weeks was expensive, and it was anticipated that it would require an audience of at least 180,000 in the course of the nine-day show to cover the costs.

The floor of the great hall was covered with 30 cm (12 in) of earth so that tents could be pitched. In addition to showing objects made by Scouts, such as toys, rugs and walking sticks, there would be working models of steam engines and aeroplanes. One part of the building was given over to a zoo, which included a lioness cub

⚜ Countries represented at the first World Scout Jamboree

Australia	Luxembourg
Belgium	Malaya
Ceylon	Malta
Chile	the Netherlands
China	New Zealand
Czechoslovakia	Norway
Denmark	Portugal
England	Romania
Estonia	Scotland
France	Serbia
Gibraltar	Siam
Greece	South Africa
India	Spain
Ireland	Sweden
Italy	Switzerland
Jamaica	USA
Japan	Wales

from Rhodesia, an alligator brought over from Florida, a baby crocodile from Jamaica, monkeys from South Africa, a baby elephant, a camel and other smaller animals and birds.

Competitions were planned for stamp collections, scrapbooks and bugle playing, and throughout the jamboree there were to be displays of all kinds – boxing, wrestling, dancing and physical training – as well as showing how Scouts would deal with accidents and natural disasters.

Above: The word 'jamboree' already existed as American slang for a 'noisy revel, a carousel or a spree'. When asked why he chose it, B-P said: 'What else could you call it?'

Right: The main arena at Olympia during one of the pageants held as part of the first World Scout Jamboree.

The event

The jamboree was officially opened on Friday, 31 July 1920. When the Grand Procession of Nations took place the following day, there were 15,000 people present to witness the pageant of colour.

By Monday the weather had changed for the worse, and torrential rain left parts of the campsite at Richmond under water. Olympia, on the other hand, was flooded with people – 14,000 on this day alone.

One popular feature of the programme was a novel long-distance dispatch-carrying competition. Eight routes were selected with the purpose of encouraging Scouts to carry written messages over long distances by means of relays. Five of the journeys were known as the Giant's routes – from the north and south-west of England and from Wales – and three others, the Pilgrim's routes, were from the south and east of England.

The idea was that each Scout should go no more than a few miles from home, but because of school holidays and Troop summer camps, the Scouts who carried the dispatches had to go longer distances, sometimes up to 16 kilometres (10 miles) from home. The Scouts were not

⚜ World Jamborees

Date	Venue
1920	London, UK
1924	Ermelunden, Denmark
1929	Birkenhead, UK
1933	Godollo, Hungary
1937	Vogelenzang, the Netherlands
1947	Moisson, France
1951	Bad Ischl, Austria
1955	Niagara-on-the Lake, Canada
1957	Sutton Coldfield, UK
1959	Laguna, Philippines
1963	Marathon, Greece
1967	Farragut State Park, USA
1971	Asagiri Heights, Japan
1975	Lillehammer, Norway
1979	World Scout Jamboree Year*
1983	Kananaskis, Canada
1987	Sydney, Australia
1991	Mount Sorak National Park, South Korea
1995	Flevoland, the Netherlands
1998–9	Picarquin, Chile
2002–3	Sattahip, Thailand
2007	Chelmsford, UK

* The 15th World Scout Jamboree was scheduled to be held in Iran in 1979. However, the Shah of Iran was toppled in a coup in that year, and the event was cancelled. The year was designated World Scout Jamboree Year, and at short notice a series of events was organized in different parts of the world so that no one would miss out on an international experience.

allowed to accept lifts, and much of the journey was done in pouring rain.

Another event was the long-distance ride in which teams of three Scouts had to start from a point over 160 kilometres (100 miles) from Olympia and carry all their food, utensils and sleeping equipment on their bicycles. They were also required to take 48 hours over the route, camp for two nights and make a log of the journey.

One of the exhibitions was on woodcraft, with hike tents and equipment, rafts and other outdoor Scouting objects. At the time these were novel items to most people, but they have long since become part of normal Scouting practice.

As the days passed the significance of the jamboree became clear. What had started off as a Scout rally had developed into a demonstration of international goodwill. The Scout Movement had come into its own, and the public recognized it for what it was meant to be – a new brotherhood that knew no boundaries of race, creed or colour. The national press gave unprecedented coverage to the jamboree, which attracted more spectators than the building could cope with, and many had to be turned away.

On the last evening, 7 August, Baden-Powell was acclaimed as Chief Scout of the World in what must have been an electrifying atmosphere. After a rousing speech, the 'Last Post' was sounded in memory of those Scouts

who had fallen in the war. There was then a two-minute silence before 'Auld Lang Syne' was sung, after which Baden-Powell was lifted up, shoulder high, and carried across the arena to great cheers.

After the jamboree

The first World Scout Jamboree came to a rousing end, but there were lessons to be learned for the future. An indoor exhibition limits the activities that can be carried out and prevents a full demonstration of genuine outdoor Scouting. As a result, all subsequent jamborees have been held in camps. It was noted, too, that the public is chiefly attracted by the happiness of the participants rather than by spectacular displays and that, above all, a jamboree is a manifestation of friendship between young people of many nations. The more this aspect could be stressed, the more successful the jamborees would be.

One result of the jamboree was the establishment of the International Conference (or the World Scout Conference as it later became). Two days before the jamboree opened a meeting was held at which it was decided that an international organization should be set up with an International Conference as the governing body, meeting every two years. A gift from an American, F. Peabody, enabled an office to be set up, initially at the UK Scout Headquarters in Buckingham Palace Road, London, and one of its first actions was to publish *Jamboree*, a quarterly magazine about world Scouting.

Another result of the jamboree was the deficit, which left the Movement almost bankrupt. What had been a potential goldmine had turned into a financial crisis. The number of Scouts also declined in the following year, although the number of leaders increased. However, these factors did not deter Baden-Powell from pressing ahead with plans for similar and more ambitious events.

⚜ The final speech

Brother Scouts, I ask you to make a solemn choice. Differences exist between the peoples of the world in thought and sentiment, just as they do in language and physique. The war has taught us that if one nation tries to impose its particular will upon others, cruel reaction is bound to follow. The jamboree has taught us that if we exercise mutual forbearance and give and take, then there is sympathy and harmony. If it be your will, let us go forth from here fully determined that we will develop among ourselves and our boys that comradeship, through the world-wide spirit of the Scout Brotherhood, so that we may help to develop peace and happiness in the world and good will among men. Brother Scouts, answer me. Will you join me in this endeavour?

Baden-Powell's speech at the close of the first World Scout Jamboree, Olympia, London, 7 August 1920.

Above right: As at all subsequent events, there was a newspaper, *The Daily Scout*, seen here with some jamboree name tags, an invitation card and a plaque.

Above left and left: Around the main arena at Olympia were numerous exhibitions where Scouts showed off the things they had made, while others could try out their skills.

Scouting for Boys was written primarily for boys between 11 and 14 years of age, and younger boys were catered for by the introduction of Wolf Cubs. The questions now were how to retain more boys in the Movement once they had left school and how to find a place for those who did remain as they grew through their teenage years.

Rover Scouts

In September 1918 *Headquarters Gazette* reported that a new section must cater for the 'returning heroes'. Senior Scouts, an existing and rather unpopular scheme, was dropped and replaced by Rovers, a word that suggested adventure and freedom. By November 1919 the Rover Scout section was firmly established, as Baden-Powell wrote:

The Rover stage is the third progressive step in the education of the Boy Scout. But you can't hold a lad without giving him some definite objectives and activities. So we offer Service.
1. Service to self, career, health
2. Service to the Scout Movement
3. Service to the Community.

According to B-P, service was the means by which a Rover Scout fulfilled his promise of duty to God. Thus the concept of 'Brotherhood and Service' became the Rover Scouts' motto. Other new words and terms were coined as the section developed. Rover Patrols became known as Crews, and the leader was a Rover Mate. Finally, a gathering of Rovers from different places was called a moot, an Anglo-Saxon word for an assembly that appealed to Baden-Powell.

By choosing terms such as 'Squire', 'Vigils' and 'Quest', Baden-Powell helped construct a symbolic framework for the Rovers that was based on Arthurian legend. The legends of King Arthur and his Knights of the Round Table provided a rich vein of popular symbolism. Scout shops began to sell small bronze replicas of a statue that had been sculpted by Baden-Powell himself – that of a kneeling knight offering up his sword in an act of self-dedication.

Below: A new Rover spending a night in prayer in the chapel at Roland House, a Scout hostel in Stepney, east London, before his initiation into a Rover Crew.

Rovering to Success

B-P's book for Rover Scouts, *Rovering to Success*, was first published in 1922. It became another bestseller, offering advice on a range of topics, and it was so successful that he received letters from parents asking for advice on the problems they were having with their teenagers. There was also a magazine, *Rover World*.

The Chief Scout believed that Rovers Scouts were 'a brotherhood of the Open Air and Service. They are hikers on the Open Road and Campers of the Wood.' Their uniform was identical to that of the Scouts, but they had their own badges, red garter tabs and epaulettes, and a thumb-stick instead of the Scout stave.

A Rover's duty

After an elaborate initiation ceremony, involving a knight mentor and a St George's Cross flag, the Rover Scout could embark on his quest, like Arthur's knights. There were quests for truth, world Scouting, Rover errantry, younger sibling, beauty, kindness to animals, conscience, happiness, personal efficiency and the spiritual.

The idea of quests inspired Rover Scouts to undertake community service projects. Some crews specialized in first aid or voluntary work in local hospitals. Rovers in Leyton, east London, ran an early type of Citizens' Advice Bureau, while in other places they looked after young people on probation.

Rover Scouting had few rules to start with, as its members did not need or want to be 'ordered about'. But with no clear ground rules diversity became increasingly apparent. Eventually, it was decided in October 1921 that the minimum age for Rovers should be 17 and that the section's objective was to retain older Scouts with a view to their becoming leaders. As Baden-Powell put it in 1928: 'Rover Scouting is a preparation for life, and also a pursuit for life.'

The first Rover moot

Rovers had their own versions of the World Scout Jamboree, and the first World Scout Moot was held in 1931 at the International Scout Chalet at Kandersteg, Switzerland, which had opened some eight years previously. It was attended by Rover Scouts from 22 countries. Baden-Powell was present for both this and the second moot in 1935, when he expressed the hope that the moots would generate enough goodwill to avoid future conflict among nations, a hope that would be shattered just a few years later.

Rovers and the Second World War

The Second World War caused considerable difficulties to Scouting, especially to Rover Scouts. They were not only among the first to be called up, but also suffered the greatest loss of life. Many Crews were suspended for the duration of the war and some never reopened. In Britain the number of Rovers slumped from a pre-war high of 38,000 members to 7,291 in 1945.

An end and new beginning

In the 1950s the age range for Rovers was changed to between 17½ and 24 years, and a new training scheme was introduced. However, the new ideas were not warmly welcomed. In 1966–7 the Rover Scout section ceased to be – at least in Britain. In its place came Venture Scouts, a section for those aged between 16 and 21, while those over 21 could join the B-P Scout Guild (renamed in 1976 as the Scout Fellowship). In turn, Venture Scouting was replaced in 2002 by Explorer Scouts, aged between 14 and 18 years, and the Scout Network, for those between 18 and 25 years, both of which are growing in numbers.

Rover Scouting continues to flourish in many countries, however, giving valuable service to Scouting and the wider community.

Below: Over 2,600 Rover Scouts from 22 countries attended the first World Scout Moot in 1931. It was held in the grounds of the International Scout Chalet at Kandersteg, Switzerland.

⚜ Rover Scouts Moots

Date	Venue
1931	Kandersteg, Switzerland
1935	Ingaro, Sweden
1939	Monzie, Scotland
1949	Skjak, Norway
1953	Kandersteg, Switzerland
1957	Sutton Coldfield, UK
1961	Melbourne, Australia
1990–91	Melbourne, Australia
1992	Kandersteg, Switzerland
1996	Ransäter, Sweden
2000	Mexico City, Mexico
2004	Hüalien, Taiwan
2008	Mozambique (planned)

Left: In his travels as Chief Scout of the World Baden-Powell met and encouraged the growth and development of Scouting among all people.

B-P's travels

In the course of promoting Scouting, Baden-Powell travelled thousands of miles around the world, and after his appointment as Chief Scout of the World in 1920 he took his responsibilities even more seriously.

Baden-Powell's first trip abroad after the experimental camp on Brownsea Island was intended to be a holiday. He had not had a break for two years and wanted to escape from the English winter weather, but his funds were low, so he managed to persuade a shipping company to give him a free ticket to South America in return for writing about the trip in *The Graphic* magazine. His choice of destination was decided upon while he was at Southampton docks waiting to see his old regiment return from India: he smelled the aroma of coffee and spices in a shipment from Brazil. He sailed in February 1909 to Rio de Janeiro and on to Buenos Aires, where, much to his embarrassment, he was fêted as the hero of Mafeking by the British colony and the Argentine government.

Onwards to Chile

When it became known that B-P also wanted to go to Chile, he was given a free railway ticket and his own carriage. He was met by the head of the railway company with horses and mules and escorted over the Andes, where he was received as warmly as he had been in Argentina. He stayed for three days and addressed a meeting of Chilean educators and boys about Scouting. When he left for home the town's population turned out to see him off, and two bands played 'God Save the King' for half an hour without stopping. Given the warmth of the welcome and his fame, it is not surprising that later that year Chile became the first country outside Britain and British territories to start Scouting.

Travels within the empire

Baden-Powell began to receive invitations from different parts of the world to give lectures and to inspect Scouts. The first invitation he accepted from within the British Empire was from Canada, and the first invitation from a non-empire country was from the United States of America, which he covered in a single trip in 1910. For

Denmark, the Netherlands and Belgium as he travelled back home. Everywhere hundreds of Scouts turned out to meet him. On his return he noted in *Headquarters Gazette* that there was a need for some form of international alliance – it would come in 1920 with the first World Scout Conference – and he established an international office at Scout headquarters.

Another lengthy lecture tour of the USA followed in 1912, and on the outward journey he met and fell in love with Olave St Clair Soames, who was to be his wife within a few months. On the return leg he visited Japan, China and the Philippines and travelled on to Australia and New Zealand for a seven-week tour. If the reception he received here was enthusiastic, on his next stop, in South Africa, it was overwhelming. Everywhere he went he was welcomed by large crowds, civic authorities and, of course, Scouts.

War and diplomacy

Apart from a belated honeymoon in 1913 with Olave to Algeria, foreign travel became almost impossible with the outbreak of the First World War and the birth of their three children, although they did travel to France (see page 53). After the success of the first World Scout Jamboree and now with the title Chief Scout of the World, Baden-Powell was able to visit Scouts all over the world and sort out international issues.

the first part of the journey he was accompanied by 16 British Scouts, who had won the trip as a prize in a competition in *The Scout*, which had been part of an initiative to encourage young people to emigrate to Canada. He stayed longer than planned, because he could not resist the opportunity to spend a week camping and fishing in the Canadian wilderness north-west of Ontario. He then moved on to the USA, where he was warmly welcomed by the leaders of the newly formed Boy Scouts of America.

Meeting the tsar

At the end of 1910 the Russian minister of war invited him to St Petersburg, and he was taken to meet Tsar Nicholas II at Tsarskoe Selo. It was a warm and informal meeting, in which the tsar, speaking in English, asked about Scouting. He had read *Scouting for Boys* and had arranged for it to be translated into Russian, and his son and heir was a Scout. A school in south Russia had taken up Scouting, and the tsar arranged for some of the boys to be brought to Tsarskoe Selo to meet Baden-Powell, because he hoped that other schools would adopt Scouting. In Moscow Baden-Powell learned more about the expansion of the Movement in Russia from the Russian Boy Scouts committee. In that city alone there were already of 3,000 members.

Scouting in Scandinavia

A working holiday in Norway in 1911 allowed B-P to see something of Scouting in that country and in Sweden,

Above: Baden-Powell prepares for an elephant ride during a visit to India in 1937. This was one of his final trips abroad before his retirement from public life.

Right: Tribal chieftans met with Baden-Powell in Canada in 1923 and called him 'Chief Spotted Eagle'.

One such visit was to India in 1921, where Scouting existed for British-born and Anglo-Indian boys only. The Indian government had expressly forbidden Indian boys from joining the Scouts, fearing that they might be trained to become revolutionaries. As a result, a number of unofficial organizations had sprung up. After several meetings with government and Scout officials, agreement was reached to blend British and Indian Scouting into a single association.

The second World Scout Jamboree

In 1924 Olave and B-P went to Denmark for the second World Scout Jamboree, and they took their son, Peter, with them on his first trip abroad. Attended by Scouts from over 35 different countries, this event was noted for the hospitality offered by the Danes. Visiting Scouts were hosted by Danish families for a further week and for the large number of competitions of one sort or another

(something that was never repeated). One of the competitions – for dancing – was won by the British contingent, which received the magnificent silver trophy presented by *Sontag*, a Danish magazine. Among many personal gifts to Baden-Powell was a statue of a Scout from the Chile contingent.

Meeting the president

During another trip to the USA in 1926 Baden-Powell and Olave were entertained at the White House by President Calvin Coolidge, and B-P received the first Silver Buffalo, the Boy Scouts of America's highest award for good service.

A six-month trip to South Africa with the entire family followed at the end of the same year. It was his ninth visit to the country. When he first came in 1896 it was to fight; now, as Chief Scout of the World, it was to help Scouts realize their place as part of a peaceful

Above: A gift to Baden-Powell from the Scouts of Chile in 1924.

worldwide family and the importance of Dutch and British cooperation in the training and support of the country's youth.

As well as participating at the World Scout Jamborees and World Scout Conferences, Baden-Powell also attended the world moots, gatherings for Rover Scouts. The first was held in 1931 at Kandersteg, Switzerland, a chalet and grounds that had been bought for world Scouting in 1923. Some 2,600 Rover Scouts from 22 countries, including B-P's son, Peter, himself now a Rover Scout, took part, helping to further the understanding of the worldwide Scout family.

Promoting unity

In 1933 Baden-Powell visited Italy to try to solve two important problems. There was talk in some countries of Roman Catholic Scouts breaking away from established national associations and forming their own groups. B-P believed that Scouting overcame all religious barriers, and he even had an audience with Pope Pius XI in the Vatican, during which the pope expressed his full support for the Movement and its work. Papal endorsement had the required effect in a number of European countries, although in Canada Catholic Scouts went on to form a separate association, although with Baden-Powell's acceptance.

While he was in Rome he also met the Italian dictator, Benito Mussolini, and discussed youth training with him. The Italian fascists' own youth wing, the Balilla, had replaced Scouting since 1927, and he was interested to see what was happening. The Balilla's programme was similar to Scouting but was obligatory, nationalistic and purely physical. There was no spiritual balance, and it aimed to develop mass cohesion instead of individual character.

The goodwill cruises

Another opportunity to visit more of the worldwide Scout family came later in the year with a goodwill cruise to the Baltic countries in the *Calgaric*, a chartered ship. This cruise arose from an idea of Olave's as a means of bringing British leaders into personal contact with their counterparts in other countries. But it did much more than that. Accompanied by 620 Guiders and Scouters, the Chief Scout and the World Chief Guide spent 18 days visiting and encouraging the Scouts and Guides in the Netherlands, Norway, Sweden, Finland, Poland, Latvia, Lithuania and Estonia. Their presence gave new impetus to the Movements in those countries and caused some world leaders, previously not committed, to take a public stand behind the two Movements. In each country they visited on the cruise B-P and Olave were honoured and received by presidents and prime ministers.

The event was so successful that a second cruise, this time to the western Mediterranean, took place in 1934 on the *Adriatic*, calling at Malta, Gibraltar, France, Algeria and Portugal.

A third and final cruise on the *Orduna* in 1938 visited Iceland, Norway, Denmark and Belgium. But by now

Above: Baden-Powell and Olave with their children (from left to right, Heather, Peter and Betty) during the *Calgaric* cruise in 1933.

Far left: For over 30 years Baden-Powell travelled widely. Here, the Scouts of the world meet the Chief Scout of the World.

Baden-Powell was a tired, sick man, and his days of world travel were nearly over. He didn't leave the ship when it docked, instead greeting the assembled crowds from the deck or a cabin window. A final visit to India in 1937 for the first All-India Jamboree had convinced him that the time had come for him to abandon his active role in the Movement at the earliest opportunity.

Passing on

He was pleased to see the Scout Associations in South Africa and India, at that time still dominions of Britain, recognized by World Scouting and achieving their independence. In 1937 he was awarded the Wateler Peace Prize by the board of the Carnegie Institute for his services to world peace and promoting international goodwill through the Scout Movement. Now that Scouting was in good shape internationally and in good hands, and now that his own children were grown up, he could rest.

Coming of age and the 1929 Jamboree

Scouting reached its 21st birthday in 1928, a milestone traditionally seen as a coming of age. During this short period it had grown from its small beginnings of 20 boys on Brownsea Island to become a worldwide movement with some two million members.

Instead of marking the anniversary in 1928, it was decided to wait a year and celebrate the 21st anniversary of the publication of *Scouting for Boys*, the book on which the Scout Movement had been built and by which it had spread. Such an anniversary required a special celebration, so it was planned to hold the third World Scout Jamboree in that year and in the country where Scouting began.

Arrowe Park is chosen

The question of a suitable venue was quickly settled when the mayor of Birkenhead, near Liverpool, offered the use of Arrowe Park. It was a site of 182 hectares (450 acres), with undulating woods, a hall for meetings and receptions, good transport facilities and a nearby port. By happy chance the very name of the place gave Baden-Powell an idea of a symbol for the jamboree: a Golden Arrow. More than 65 countries were represented and over 30,000 Scouts and 320,000 visitors

took part, despite the heavy rain and gales that caused the site to become extremely muddy. The French camp suffered most, but their model of the Eiffel Tower made out of Scout staffs rose above it majestically. The mud and rain strengthened rather than dampened the spirits of those present.

The opening ceremony

The Duke of Connaught, the President of the Scouts in Britain, performed the official opening on 31 July 1929. As a prelude to the ceremony Baden-Powell blew a blast on the kudu horn that he had used at the Brownsea camp in 1907 and on other major occasions. In a speech later he joked about the poor weather and noted that whenever he went to a jamboree it rained: 'I don't like you all to feel too happy so I turned on the rain. You see, any ass can be a Scout on a fine day, but the thing is to make the best of conditions on a bad day.'

Above: The poor weather for much of the jamboree did not dampen the enthusiasm of the participants from more than 65 countries.

Far left: Despite the rain, which caused the site to become very muddy, a parade of flags by the world Scouts took place before an act of worship.

Below: These girls hitch a lift on a trek cart at the 1929 Jamboree site at Arrowe Park.

'All the world in miniature'

There was then a march past of the Scouts present with their flags, the youth of the world, representing its many races and colours. As one journalist wrote:

There were South Africans in grey shirts, Arabs from Palestine, Morocco and Algeria in white robes, Indians in green turbans, boys from the Gold Coast and Nigeria, natives from Jamaica, Kenya, Barbados, Ceylon and other far countries of the British Empire. Latin America was there with splendid contingents from Brazil and Chile. The old countries of Europe – Spain, France, the Netherlands, Denmark, Norway, Germany – had sent their young people, and new nations like Czechoslovakia, Estonia, Latvia and Lithuania were strongly represented. I saw the glory and splendour of the world's boyhood in that English park – all the world in miniature – and tried to peer into the unknown future toward which they go, so keen ... so gallant ... without fear.

A grey, lean old man, with a tanned, leathery face and twinkling eyes under his Scout's hat, watched this living pageant of an idea that had come into his head. The world is moved by ideas and this one of Baden-Powell's has in it the eternal spirit of boyhood and some touch of magic which is helping to exorcise old ghosts and demons and to draw the human family closer together in comradeship and service.

As I write, I still hear the storms of cheers which are rising up to the Chief Scout as the homage of the young knights of all nations to the veteran who knew their secret, their passwords, and the game of life. Tonight, round the campfires, they will sing their national songs and dance their old folk dances. It is a fairy-tale come true.

Above: Baden-Powell and the Prince of Wales (on his left) at the gateway constructed by Hungarian Scouts during the 1929 Jamboree.

Left: The official document with the king's seal conferring the title Lord Baden-Powell upon the founder of the Scout and Guide Movements.

Bringing nations together

The British leaders of the world's different religious faiths visited to conduct acts of worship and to meet together, causing one of them, Cardinal Bourne, the Catholic Archbishop of Westminster, to declare that at this time only Scouting could bring about such a remarkable achievement.

There were various ceremonies and displays in the arena every afternoon. So, for example, there was a Wolf Cub rally; the French enacted scenes from the life of St Joan of Arc; the Belgians staged the story of St George and the dragon; and the Boy Scouts of America told the story of Native Americans and life on the prairies. One of the more unusual ceremonies was when the University of Liverpool awarded an honorary degree of Doctor of Laws to Baden-Powell.

Above: The presentation to Baden-Powell of a Rolls-Royce motorcar (nicknamed 'Jam Roll') and a caravan (nicknamed 'Eccles') from the Scouts of the world.

News from the palace

The Prince of Wales (later King Edward VIII) attended in his capacity as Chief Scout of Wales. He arrived on 1 August, staying for several days, and in a speech to the entire jamboree he was able to bring a message from his father, George V, announcing that to mark this great event in Scouting's history Baden-Powell was to be made a baron. The news was received with enthusiastic cheers. Initially Baden-Powell wanted to refuse the honour, but he was persuaded to accept it as a recognition of the Movement's work as well as of his own achievements. He consulted with the World Scout Committee about the precise title he should adopt and, after hearing their advice and considering alternatives, chose to be Lord Baden-Powell of Gilwell, in recognition of how much Gilwell Park meant to him and to the Movement.

'Just a pair of braces'

In order to mark Scouting's 21st birthday it had previously been decided to invite Scouts to contribute to a collection to buy a present for Baden-Powell. When Olave had asked if there was anything he needed, he had replied 'a pair of braces' to hold his trousers up. However, the money raised was such that on 10 August, after an arena display, Baden-Powell was given a Rolls-Royce motorcar (which they nicknamed 'Jam Roll', a play on the words jamboree and Rolls-Royce), a caravan (named 'Eccles', after the caravan's manufacturers), a cheque for £2,800 and an oil painting of Baden-Powell by David Jaggar. Much to his delight, the Irish Scouts later gave him the new pair of braces that he had desired.

Ambassadors for peace

At the close of the jamboree Baden-Powell stood in the centre of the arena as Scouts formed lines like the spokes of a wheel, stretching away from their founder, who represented the hub of a great wheel. 'Here is buried the hatchet of war, of enmity, of bad feeling, which I now bury in Arrowe,' he said as he buried an axe. Then, as large, wooden, gold-coloured arrows were handed out down the lines of Scouts to the heads of the international contingents, he added:

From all corners of the world you come to the call of brotherhood and to Arrowe. Now I send you forth to your homeland, bearing the sign of peace and good will and fellowship to all your fellow men. From now on the symbol of peace and good will is the golden arrow. Carry that arrow on and on, so that all may know of the brotherhood of men.

I want you to go back from here to your countries in different parts of the world with a new idea in your mind of having brothers in every country. You have seen them and you know them now, personally. I want you to remember the good points in us and forget the bad ones.

Tell your friends in your own countries all the good you can about us, so that we can all think better of one another. Go forth from here as ambassadors of good will and friendship.

In 1929 the Rover Scouts of Holborn in London staged a one-night revue, written and produced by an anonymous 'Holborn Rover', entitled *Good Turns*. Similar productions followed over the next two years, and, by the third year, the shows had gained a considerable reputation. In 1932 Admiral Phillpotts, the County Commissioner for London, suggested to the 'Holborn Rover' that a larger production, sponsored by the London Scout Council, might be put on that autumn in a West End theatre to raise money for a swimming pool at Downe Scout campsite in Kent. The idea was accepted.

A cast of 120

Within an hour of the proposal being made, a programme had been hastily compiled, and within the next few days a cast of 120 people had been recruited. The Holborn Rover Scouts were to carry the main burden, and they would be assisted by the 4th Harrow Rovers. At the first rehearsal they were told that everyone who took part did so on an equal basis, and that anyone with lines or a song was just fortunate. This remains the tradition today, and although 'stars' may emerge they join in with the chorus as the occasion demands.

One night during rehearsals the cast came together after a break, and the producer asked, 'Are they all back?' to which a piping voice answered, 'Aye, aye, Skip, the gang's all 'ere.' A young cockney Scout had given the

The Gang Show captures something of the unique spirit of Scouting: it is an ensemble performance of verve, enthusiasm and teamwork. After Baden-Powell saw a production he declared, 'It must go on and on.'

The Gang Show

Above: Before his
involvement and
success with Gang
Shows, Ralph Reader
had four productions
playing on Broadway
at the same time.

Left: An original score
in Reader's own hand,
along with some of the
music and programmes
for many of the shows
that played in London
theatres.

Far left: Some of those
who took part in Gang
Shows over the years
went on to become
famous entertainers in
their own right.

first West End show its title, and it was the one that gave
the name to all Gang Shows ever since.

For *The Gang's All Here* the Scala Theatre was booked
for three performances. The challenge of having to sell
nearly 5,000 tickets for a Scout show was formidable –
some thought it would be impossible – but they went
ahead, despite many problems and unsold tickets. The
three performances were momentous evenings. Songs
such as 'Steer for the Open Sea' and 'There'll Come a
Time Some Day' were highlights, and the end of the
show brought cheers and many curtain calls. Everyone
wanted to organize another show the following year,
especially since, to their surprise, they had made a profit.

Sold-out success

A second show, *The Gang Comes Back*, was planned
for 1933, and the same theatre was booked for six
evening performances and a matinée. Every seat was
sold within a few weeks of the box office opening. The
drama critics of the national newspapers took notice,

and theatre professionals were encouraged to see it. They came out of politeness; they left asking for more seats for the following night. By the time the production finished, Gang Shows were an established part of the Scouting landscape, and Scouts outside London began to stage their own versions, using material from the London shows but with local casts.

For the next London show in 1934, every seat was sold before the opening performance.

Baden-Powell's enthusiasm for the Gang Show ensured that it would continue. He wrote, 'You have made a big success – may we have more', and later, 'I am not merely thinking of the acting, good though it was, but of the splendid teamwork of the whole lot. It must go on and on.'

The mystery writer revealed

It was not until 1935 that the identity of the Holborn Rover became public knowledge – he was Ralph Reader, Broadway star, the West End producer and an active Scout. He did not own up willingly, and becoming known for his work with Gang Shows nearly destroyed his professional career, because many of his colleagues in the theatre could not accept someone who worked with amateurs.

Nevertheless, in 1936 Reader staged *Boy Scout*, a musical pageant, at the Royal Albert Hall in London. It told the story of a boy who joined a Scout troop and of his life with his fellow Scouts, and it ended with a jamboree. With a cast of 1,200, a choir of 250, catchy music and colourful costumes and scenery, it became a spectacle that played to packed houses for three performances. It was revived the following year and was even more successful.

In time he would produce more than 150 other events at the Royal Albert Hall, including at the British Legion Festival of Remembrance, but for millions, Reader would always be 'Mr Gang Show', to whom the Movement owes an enormous debt.

During the Second World War Reader joined the Royal Air Force and staged many RAF shows. Some of those who took part in his Scout or RAF shows went on to become famous in their own right, including Tony Hancock and Peter Sellers.

The London Gang Show was revived after the war and continued with a new production every year, often playing to members of the royal family.

A worldwide phenomenon

But the Gang Show concept was too exciting to be limited to Britain alone, and Gang Shows have sprung up across the Scouting world.

A scarlet scarf has become internationally accepted as the symbol of Gang Shows, along with an identifying badge in gold on the point of the scarf, which can be worn only after the production has completed three annual performances and achieved a high standard.

Today a Gang Show is being performed somewhere in the world every night of the year.

Right: The musical pageant *Boy Scout*, staged at the Royal Albert Hall in 1936 with a cast of over 1,200 performers and a choir of 250.

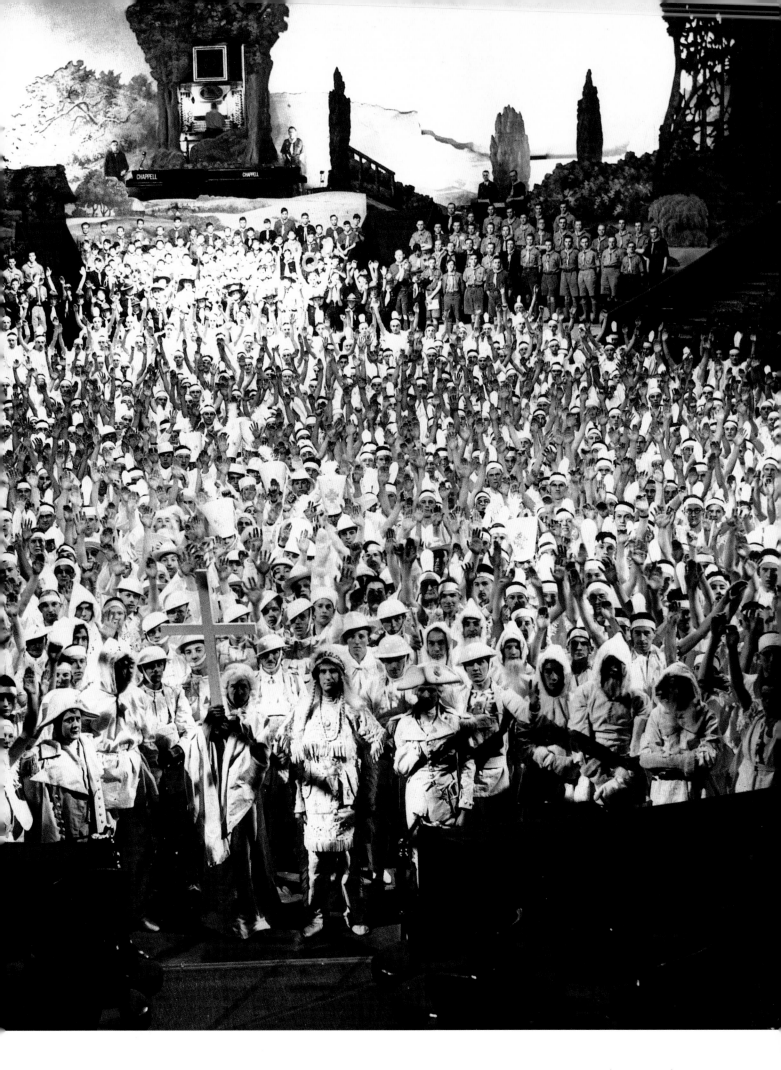

Far left: The earliest British Scout uniforms included dark green flannel shirts or jerseys as well as shorts and a staff.

Left: By the 1950s the flannel shirt or jersey had been replaced by more practical material.

Scout uniform

Scout uniform was not the first uniform that Baden-Powell had designed. His somewhat flamboyant designs for the South African Constabulary had drawn considerable attention, and several aspects were modelled by the first Scouts. However, the Scouts' uniform had to be both simple and practical, and within the reach of every pocket.

The boys at the Brownsea Island camp had worn their everyday clothing, apart from a shoulder knot of coloured ribbon to indicate their Patrol and a metal 'Scout' badge. At first, boys who already belonged to an existing youth organization or corps were told to 'dress in that uniform, but on passing the tests for a Scout given here, you wear the Scout badge, if your commanding officer allows it, in addition to any of your corps badges that you may have won'.

'Not a showy uniform'

The first edition of *Scouting for Boys* also stated that 'a scout does not use a showy uniform, because it would attract attention; but Scouts in a Patrol should, as far as possible, dress alike, especially as regards hats, or caps, and neckerchief'. Further on in his book B-P's stipulation about shorts – 'trousers cut short at the knee' – prompted a new fashion. At that time, only soldiers in hot climates wore shorts. However, it would seem that mothers up and down the land reached for their scissors in an effort to kit out their sons with the ideal Scout uniform.

A formal uniform

The uniform requirements became more detailed and the first official 'rules' were published in Britain in *Policy, Organisation and Rules* in 1910. They specified the hat, the colour of shirt, shorts and socks, and a stout staff marked in feet and inches. Several of these items had first featured in the uniform of the South African Constabulary. For instance, the hat was already in existence, known as a Boss

one seen on printed maps since 2000 BC to indicate compass directions. These brass badges were worn on the sleeve.

A metal arrowhead badge with a bar bearing the motto 'Be prepared' was given to the boys who went to Brownsea Island, and in *Scouting for Boys* Baden-Powell gave the reason for his choice of design:

The scout's badge is the arrowhead, which shows the north on a map or compass. It is the badge of the scout in the army, because he shows the way; so, too, a peace scout shows the way in doing his duty and helping others.

The World Scout Badge

Great symbolic significance is given to the World Scout Badge, which was introduced by the World Scout Conference in 1969. The three parts of the central symbol remind Scouts of their duty to God (centre), service to others (left) and obedience to the Scout Law (right), with the joining ring representing the family of Scouting bound together. The two five-pointed stars stand for truth and knowledge, with the ten points of the stars representing the points of the original Scout Law. The reef knot encircling the whole cannot be undone, no matter hard it is pulled, reminding all Scouts of the strength of world Scouting's unity and family. The badge is white, representing purity, while the purple background denotes leadership and service.

of the Plains hat – it naturally became known as a B-P hat once it was Scout uniform. Each item of uniform was meant to have a practical use.

The woggle first appeared in the early 1920s as a means of fastening the scarf, invented by Bill Shankley, a member of staff at Gilwell Park.

World uniform

The first really fundamental change to Bristish Scout uniform came in 1966, when shorts and the hat were abandoned. Another review, which sought opinions from the entire Association, took place in 2000 and resulted in the current activity-based uniform.

Throughout the world, Scouts can be recognized by the neckerchief and the World Badge. Although the uniform changes from country to country, according to climate, culture and national dress, these are the common elements. The distinctive purple badge and an often brightly coloured 'necker' are key parts of the Movement's identity.

The first uniforms worn by American Scouts and other emerging associations looked rather like First World War army uniforms, but they gradually became more diverse. A more formal uniform is usually worn during parades and on special occasions, and there are specialist variations for Scout bands and the Sea and Air branches. Fashion has also played its part in the Scout uniform story – the shorts and shirt dominated boys' fashion right up to the 1950s throughout the western world. Since then, however, the relationship has been reversed, and it has been young people who have put pressure on the Movement to move with the times. Many of the world's top fashion designers have dabbled with uniform, and the results can be seen in the richly varied uniform worn by the world's 28 million Scouts.

The Scout Badge

While he was serving in India Baden-Powell began to train his men in the arts of scouting and tracking. This training finished with a proficiency test and those who passed were allowed to call themselves scouts. Training exercises included the use of a map and compass, and Baden-Powell chose a spearhead- or arrowhead-shaped badge as an award for his new scouts, using a design not unlike the

Above: A revised British Scout uniform introduced in 1966 included long trousers and a beret. It lasted with little variations for 35 years.

Below: The present British Scout uniform, launched in 2001, is practical for today's adventurous programme, but the scarf still remains.

Grassroots Scouting

Part of the attraction of Scouting lay in the fact that it offered something for everyone, no matter who they were. The first Scout Patrols were started by the boys themselves, who then sought out older brothers, Sunday school teachers or any other adult they could find to become their leader.

In its early years people quickly saw Scouting's potential wherever they came across boys with poles and haversacks, playing games, doing errands or camping in farmer's fields. Teachers started Patrols and Troops in schools and local religious leaders began to see Scouting as a way to reach out to young people in an exciting and different way. In these formative years Scout Troops were less insular, performed more civic functions, entered local competitions and helped at many fêtes and fairs. In return for this community involvement, they were rewarded with access to private land for camps, the provision of premises for meetings or financial support for equipment. Joint activities with other youth organizations took place at first, but eventually such things as swimming galas and sports fixtures became Scout-only events.

Military or religious?

A common idea – but totally untrue – was that the Scouts were another military organization. Some people

Left: An early Scout Troop in a variety of uniforms gather for some instruction before that day's adventures, providing escape from normal routine.

Right: The concept of providing help for others has been one of the fundamental principles of Scouting from the outset.

believed that it was too military, but others thought it was not military enough and that Scouts were only playing at being soldiers and devalued the role of the army. Others argued that Scouts were pretending to be pacifists but really had other, secret motives. Similar arguments were made about the Movement's attitude to religion: it was too formal, too liberal or not religious enough, or it failed in its moral duty to instil strict religious principles. However, it was Scouting's broad appeal and flexibility that proved to be its greatest assets.

Many early Troops were sponsored and supported by their local churches, which allowed them to meet in church halls, usually in return for taking part in a Sunday service once a month or so and for doing all manner of odd tasks as and when the need arose. Other Troops took advantage of any available philanthropic help to gain their own premises, and all sorts of buildings became homes for Scouts.

Why join?

The reasons boys joined were many and varied. The uniform, the activities and badges, the responsibilities and the fact that friends had already joined played a part, but above all boys were drawn by the adventure of camping and other outdoor activities. For them and their adult leaders, Scouting was a form of escapism, a world away from life's normal routines. By day Scouts were at school, but by night they could let their imaginations run wild and be attacking an enemy fort in nearby woods, sleeping out under the stars or captaining a boat looking for pirates and buried treasure. They did not need to go into the wilds of Africa; they could find adventure on their own doorsteps. But they were also part of a team of boys of the same age who shared the same dreams.

Through training and acquiring new skills, all boys could progress from being a Tenderfoot, a raw recruit, to being a Second Class and then a First Class Scout – from a nobody to a somebody.

It was much the same for Scoutmasters, who might be holding down dull jobs in a local shop or business by day but who in their spare time were commanding their own Troops, giving orders and making the decisions.

A day-long commitment

The motto, the Scout salute, the left handshake and the uniform all help to create a ritual framework, while the

Left: Community involvement, such as mending fences for a farmer, was rewarded with fields for camping or places for the Scout Troop to meet.

Below: The same then as now – young people joined Scouting for fun activities out of doors, such as cooking a meal over an open fire.

Law and Promise provided a way of life. All Scouts had to learn and remember these two key texts and put them into practice, for, unlike in other organizations, a Scout was a Scout all day, every day. Daily good turns had to be carried out, giving rise to opportunities for displays of individual gallantry and bravery. Medals were awarded for significant acts of heroism – such as stopping a runaway horse (then a means of someone's livelihood and more common than now) or saving someone from drowning (at a time when the ability to swim was not widespread).

Rituals develop

Ceremonies of one kind or another evolved, including the formal opening or closing of the Troop meeting, the presentation of badges and the 'going up' from the Cub Pack to the Scout Troop. The most significant of these was the enrolment or investiture, when, with his complete uniform and knowledge of the Scout Law and Promise and with due ceremony, each new recruit became a Boy Scout and a member of this special 'gang' of brothers.

Although it was originally common for a Scout to be sworn in by one of his peers, it soon became the practice for this role to be carried out by the Scoutmaster. Such ceremonies were often held in a church – many leaders were clergymen – and may have involved several Scouts being enrolled together. All these factors helped to create a significant and memorable moment in a Scout's life. Large and highly colourful certificates marking this moment could be bought, as were ones to record the formation of a Troop or the award of a gallantry medal.

Getting organized

Scout Troops varied in what they did and how frequently they met. Patrol Leaders, who could be up to 17 or 18 years of age, were usually older than their Scouts. Each

Patrol of about eight boys would meet on separate nights as a Patrol and then once a week together as a Troop. Many early Patrols specialized in some activity, such as first aid or cycling, and there were also different kinds of Troops – for working boys or for schoolboys, while others were attached to institutions or businesses.

Wide games

On Saturday afternoons troops would frequently meet for sham fights, raids and to send messages. These exercises, later called wide games, were taken rather seriously and were sometimes played between different Troops or Scout Districts, at times involving anything up to 250 Scouts. For variety, visits were often arranged to telephone exchanges, printing works or the town hall. But what the Scouts enjoyed most of all – and for many the main reason they joined – was the chance to go camping.

Going to camp

Tents and the other equipment needed for camping were rather bulky, probably second-hand and had to be pushed in trek carts, a skill in its own right. Sites were found in muddy fields, water was fetched in buckets and primitive earth toilets were constructed by digging trenches. Unless the Scoutmaster had a military background, he too learned the hard way with his Scouts.

At the time camping was a relatively uncommon activity, certainly for children, and it was perceived as being risky and unhealthy, so parents needed some reassurance that it was safe. Even if their sons did not die of starvation or food poisoning, the cold damp air, many people thought, would lead them to an early grave.

Once a year most Troops would hold a big summer camp lasting a week or two. Some Scoutmasters employed a camp cook (usually ex-army) to make sure that the food was acceptable. Other camps were quite formal, with lots of drill, daily inspections and worship. But no matter what it entailed, camping was the ideal way for the Scoutmaster to get to know his Scouts and for all Scouts to appreciate the 'great outdoors', to live the dream of being pioneers or adventurers and to put into practice their skills.

It was the times like this that forged lasting friendships, created enduring memories and helped make these early years an unforgettable experience.

Below: From its small beginnings Scouting quickly was accepted by society to become as much a part of growing up as school.

Family life

Despite his busy life, Baden-Powell was a great family man. After their marriage in 1912 he and Olave lived at Ewhurst Place in Sussex until 1917, when they started to rent a 15th-century farmhouse near Horley, Surrey.

When the owner of the farmhouse was killed in the war, they found themselves looking for a new home for their growing family, and in 1918 they bought Blackacre Farm in Bentley, Hampshire. They changed its name to Pax Hill to mark the end of the war, *pax* being the Latin word for peace.

In the years that followed they had two new wings built for servants and guests, as well as a large music room, known as the Barn, where Baden-Powell displayed his souvenirs and awards, records of past achievements and gifts sent by admirers and friends. Because he suffered headaches when he slept indoors, Baden-Powell's bed was on a bedroom balcony, open to the elements all year round.

The morning routine

When he was at home B-P usually rose at about 5 a.m., a habit persisting from his army days in India and one that allowed him to do a couple of hours' work while everyone else was still asleep and he would not be interrupted by the telephone or callers. In this way he reckoned 'to get 13 months of life into each year instead of 12'.

After a cup of tea he would paint for a couple of hours until 7.30 a.m. when he would wash and dress. Then, after he and Olave had taken their pet dogs for a walk in the surrounding countryside, they would breakfast with the family and any guests who might be staying at the time.

Keeping on top of the paperwork

Baden-Powell's private secretary, Eileen Wade, who lived in a nearby cottage, usually called early to help him deal with the mountain of mail that would arrive each day. The correspondence might include a letter from a former sergeant in his regiment asking for help to get work, demands from the Girl Scouts in America for an opinion on a memorial, invitations from a magazine for an article,

Above: When he was at Pax Hill, his home for 19 years, Baden-Powell slept on the open bedroom balcony.

Above right: For relaxation and sport Baden-Powell loved salmon fishing. He also founded a local angling club.

Right: Baden-Powell's campfire blanket, decorated with badges from World Scout Jamborees and other events, along with his travel wash kit and woollen socks, complete with name tags.

appeals for suggestions for raising funds for South African Scouts and requests for drawings to be displayed in an art gallery.

An hour or two in the afternoon were spent tending the garden and exercising the dogs before tea, which was the main occasion when the family would gather each day. Even if he had a day free from meetings or visits, there were always letters to answer, articles to write or reports to read. And, of course, Olave received her own large bag of mail to deal with.

The garden at Pax Hill was another source of pleasure, and visitors often found themselves trimming hedges or pruning B-P's beloved roses. In the evening he would often show films of his tours, which he made himself and which was another favourite hobby, before retiring to bed at about 10 p.m.

A thrifty household

Baden-Powell made no money from Scouting, and he wrote frequently to supplement his army pension. But they were a family of simple needs, and even his many tours at home and overseas were not a charge on Scout funds, as he liked to be self-dependent. In the Movement's early days he did do some lecture tours, most notably in America and Australia, the proceeds of which were used to defray the costs incurred.

Baden-Powell wrote his own articles for every issue of *Headquarters Gazette* (later called *The Scouter*) and *The Scout*, compilations of which were republished in books such as *Adventures and Accidents* in 1934 and *Scouting round the World* in 1935.

Winding down

His sketchbook was his constant companion. Whatever caught his eye was recorded quickly and simply, and he

later worked some sketches into finished pieces. His other passion was fishing. When he needed to get right away from everything and everyone he would go off for a few days with his rods and tackle. Olave loved playing tennis and hockey, and she even organized her own team of family and servants to play teams from nearby villages. But apart from polo, Baden-Powell was not keen on ball games, so he needed a sport that he could enjoy alone. He only fished for sport, however, always returning what he caught to the river. He especially enjoyed salmon fishing, taking a break in Scotland and the West Country for this each year.

Visitors to Pax Hill

Guests were always welcome at Pax Hill, and they were frequent, ranging from distinguished men and women to old friends and people from Scout and Guide Headquarters. Scouters and Guiders in need of a rest would come, and in summer campers would pitch their tents in the front garden. There was no ostentation or ceremony – just a warm welcome, no matter who you were or why you had come.

Family holidays

He also enjoyed travelling, particularly with his family. After the 1929 Jamboree they would take frequent camping holidays together in the south and west of England, appreciating the beauty of the countryside and making good use of the caravan and car he had been given. Because the caravan was big enough for only one person to sleep in, he usually did so, while Olave and the children camped outside, sleeping under an awning attached to the side or in lightweight tents. They frequently visited Gilwell, particularly each September for the Gilwell Reunion, the annual gathering of the Scouting family of leaders from around the world. As father of this worldwide family, Baden-Powell addressed the hundreds of people present with a yarn or story during the traditional Saturday night campfire.

Other interests

Despite his heavy workload as Chief Scout, Baden-Powell found time to belong to other bodies and societies. Some of these were honorary, such as being president of the Camping and Caravanning Club, but others required more commitment, such as his involvement with the Mercers' Company.

The Mercers were, and still are, one of the City of London's livery guilds. Not only does the company represent people in the cloth trade, but its members also carry out a wide range of charitable activities. The Baden-Powell family had had connections with the Mercers for centuries, and in 1913 B-P was elected Master of the Mercers. This was a high honour and one that not only carried significant responsibilities but also required his attendance at committee meetings and official functions.

A close family

Baden-Powell and Olave spent as much time as they could with their children, Peter, Heather and Betty, playing with them in the garden at Pax Hill or picnicking in the nearby countryside. The children all learned to ride, causing their father much pleasure to see that they had inherited his skills on horseback. They also had a large collection of pet dogs, rabbits and pigeons. Of the three children, Heather, the tomboy of the family, was closest to her father, sharing his sense of adventure and daring. Betty, the youngest, took after her mother and was Olave's favourite. A somewhat frail boy, Peter, as the son and heir of the Chief Scout, had great pressures placed on him to live up to his father's name and reputation.

Above: Heather, Olave, Baden-Powell, Betty and Peter with their dog Shawgm outside the front of the White House during a visit to Gilwell Park in 1929.

Above right: Frequent use was made of 'Eccles', the caravan, for holidays in the south and west of England with family and for overnight visits to Gilwell.

Right: Examples of the Christmas and other greetings cards that Baden-Powell designed and had printed to send to his wide circle of friends and associates.

⚜ B-P as Artist

Had he not made his name in other ways, it is possible that Baden-Powell could have earned a living as an artist. He inherited his mother's talent for painting and from an early age displayed his skills with brush and paints. He was completely ambidextrous, painting, drawing and writing with both left and right hands. Almost all his books and many of the newspaper and magazine articles he wrote carried his own illustrations, either in black and white or in colour, and many of these survive. Even during his retirement in Kenya he painted scenes of African wildlife, revealing an eye for detail and confidence with colour that seems remarkable for someone in their 80s.

From at least 1906 onwards he produced the designs for each year's Christmas card, which were printed for him to send to a wide circle of friends and associates. The cards usually showed a photograph of the family or a clever sketch with a morale-boosting message or some light-hearted fun. His last card, the largest in terms of size and sent just a few weeks before his death, took the form of an illustrated message encouraging the recipients to continue whatever they were doing for the war effort.

His artwork also provided an opportunity to show off his keen sense of humour. He produced a number of thank-you cards over the years, one of which depicted a large bee and three peas in a pod, drawn to represent his children. Even while he was attending important meetings, B-P would often draw caricatures, including those of the other people present, and his staff would have to search through his papers or blotting paper to collect them up after the meeting.

Baden-Powell was also gifted as a sculptor, and three of his works survive. He created the head of an African, a delightful piece of character work, showing his sharp eye for detail. As a homage to one of his childhood heroes (to whom he thought he was distantly related) he made a bust of Captain John Smith, the pioneer who married Pocahontas. Several copies of this bust were subsequently made and presented to various places. Finally, there is the kneeling knight, sculpted by Baden-Powell to celebrate the Arthurian legend of the Knights of the Round Table and the concept of total dedication embodied by the Rover Scouts. Smaller bronze copies of this statue were cast and sold to Rover Crews by Scout shops in the 1930s.

By now Scouting was firmly established as a world movement, but the 1930s proved to be a decade of difficulty, especially with the rising tide of nationalism.

Despite this, the Movement continued to expand in numbers, usefulness and standing, rising from a world membership of 2,251,726 in 1933 to 3,305,149 in 1939. The economic depression and consequent unemployment that afflicted many western countries in the 1930s led to close attention being given to the Rover Scout section and to the revision of its programme (see page 68). At the same time attention was directed towards leisure pursuits, and more emphasis was placed on proficiency or merit badges and handicrafts skills in general to boost Scouts' chances of gaining work.

World recession

The first Rover Scout Moot, held at Kandersteg in August 1931 and attended by 2,500 Rover Scouts from all over the world, focused on some of these issues and suggested possible remedies. The relationship of Scouting to modern trends and inventions, such as radio, and to education and school curricula occupied the attention of the World Scout Conference held in Austria shortly before the moot, on

the principle voiced by Baden-Powell that 'Scouting divorced from life is an impossibility'. Only by continuing to change and be relevant to young people would Scouting survive.

Fourth World Scout Jamboree

Two years later the fourth World Scout Jamboree was held in Hungary. The financial controls imposed as a result of the worldwide economic troubles, as well as growing unrest in central Europe, meant that this was not the most appropriate time for an event of this nature. In Britain, for example, the prime minister's permission was needed to send a contingent to Hungary, but Ramsay MacDonald agreed that, despite the need for financial stringency, the country had to be represented.

Obstacles of this nature were overcome to allow nearly 26,000 Scouts from 46 countries to be present when Baden-Powell opened the jamboree on 2 August 1933. He told the Scouts: 'You have come together here to make personal friendships with your brother Scouts of other nations, as peacemakers in the world. There is no time to waste.'

B-P's health was not at its best, and he left before the jamboree ended. In a departing speech to the participants he referred to the jamboree logo of a white stag:

Below: An ornamental gateway to a sub-camp at the Fourth World Scout Jamboree where Scouts were told they were 'peacemakers of the world'.

Scouting in the 1930s

You may look on the white stag as the pre-spirit of Scouting, springing forward and upward, ever leading you onward and upward, to leap over difficulties, to face new adventures in your active pursuit of the higher aims of Scouting – aims which bring you happiness. Those aims are to do your duty to God, to your country, and to your fellow men by carrying out the Scout Law. In that way you will each one of you help to bring about God's kingdom on earth, the reign of peace and good will. Therefore before I leave you, I ask you Scouts this question: will you do your best to make friends with others and peace in the world?

They roared back, 'Chief, Chief, Chief,' in answer to his question. They would do their best.

Scouting and fascism

Baden-Powell, too, tried to make friends, for among the observers in Hungary were members of the Italian Balilla and the German Hitler-Jugend (Hitler Youth). The principle in the Scout Law that 'a Scout ... is a friend to all' was being rightly observed. However, like its Italian counterpart (see page 70), the German organization was not voluntary. Indeed, to a certain extent it was selective, because those who were unlikely to be good party members when they grew up were rejected.

The Hitler Youth, both a political and a pre-military organization, was introduced in 1926, and in 1933 it took over all other youth organizations in Germany. There had been many efforts to establish Scouting in Germany since 1910, but misunderstanding about its real purpose led to the formation of a number of rival bodies. An application for world recognition in 1924 was rejected because of the political situation, and the formal recognition of Scouting was impossible for the rest of the decade. However, some members of the Hitler Youth were invited to the 1929 and 1933 jamborees as a gesture of goodwill, and in return they made efforts to make friends and arrange visits to Germany.

Resisting pressure from some of his colleagues to have nothing to do with the Hitler Youth, Baden-Powell sought to keep in contact. This was not because he admired them but because he believed that peace could be assured only if young people in all countries came to know each other as friends. Channels of communication

Above: Danish Scouts present at the 1933 Jamboree enjoy a meal around the grass table they have constructed by digging trenches.

Below: Children in the Balilla, the Italian fascist youth, playing hoops, c. 1930.

and contacts had to be kept open, he believed, even though he was wary of Hitler's astonishing hold over German youth and his methods of indoctrination.

When he met the German ambassador in London Baden-Powell proposed various ways of bringing British and German youth together. For his part, the ambassador saw no reason why relations between the youth of Britain and Germany should not continue to be friendly. Baden-Powell was sceptical even though he said, 'It makes us at Headquarters look ridiculous if we decree against fraternizing while our boys are keeping up and extending friendships with the German boys through Scouts, school journeys, gliding clubs, YMCA, camping clubs, etc.'

The agreement signed in Munich in 1938 by Neville Chamberlain convinced Baden-Powell that the policy of appeasement had been right, but the widespread attacks on Jews and Jewish property in Germany and Austria on the night of 9 November 1938 changed his views forever. Members of the Hitler Youth had been prominent participants in these assaults, and all contact with the organization now ceased as Baden-Powell realized that reconciliation was impossible.

Royal approval ...

Early in 1934 Baden-Powell's health had become a cause for concern as he underwent two operations for the removal of his prostate gland. He remained seriously ill for some months, and a cruise on the *Adriatic* was part of his convalescence programme. This meant that he missed the first national service and parade of British King's Scouts and Scout gallantry award holders at Windsor Castle.

Ever since he had first suggested it in *Scouting for Boys*, Baden-Powell had encouraged Scouts to reaffirm their Promise each year around 23 April, the feast of St George, the patron saint of Scouts. It was felt that more emphasis could be given to this by a central celebration with representatives from each county. An invitation came from the clergy of St George's Chapel, Windsor Castle, for a service to be held there. Afterwards the Scouts would gather outside to hear a short speech from the Chief Scout. When the details had been arranged, George V expressed a wish to see the Scouts on their way to the chapel. So those who had gained the King's Scout Award in the preceding year assembled in the castle quadrangle to march past the king before proceeding through the grounds and on to the chapel. This was the first instance of a unique annual privilege for Scouting and a sign of its royal approval and patronage.

Ill health and foreign tours meant that Baden-Powell only ever attended this event in 1937, but except for the war years the privilege has continued to this day, and Queen Elizabeth II or another member of the British royal family regularly reviews the hundreds of young people in the parade.

... and state occasions

The coronation of King George VI on 12 May 1937 gave Scouts an opportunity to play a part in a major state

Left: Efforts were made to keep in contact with the members of the Hitler Youth, some of whom are seen here at a rally near Rheinsberg, Germany, in July 1935.

Right: There has been an annual parade of King's and Queen's Scout Award holders at Windsor Castle every year since 1934, excluding 1939–45.

occasion. Although the new king's older brother, Edward VIII, had been a personal friend of Baden-Powell – not only was he a great supporter of Scouting, but he also occupied the unique role of Chief Scout of Wales – his abdication in December 1936 cost him this friendship. Baden-Powell did not think much of Wallis Simpson, and he believed that the king should have put his duty to his country above that to his lover. The new king, George VI, and his wife showed themselves over many years to be firm supporters of both Scouting and Guiding.

At the 1937 coronation Scouts throughout the Commonwealth sold copies of the official souvenir programmes, and London Rover Scouts helped erect and staff crash barriers erected along the processional routes. Other Rovers were on duty outside Westminster Abbey itself, helping with guests' cars and acting as messengers. Scouts seemed to be everywhere, so much so that Baden-Powell wrote later: 'Everyone I spoke to was impressed by the businesslike way in which they applied themselves to the various jobs for which they were detailed, and I heard it frequently said that the boys of this Association, more than any other, seem to know what to do on these occasions.'

Scouting and South Africa

Issues of race and colour presented a particular problem for Scouting in South Africa, where four separate sections had been formed: the Boy Scouts Association of the Union for white boys, the Pathfinders for natives, the Coloured Boy Scouts for half-castes and the Indian Boy Scouts. For a long time these four associations had nothing to do with each other, but as this country held such a special affection for him, Baden-Powell wished that Scouting could do something to weld the various races into a single community. He was disappointed that Scouting was not open to all boys, regardless of race, creed or colour, but he remained a realist and accepted that progress on this most difficult of subjects had to be slow and cautious.

At a conference of the South African Scout Council held in Durban in 1936 under his guidance the various arguments were discussed thoroughly and openly. After two days of deliberations it was agreed to form a federation of the four sections under the Boys Scouts Association of the Union. It was not all that Baden-Powell could have hoped for, but it was far more than he had expected, and it was a foundation on which to build for a future when mixed Scouting was not only possible but able to continue throughout the years of apartheid.

Honouring the Founder

In 1936 and 1937 Baden-Powell received several honours. In his coronation honours list, George VI awarded B-P with the Order of Merit, the highest gift that the British sovereign can give and limited to no more that 24 holders at any one time. The French president conferred on him the Grand Cordon of the Legion of Honour, while from the United States came the award of the newly created Wateler Peace Prize from the Carnegie Institute, a fitting recognition of 'his services to world peace and promoting international goodwill through the Scout Movement'. This meant that since 1907 he had received some 32 honours and awards, six honorary degrees and the freedom of 11 cities. But his greatest satisfaction was in knowing that Scouting would continue to grow and exist long after his life was over.

Above: The first King's Scout parade at Windsor Castle in 1934 was reviewed by King George V and Queen Mary, accompanied by the young princesses Elizabeth and Margaret.

Right: Baden-Powell buys a souvenir programme from some of the Scouts involved in preparations for the coronation of King George VI in 1937.

Handing on

In 1937 Baden-Powell was warmly welcomed at the World Scout Jamboree held in the Netherlands. Now aged eighty, B-P knew that the end was close, and his thoughts were turning to retirement and handing over responsibility for his beloved Movement.

In his closing speech the founder recognized that he would not be present at another jamboree:

The time has come for me to say good-bye. You know that many of us will never meet again in this world. I am in my eighty-first year and am nearing the end of my life. Most of you are at the beginning, and I want your lives to be happy and successful. You can make them so by doing your best to carry out the Scout Law all your days, whatever your station and wherever you are.

At the end of his speech he bade the Scouts a moving farewell: 'Now good-bye. God bless you all!' His voice then faltered, but after a brief pause he swung his Scout hat over his head, repeating loudly and strong, 'God bless you all!'

Failing health

He was right – this was the last time he would appear on the world stage. His health was already failing, and his spirits were especially low when his brother Baden died in early October, although they rose at the end of the

Above: Their first grandson, Robert, then aged three, visited Baden-Powell and Olave at Paxtu in February 1940.

Above right: Baden-Powell with his successor as British Chief Scout, Lord Somers, who died in 1944 after only three years in office.

Right: Baden-Powell's coffin is taken on a gun carriage to St Peters's Churchyard, Nyeri, for burial on 9 January 1941, the day after his death.

month when he and Olave celebrated their silver wedding. Among the many telegrams and letters two were of particular interest. His son, Peter, had married the year before, and they now had their first grandson, Robert. Their daughter Betty, had also married and now living in Northern Rhodesia, had given them their first granddaughter.

A silver wedding surprise

To mark the silver wedding a dinner party for over 300 Scouters and Guiders was held in London. The couple received a collection of silver plate plus a cheque for £2,600 from the two Movements to be used as they wished. Shortly afterwards, B-P's medical check-up showed no sign of disease but a 'tired heart', and hearing his punishing schedule for the months ahead, his doctor prescribed complete rest for a year. It was therefore decided to use the silver wedding money to build a small cottage in Kenya in the grounds of the Outspan Hotel and in the shadows of Mount Kenya. They named the cottage Paxtu, a play on the fact that it was their second home to be called Pax and that the word in Swahili means 'complete peace'.

He and Olave left Pax Hill and Britain together for the last time in October 1938 to begin a new life.

A fruitful retirement

The couple settled in to their new home and surroundings. The children and grandchildren visited from time to time, and B-P resumed his love of painting, producing some striking scenes of African wildlife.

In 1939, without his knowledge, he was nominated for the Nobel Peace Prize in recognition of his work and achievements over 30 years in promoting the cause of world peace through the Scout Movement and through jamborees in particular. Unfortunately, the prize was not

Pax Hill
Bentley
Hampshire

My dear Scouts

If you have ever seen the play 'Peter Pan' you will remember how the Pirate Chief was always making his dying speech because he was afraid that possibly when the time came for him to die he might not have time to get it off his chest

It is much the same with me: and so, although I am not at this moment dying, I shall be doing so one of these days, and I want to send you a parting word of goodbye.

Remember it is the last you will ever hear from me.. so think it over.

I have had a most happy life, and I want each of you to have as happy a life too. I believe God put us in this jolly world to be happy and enjoy life.

Happiness doesn't come from being rich nor merely from

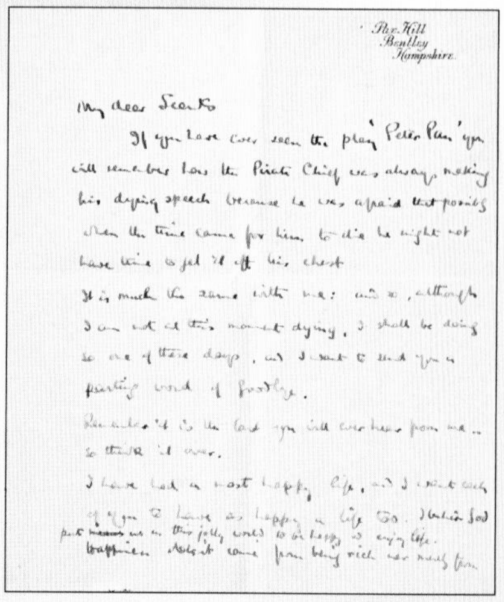

Baden-Powell's final message

Dear Scouts

If you have ever seen the play Peter Pan you will remember how the pirate chief was always making his dying speech, because he was afraid that possibly, when the time came for him to die, he might not have time to get it off his chest.

It is much the same with me; and so, although I am not at this moment dying, I shall be doing so one of these days, and I want to send you a parting word of goodbye.

Remember, it is the last time you will ever hear from me, so think it over. I have had a most happy life, and I want each and every one of you to have as happy a life too. I believe that God put us in this jolly world to be happy and enjoy life.

Happiness does not come from being rich, nor merely from being successful in your career, nor by self-indulgence.

One step towards happiness is to make yourself healthy and strong while you are a boy, so that you can be useful, and so can enjoy life when you are a man. Nature study will show you how full of beautiful and wonderful things God has made the world for you to enjoy.

Be contented with what you have got, and make the best of it; look on the bright side of things instead of the gloomy one. But the real way to get happiness is by giving out happiness to other people. Try and leave this world a little better that you found it, and when your turn comes to die you can die happy in feeling that at any rate you have not wasted your time but have done your best.

'Be Prepared' in this way, to live happy and to die happy; stick to your Scout Promise always – even after you have ceased to be a boy – and God help you to do it.

Your friend
Baden-Powell

awarded that year because of the outbreak of the Second World War.

Baden-Powell's first reaction to the declaration of war was to write to his successor as Chief Scout, Lord Somers, offering to return home if it would help. Somers declined the offer of his services, assuring him that the Movement would live up to every expectation.

After the marriage of his daughter Heather, Baden-Powell knew that his life's work was drawing to a close. His health slowly deteriorated and he contracted a slight form of skin cancer. Slowly he grew weaker, rallying occasionally, with Olave constantly at his bedside, day and night.

Olave wrote in her diary for 8 January 1941:

At 2.30 a.m. Sister woke me, saying 'he is going'. I went to his room and just sat on his bed. He was quite unconscious and still, breathing slowly ... At 5 a.m. I thought he would still see the day through and went back to bed to get warm. I kissed his dear forehead and Sister Ray stayed by him. And as I lay listening she suddenly came at 5.45 – 'He is gone'. He look so sweet and perfect in death as he was in life – utterly, utterly noble and good and dear and wonderful, great and faultless.

B-P's final messages

Baden-Powell left behind a number of written final messages – to the Scouts, the Guides, to Rover Scouts, to Scouters and Guiders and to the general public. Some of these were certainly written in the 1920s and kept sealed until his death. He also left a final letter for Olave, expressing his love and hope that her courage would ease her loss. His final letter, written only a few days before his death, was to King George V's private secretary, asking him to assure the king of his loyalty and express his thanks.

The nation's final tribute to Baden-Powell was refused by Olave – a grave in the central aisle of the nave of Westminster Abbey, between those of the Unknown Warrior and David Livingstone. She did not like the abbey, considering it dull and gloomy. Instead she wanted him laid to rest among 'the quiet of Gilwell with birdsong and wind in the trees'. In the event he was buried in Nyeri, Kenya, where she could be near him.

Olave continues the Founder's work

Baden-Powell's funeral, planned in secret for some time, was held with full military honours in St Peter's Churchyard, Nyeri. Olave returned eventually to England and threw herself back into her role as World Chief Guide. Pax Hill now had other owners, so Olave accepted a grace and favour apartment at Hampton Court Palace, a gift from a grateful king, which she used as her home for most of the rest of her life. When she died in 1977 her ashes were flown to Kenya and buried in the same grave as B-P, reuniting them again.

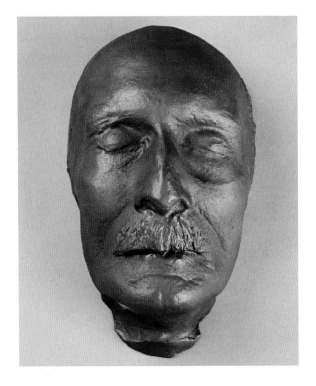

Above: The offer of a grave in Westminster Abbey was declined. Baden-Powell was buried in his beloved Kenya and Olave's ashes were also placed there in 1977.

Right: As was the custom at the time, a death mask was made shortly after Baden-Powell died on 8 January 1941.

The outbreak of the Second World War found the worldwide Scout Movement ready to help in any way it could. Although its founder and chief was now frail and living in Kenya, Scouting rose to the occasion as only it could.

A national service badge, laying emphasis on the work of civil defence, had been introduced in Britain well before the declaration of war, and during the course of the Second World War over 60,000 Scouts in Britain over the age of 14 were awarded this badge for sustained work of every description. The whole Movement took part in hundreds of activities. Scouts worked as air-raid messengers, first-aid orderlies and telephonists, instructors to the Home Guard and assistants in rest centres. They made thousands of camouflage nets and also turned coal dust into briquettes for the Ministry of Fuel and Power. In addition, they played a major role in helping with children evacuated from the cities.

Many Scouts worked on the land, planting cabbages or harvesting plums, while other collected seaweed. They also collected rubbish for pig food, using the slogan 'Rubbish makes rashers'. Scouts raised money for a minesweeper and an evacuated Wolf Cub helped to raise funds towards the cost of a Spitfire aeroplane. Scouts in London raised over £57,000 during four years of war savings, and on just one day in 1944 Scouts from across the country raised over £32,000 through the Bob-a-Job scheme. The money raised was used to send Red Cross relief teams into north-west Europe. Scout property, premises and equipment were lent to the services and used for dealing with refugees. Scouts also assisted with milk rounds, found and treated injured animals and even converted their trek carts to animal ambulances.

Scouting in the Second World War

1st MOLESCROFT SCOUTS FIRE SERVICE.

Above: The 1st
Molescroft Scouts,
Yorkshire, provided a
fire-fighting service
using their own
homemade mobile
equipment.

Left: Scouts trained
members of the Home
Guard in such skills
as how to roll over
railway lines without
being observed.

Civil defence

But it was during the air raids that many Scouts provided outstanding service. Scouts over 14 could be used as indoor messengers or for other duties connected with civil defence, provided that they went to shelters in the event of an air-raid warning. In some places, including Glasgow, the under-16s were formed into 'after-the-raid-squads', who set to work the moment the 'all clear' had sounded after a raid. They would help rescue victims buried under the debris of bombed houses, salvage furniture, look after helpless children and assist at rest centres and canteens, as well as running messages for the civil defence services.

Scouts erected over 40,000 air-raid shelters, manufactured homemade torch batteries and assembled, distributed, repaired and disinfected gas masks. They painted street corners and kerbs white, blacked out private and public buildings and provided film shows and other entertainments in the air-raid shelters. Many householders who had been indifferent to the ideas of Scouting now began to see the point of the training.

During the London Blitz calls went out to fire brigades in all surrounding areas. Scouts met the fire

engines on the outskirts of the city and guided them by the quickest route to where they were needed. Scout messengers were often found cycling amid falling shell fragments, carrying information from fire engine to control points. Scouts worked in hospitals alongside the medical staff, equipped and manned ambulance tents and even assisted with X-rays. During the evacuations, they acted as escorts and guides, erected temporary latrines, distributed clothing, packed and distributed rations and cleaned and repaired houses as billets. Scouts were to be found in the Observer Corps, as balloon barrage orderlies, manning listening posts and entertaining troops.

Many lives were saved by Scouts, but some lost their own lives while on air-raid duty. Scout awards for gallantry were made to over 80 members, and 26 members of the Scout Movement were awarded the Victoria Cross for acts of gallantry during the war.

While all this was going on, 'normal' Scouting continued, despite the absence of thousands of leaders on war service and all the other difficulties of the period. But they managed, camping with camouflaged tents and extinguishing their fires after dark. By September 1941 the numbers of warranted leaders

Left: Scouts provided valuable help in an east London hospital, ranging from carrying the injured to working in the operating theatre.

Right: Among their many activities Scouts joined in with fire-watching duties from vantage points in many towns and cities.

☙ Sir Winston Churchill's message to Scouting

During a conference held in 1942 to help shape the future of Scouting in Britain, a message was received from the prime minister, Winston Churchill, who wrote:

I first met B-P many years before the birth of the Scout Movement. He was a man of character, vision and enthusiasm and he passed these qualities on to the Movement which has played and is playing an important part in moulding the character of our race. Sturdiness, neighbourliness, practical competence, love of country and, above all, in these times, indomitable resolve, daring and enterprise in the face of the enemy, these are the hallmarks of a Scout. You have many practical difficulties under war-time conditions in carrying on your work but with persistence and ingenuity these can be surmounted in Scout fashion and I have no doubt that in your hands the Movement will carry on its task with the steadfast will and high courage with which it was founded. 'Be prepared' to stand up faithfully for Right and Truth however the winds may blow.

had dropped by more than half, from 44,000 to 21,000. This meant added responsibility for Patrol Leaders and many Troops were run entirely under boy leadership.

Scouting in occupied Britain

One part of Britain – the Channel Islands – was, of course, occupied by the Nazis. Although the invaders banned Scouting, at least one Troop did continue to meet, right under the noses of the occupying power.

In *The Scout* of 21 June 1945 Patrol Leader Vernon Carey of the 11th Jersey Scout Troop wrote about the experience:

In July 1940 we were occupied by the Germans and, of course, all Scouts were forbidden. At that time I was in the Wolf Cubs. But our Assistant Scoutmaster – Mr Guy – carried on for about a year and a half with four Scouts, keeping very secret all the time, for we did not know what the Germans were going to do with us ...

We met at one of the Patrol Leader's houses and made a little hut outside our headquarters. We were there for about a year and a half, when one day the Gestapo raided the house. Luckily we were not there at the time, but they found wireless, ammunition and photographs, all forbidden by the Germans. On VE Day we had a hurried meeting, dragging out old uniforms, and went into town, a very happy and jubilant band.

British Scouts visit Canada

In 1942 the Canadian Boy Scouts Association invited four King's Scouts from Britain to tour Canada, to tell the Scouts of that country something of the part played by Scouts in Britain's civil defence. From a list of recommended King's Scouts the names of four boys from all over Britain were selected. All had served during the heavy air raids and were qualified to speak from first-hand experience. The tour was extended to include the USA and lasted 14 weeks, during which the party covered 48,000 kilometres (30,000 miles) and visited 135 cities and towns. They broadcast on 60 occasions, addressed 220 public meetings and rallies, were guest speakers at 17 service club meetings, spoke at 125 school assemblies and gave talks at 50 civic receptions and 80 lunches and dinners. On their return the party divided into pairs and, under the aegis of the Ministry of Information, toured Britain telling of their experiences in North America.

A living memorial

Two days after the Westminster Abbey memorial service for Baden-Powell, on 29 January 1941, the Council of the Association met to appoint Lord Somers as Chief Scout, the man that Baden-Powell himself had chosen as his successor. Somers wasted no time in making his mark. A few months after Baden-Powell's death the new Chief Scout wrote in *The Scouter*:

We propose to build a Memorial House to commemorate our Founder. This will be a great centre in London, dedicated to the B-P way of life; a house where Scouts from all parts of the world will be welcome and feel at home; a common meeting ground where the Fourth Scout Law can be seen in practice ... We all owe so much happiness and our ability to be useful to our Founder that we shall do all we can to build a worthy memorial to him. I should like to stress, however, that we are not out for something to look at, but something for Scouts to use.

A fund was opened on St George's Day, 23 April 1942.

Lord Somers commissioned a far-ranging review of Scouting and consulted widely on the sort of Scouting young people and adults wanted to take part in after the war. With all this activity going on, Scouting certainly had its hands full carrying out its normal programme plus its numerous war service tasks, but there was still time for experimentation and development.

Air Scouting takes off

At the time that the Battle of Britain was in progress in the skies above London, it was decided to introduce an Air Scout branch and to prepare a scheme as soon as

Above: Like their British counterparts, American Scouts joined in salvage operations. These boys in New York helped collect old rubber toy train track.

possible. Introduced on 31 January 1941, this scheme was, of course, based on ordinary Scout training but with an air bias. Interest was immediate and there was a steady demand for literature and advice.

Gilwell at war

With the requisition of Gilwell for the duration of the war and the call-up of J. S. Wilson, its Camp Chief, the prospect of an early resumption of Wood Badge training courses was remote, yet the demand and necessity were still there, despite all other pressures of the time. Under the able leadership of A. M. (Tiny) Chamberlain, Gilwell's Assistant Camp Chief, courses resumed at Youlbury, Scout Campsite, near Oxford.

The war had, of course, reduced the full-time staff to a minimum. By the end of the first year 57 members of staff were serving in the armed and civil defence services, and before the war ended that figure had nearly doubled. Wartime bravery was not, of course, confined to Britain.

Denmark

In Denmark Scouting went underground during the Nazi occupation. Although the Movement was not officially banned until 1944, many Scouts acting in the Resistance or on behalf of others were killed before that time. Scouts were instrumental in smuggling out of Denmark more than 90 per cent of its Jewish population, rescuing them from certain death. Four of the 11 secret radio operators found and shot by the Gestapo in a Copenhagen basement were Scouts.

Many Danish Scouts acted as secret couriers, travelling to and from neutral Sweden. They acted as saboteurs, using Scouting skills to remain undetected, and took photographs of Nazi armaments to smuggle vital information to the Allies.

France

The French Resistance owed a great debt to Scouting, as was acknowledged at the time. Some 10,000 French Scout Leaders had joined the forces on the outbreak of war, and most of them were taken prisoner when France fell, leaving the country largely without its Scout Leaders. Many Rover Scouts and older Patrol Leaders took on the job, which they carried out in secret.

More than 75 per cent of Resistance operatives in many areas were Scouts or former Scouts, trained to observe and take mental notes and keep their wits about them. Even the youngest Wolf Cubs played their part, helping prisoners to escape from temporary internment camps by leaving clothes and food at prearranged places and altering road signs. Scouts helped to smuggle thousands of French Jews across the mountains into neutral Switzerland, an operation led by a 21-year-old Rover Scout, and 130 Jewish children whose parents had already been taken were collected together at a 'holiday camp' and given new identities and matching papers, saving them from the death camps. One brave Scout was caught while he was smuggling for the Resistance, and

he ate the papers he was carrying before he could be searched. He later died fighting in Alsace.

The Netherlands

The story of Scouting in the Netherlands during the Second World War is a subject worth many books on its own, but it is epitomized by one famous individual, Jan van Hoof of Nijmegen, who has been held up as an example of bravery to generations of Scouts ever since. Before the Nazi occupation of the Netherlands Jan had been a Cub and a Scout, but to become a Rover Scout he was invested secretly, in woods within earshot of a Nazi barracks, because Scouting was prohibited. During the occupation the Movement carried on in secret, publishing its own underground paper and investing younger boys to make sure that the Movement survived the war. Jan first became a member of the Underground Clan of Rovers, and then he was taken on by the Netherlands intelligence department. He became a secret soldier and spy, acting entirely alone.

Jan gave himself the job of watching the bridge at Nijmegen because he knew that it would be vital to both the Allies and the Nazis. The Germans had fixed explosives to the bridge and were prepared to blow it up if they had to retreat. Jan decided that it was his responsibility to remove the detonating mechanism to save the bridge. The bridge was both high and long, and

Above: French Scouts, proud to wear uniform in public again, climb on top of a newspaper kiosk to watch one of the liberation parades in November 1944.

the detonator was right next to a Nazi lookout point. Other underground Scouts thought it was an impossibly dangerous task, so Jan told nobody about his plans.

When Allied soldiers parachuted in on 17 September 1944, the Scouts of Nijmegen put on their uniforms and their orange armbands (showing allegiance to the nation's royal house) and defied the Nazis. They worked as Guides and Scouts for the Allied forces. While the bridge was under shell-fire, Jan ran into the smoke and cut the detonator cable, narrowly escaping with his life. He was killed the next day, aged 22, guiding an Allied armoured car through Nijmegen. He had saved the bridge.

Jan's name can still be seen on a plaque under the second span of the bridge. There are many Scouting

Nederland Troops in the Netherlands named after him, and he still exemplifies the essence of Dutch Scouting.

Greece

The stories relating to Greek Scouts during the Second World War make remarkable reading. The prime minister Joannis Metaxas officially dissolved Scouting in 1939, despite the best efforts of the International Bureau in London to keep it alive. When first Mussolini and then Hitler attacked the country, Scouts appeared from every corner to help their fellow countrymen, acting as auxiliaries, first-aiders, messengers, blood donors, stretcher-bearers and guerrilla fighters. Even when Greece was completely occupied by the Nazis, Scouts grouped in secret to invest new members. Their principal focus became the survival of other children in the period of widespread starvation during the winter of 1941–2. Scouts and Guides set up soup kitchens in schools in Athens and tried to cheer up the children and raise their hopes by decorating their walls with pictures depicting Greek legends and folk tales.

Scouting publications came out in secret, under the code-name Phoenix, showing the hope that Scouting would rise again from the ashes. Greek banks and companies with funds secretly gave the Scouts and Guides money to get children away to secret camps in the summer, where they could be fed and looked after for six weeks or more. Records state that by the time Greece was liberated there were 50 first-aid units run by eight to ten Scouts each in Athens alone. The situation was paralleled in the Greek islands, where Scouts published a digest of BBC news to keep the people in touch with Allied movements. Many who were Scouts in the first year of the war were soldiers or airmen of Allied forces by the end of it. When Greece was liberated, there were many times more Scouts than there had been at the time of the occupation – and the phoenix did indeed rise again, as one might have expected.

Norway

Almost from the first moment of the Nazi invasion of Norway in 1939, Scouting dived underground and began its own resistance. Scouts acted resourcefully and responsibly when Nazi troops caused near panic in the streets, calming people down and acting as auxiliary first-aiders. The Chief Scout of Norway wrote to all Norwegian Scouts: 'There will be need for self-sacrifice and mutual help, and remember, however difficult things may be for you, there are always others who are worse off.' Scouting was officially banned here in 1941.

Thanks to the actions of one traitor, the Nazis found out exactly where every Scout Troop was based and what funds it had. Banks were ordered to transfer Scout funds to the Hitler Youth account, and all equipment and uniforms were to be seized. The courageous Scouts and Guides of Oslo came up with a plan to undermine this theft: they would divide their equipment and uniforms into two parcels, keeping back the best in the second. They then rushed to hand in the first parcels, and the

Below: Over 80 British Scouts received awards for gallantry in the Second World War for such acts as rescuing someone from a burning house.

Above: Many children who were evacuated from cities were helped by Scouts to settle into their new homes and surroundings.

Nazis were so overwhelmed by the first load that they never asked for the rest of it. However, Scout Troops in other areas had personal visits from members of the SS, who took everything.

The underground Scout Movement concentrated on assisting the Resistance, for which many were killed, and in helping others less able than themselves. It was a Norwegian Scout who first alerted the Allies to the movements of the German battleship *Bismarck* in the North Atlantic. Norwegian Cubs had special roles as messengers, and British agents grew to depend on even the youngest of them, trusting them completely.

Scouts who were marked out for extermination through their activities were helped by other Scouts to flee to England and Scotland, and many settled there. Many Resistance operations depended on communications between Norway and Scotland, which became a training base for covert operations in Norway, some of which were directed by Gilwell's Camp Chief, J. S. Wilson.

⚜ Lord Somers' message

In summarizing Scout activities during the Second World War, Lord Somers wrote:

The spirit of service is the spirit of the true Scout whatever his age or rank. The spirit of the good turn, ever present in peace time, has matured to devoted self-sacrifice in war. In writing to me recently the Prime Minister, Mr Winston Churchill, said: 'The record of the work of the Boy Scouts during the war on the Home Front is a very fine one.' I think, therefore, the world should be told of some of the acts of heroism and devotion to duty of our Scouts.

Scouting: The world story

Throughout the course of the 20th century, whenever a dictator came to power –
left-wing, right-wing, fascist, Nazi or communist – one of his first acts was to ban
Scouting and Guiding. But the Movements continued – in whatever form they could.

Reconstruction and peace

In many countries where Scouting was banned, the ruling power introduced its own (usually mandatory) youth organization, because the indoctrination of young people was seen as key to the dictator's survival. Because B-P's youth Movements were voluntary and encouraged young people to think for themselves, they were regarded as threats. When Poland was invaded in 1939, Scouting was banned by the Germans, and as other countries were occupied by the Nazis, Scouting was suppressed there too. It became a familiar pattern. By September 1941 no fewer than 14 Scouting countries were under Nazi domination and four others were allied to the Axis powers. In all these countries Scouting had to go underground to survive.

Underground Scouting

Some of the more extraordinary places where it did survive – literally under the noses of the captors – were the prisoner of war camps in Germany and the Far East. In some of these camps men who had been Scouts at home formed Rover Scout crews. They held meetings, making their own badges and Scout identity cards without the knowledge of their guards. Some of these materials have survived as proud reminders of the determination and courage of these men.

Re-emergence

A country did not have to be completely liberated before Scouting restarted. In Italy the Movement had been abolished by Benito Mussolini in 1927, but as the liberating armies moved up from the south from 1942 Scout Troops were formed, with many members wearing the uniforms their fathers had worn before the fascist regime was imposed. Shortly after the fall of Mussolini in 1945, but before the armistice was signed, the new government authorized the official re-establishment of the Scouting Movement. A similar pattern was repeated in other countries once they, too, were liberated.

In August 1944, even before the end of the war, a scheme was launched in Scotland and soon taken up enthusiastically elsewhere to enable Scout groups in one country to be put in direct contact with troops in another country. The aim of the scheme was to strengthen the idea of the world Scouting family by means of correspondence and exchange visits. Many friendships were formed as a result of this initiative, and it led to a significant growth in the numbers of Scouts visiting and camping in countries other than their own.

Above right: A flag, scarf and literature were among the things made by Rover Scouts while they were held in prisoner of war camps in the Far East.

Right: Scouts joined in the celebrations as the Second World War ended before assisting with relief projects throughout Europe.

Scout International Relief Service

Towards the end of the war, Scouting began to play a part in helping to ease the plight of the civilians affected by the hostilities. As early as January 1943 Scouters and Rover Scouts in Britain were invited to register their interest in the Scout International Relief Service. The work of the service would be directed to helping people who had suffered as a result of the war and not, except incidentally, to the re-establishment of Scouting.

The scheme was to be financed by every member of the Movement working to earn some money on 20 May 1944. The target was £20,000, but over £33,000 was raised in this way. The first team of volunteers went to the Balkans, and others soon followed to other parts of

Europe and beyond. One team at a centre in Nijmegen, the Netherlands, handled 20,000 refugees in the first 18 days there, and assisted in the evacuation of Allied civilians from Calais and Dunkirk in France and in Belgium. Scout volunteers were among the first groups to tackle the problems of relief in Greece, starting by travelling into the mountains to release prisoners of war. Working in appalling conditions, this team brought hundreds of tons of food and clothing to desperate villages.

The Scout International Relief Service had no more than a hundred members (including 26 women), but it provided aid to the distressed, the outcast and the unfortunate in many ways and in places as far afield as Egypt, Albania, Yugoslavia, Greece, Palestine, Syria, Italy, Cyprus, Austria, Germany and Hong Kong, as well as in north-west Europe.

The Jamboree of Peace

Another casualty of the war had been the World Scout Jamboree that had been scheduled to take place in France in 1941. Two years after hostilities ceased it was at last possible for this, the Jamboree of Peace, to be held, despite immense difficulties. France had been invaded and occupied, supplies of almost everything were limited, Baden-Powell had died and the strength and unity of post-war Scouting were untested and unknown. Staging this jamboree was, therefore, a huge challenge for its hosts.

The chosen site was at Moisson, about 65 kilometres (40 miles) north-west of Paris and near the banks of the River Seine. It was divided into 15 sub-camps, named after

⚜ Scouting ideals

The ideas, or ideals if you like, of Scouting are in opposition to any form of totalitarian government. The two cannot exist side by side … I myself cannot see any hope of bridging this gulf, rather would I believe the suppression of the Scout Movement by all forms of totalitarian government to be a tribute to its efficacy and its principles.

J. S. Wilson,
Scouting Round the World *(1959)*

Left: Mickey Mouse wearing the Boy Scouts of America uniform appeared in full colour on the wrapper for the 1947 jamboree newspaper.

Right: After a break of ten years it was possible to hold the sixth World Scout Jamboree at Moisson, France.

Below: Even Scout badges were made by Rover Scouts in Second World War prisoner of war camps.

Bottom: Over 25,000 Scouts from 70 countries attended the 1947 Jamboree of Peace.

French departments. In contrast to the mud of previous jamborees, this site was renowned for the dust, caused by the hot weather. It was ten years since the previous jamboree, and a whole generation of Scouts had grown up without any previous experience of such an event or the demonstration on this scale of friendship and goodwill. But the organizers need not have been worried. There were some 25,000 Scouts from 70 countries, reflecting a changed world. Many well-known countries and nationalities were missing, and little did the 200 Scouts from Hungary and 500 from Czechoslovakia know that this was the last time their countries would take part in a jamboree for many years to come.

There were signs of hope for the future, however. As if to emphasize this point, there was a sub-camp of 200 Scouts, mostly from Baltic countries, who were continuing their Scouting in displaced persons camps in Austria and Germany. For some who had lost families and homes, the problems of adapting to a new life in a new country lay ahead. These participants made the most of the meagre resources available, making camp gadgets and decorations from materials they found on the spot, and for the first few days even their cooking pots were made from old biscuit tins.

The jamboree soon took on its usual form, however, with shows and entertainments, campfires and displays, shared meals and special days. The decoration of the site – towers, stages and gateways – was on a more grandiose scale than many people had expected and was the result of the hard work of Scouters and Rover Scouts who had laboured at weekends for many months. Their workmanship and ingenuity were amazing.

A new dawn for Scouting

At the closing ceremony there were the usual final speeches, and then the Chief Scouts assembled on the arena stage and linked hands, singing 'Auld Lang Syne' spontaneously. Gradually everyone present joined in. The thousands of boys then formed a human carrick bend, a knot that was the camp's logo and the sign of the friendship that should exist between all free people. Proof of this came from India and Pakistan, which had become separate self-governing countries at the beginning of 1947 but were torn apart by continuing conflict between Hindus and Muslims. A contingent made up of Scouts from the new countries camped together at Moisson without rioting or bloodshed. The flags of the new countries were broken on flagpoles on either side of the Scout flag, and everyone joined in celebrating the new-found independence of their respective countries. It really was a Jamboree of Peace.

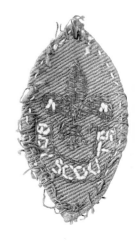

The golden jubilee

For Scouts everywhere 1957 was a special year, marking both the centenary of Baden-Powell's birth and Scouting's 50th anniversary, its golden jubilee. The jubilee year began with celebrations in every town and country where Scouting existed.

Scouting had reached its 50th birthday – and was looking as youthful as ever. Remembering the 'duty to God' aspect of the Scout Promise, there were numerous acts of worship and religious services to mark the anniversary. One was held in February in the chapel of Baden-Powell's old school at Charterhouse and broadcast on television. The school's headmaster gave an address, and then Olave Baden-Powell, World Chief Guide, led the renewal of the Scout and Guide Promises.

Thanksgiving at Westminster Abbey

A national service of thanksgiving was held in London at Westminster Abbey, which was packed with members of the two Movements that Baden-Powell had founded. It was a star-studded occasion, attended by members of the British royal family, government ministers, diplomats and the Baden-Powell family. Before the service began, wreaths were placed on Baden-Powell's memorial stone in the abbey. The Archbishop of Canterbury spoke of the obligations of the Scout Promise and how the Scout Law was:

wrapped up in doing things, doing interesting things, doing them with others and for others in a spirit of adventure and honour, each bearing his own responsibility and each bearing a bit of everyone else's load. It was not 'being good' in any repellent sense; it was enjoying life by keen living and finding friendship by helping to create it and learning responsibility by sharing it.

Remembering B-P

On the same day as the service was being held in London, in Nyeri, Kenya, 3,600 Scouts and Guides gathered at Baden-Powell's grave to pay their respects in a simple ceremony.

Above: The 35,000 participants in the 1957 Jamboree, Indaba and Moot assembled in the main arena for the official ceremonies at Sutton Coldfield, England.

Above right: There was heavy rain, but this did not deter Dutch Scouts from demonstrating their skills at country dancing.

Right: This archway was a central feature of the site at the 1957 Jamboree.

Ghana and Malaya both invited individual Scouts from Britain to be their guests for a few weeks during the summer, two instances of many such gestures of international friendship.

In London, Ralph Reader's play *Great Oaks* was revived to great acclaim. The play, about a young man who joins as a Scouter in the early days and carries on with his Troop through changing circumstances for 50 years, could hardly have been more apt. In Glasgow, Scottish Scouts mounted a magnificent exhibition in Kelvin Hall, where the magic of B-P's *Scouting for Boys* (then still in print) was brought to life for the public.

But there was much, much more. Commemorative stamps were issued, special issues of magazines and books were published, a film was released about Baden-Powell's life, and a railway steam engine was named after the British Chief Scout, Lord Rowallan.

And throughout all the celebrations, the main purpose of Scouting – the training of young people in Scouting skills within the Law and Promise – continued unabated and unaffected by the extra demands of the golden jubilee year.

World Scout Jamboree

The main celebration was, of course, the ninth World Scout Jamboree, which was held at the same time as the second World Indaba (leaders' meeting) and the sixth World Moot.

All three were held in a park of about 970 hectares (2,400 acres) with seven lakes, woods and heather-covered moorland in Sutton Coldfield on the outskirts of Birmingham. It was the ideal setting for hosting a canvas town with 35,000 people from 90 countries, complete with shops, banks, a hospital, a theatre and police and fire stations. Of these thousands of people, 5,000 Scouters were at the indaba and 5,000 Rovers were at the moot. There was also a service team of 2,700 people. The jamboree was opened on 1 August by the Duke of Gloucester, then President of the British Scout Association, and was closed by the World Chief Guide 12 days later.

An international celebration

The camp followed the now well-established pattern of jamborees – making friends, swapping badges, displays in the national arena, formal campfires and informal sing-songs. Elaborate gateways were constructed and amazing displays of Scout talent entertained and amused. The varied uniforms, the range of languages spoken and the religious tolerance shown were a microcosm of a better world. Dominating the whole site at the camp's centre was a high tower with a globe and a four-faced clock.

As seems traditional with jamborees, one night the site was hit by a sudden thunderstorm, which turned roads into rivers and hollows into lakes. Some Scouts had to be moved to higher ground, but the evacuation was completed in an orderly and controlled manner. By the following day things had returned to normal, with Scouts cooking over large fires, laughing as though nothing had

⚜ The closing ceremony

On Monday, 12 August, Olave Baden-Powell made her closing speech to the participants:

Here in this camp we are thinking more particularly today of a happy man, a man who 50 years ago had ended an eventful career in the Army; and that end was the beginning of what we see around us today, of which this great jamboree – indaba – moot and our world camps of Guides have been but tokens – millions of boys and girls, men and women, of every colour, creed and country, living together as brothers and sisters under one Promise and one Law, that Promise and Law given to us 50 years ago by our Founder.

He left this earth some 16 years ago and that end was indeed only a beginning. For you, too, as you come to the end of this wonderful jamboree tonight, the end is truly only a beginning. For these two weeks you, Scouters and Scouts of so many different lands and so many different languages, have lived in harmony together, forgetting all the differences which separate and thinking only of the ties which unite you all in the great world family of Scouting.

We celebrate our jubilee, but it is my belief that we are at the beginning of a new era in our Movement. Just as these green trees around us will soon shed their leaves in order to make room for the fresh young growth of another spring, so many of us older ones, who have come perhaps to our last world jamboree, will make way for a new and finer and even bigger generation of Scouters and Scout, a generation which will be finer and bigger because you who are sharing in the jamboree today are going away determined that your efforts will make it so.

Above: Queen Elizabeth II and the Duke of Edinburgh paid a visit to the 1957 Jamboree and toured the site in an open-top car.

Left: The activities featured at the jamboree included a demonstration by Sea Scouts of their boating skills.

happened and making a nonsense of pessimistic newspaper headlines.

On the day designated Cub Day, 30,000 Cubs arrived, with 23 special trains laid on to cope with the demand and 10,000 coming in coaches. There were also many distinguished visitors, including the British prime minister, Harold Macmillan, and Sir John Hunt, famed for his recent expedition to conquer Mount Everest.

The royal visit

Queen Elizabeth II and the Duke of Edinburgh visited the jamboree on 3 August, spending several hours touring the camp in the heat of the sun and amid the crowds and dust. Although the British royal family had been strong supporters of Scouting from the outset, it was the first time that a reigning British monarch had visited a jamboree.

To mark the golden jubilee the British contingent enacted a pageant in the main arena to tell the story of Baden-Powell and the Scout Movement. The part of Baden-Powell as an adult was played by his own son, Peter, and as a child by one of his grandsons, while Scouts from the Charterhouse School Troop took part in the school scenes.

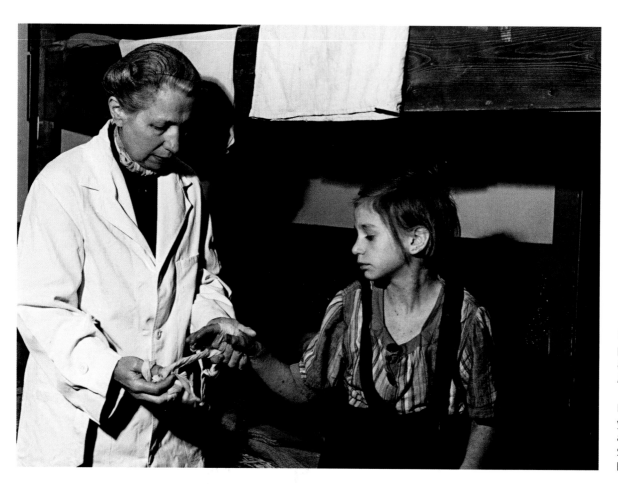

Left: A young displaced person being tended at a camp set up by the Allies in Berlin, c. 1946.

Right: General Franco's youth corps absorbed aspects of Scouting, but Scouting itself was banned.

Post-war suppression and communism

Scouting had an uneasy relationship with communism from the outset. Baden-Powell spoke out against it and was mocked for his views in the columns of several newspapers. In the 1920s young British communists sent him a small coffin made from black card, while British Scout headquarters issued a pamphlet, *Scouting and Communism*, warning of its dangers.

The years after the end of the Second World War brought new problems and challenges for Scouting. In some countries the fall of one totalitarian regime was followed by the emergence of another, and the freedom won at such great cost turned into another form of repression that brought new tensions and suffering.

Scouting and totalitarianism

Some countries in which Scouting had been deeply rooted, such as Lithuania, Latvia and Estonia, ceased to exist as independent nations, and it became impossible for the Scout Movement to survive there. In other countries, such as Albania, Bulgaria and Romania, one dictatorship was simply replaced by another and the ban on Scouting imposed in earlier years was never lifted.

In Spain Scouting had to await the death of General Franco (which did not occur until 1975) before it was able to emerge again. And in Czechoslovakia, Hungary and Yugoslavia, following a brief revival, Scouting was again prohibited, and even possessing the uniform, badges or insignia risked severe penalties. As time went by, even the very fact that the Scout Movement had existed in some of these countries was sadly forgotten.

Many nationals from these countries were among the thousands of people held in special displaced persons camps in places as far away as Australia. Among these people were Scouts, so a special displaced persons division was established at the World Scout Bureau and

by February 1950 over 30,000 displaced Scouts were being supported in Germany, Austria and northern Italy alone. In many cases these Scout groups were eventually encouraged to join the nationally recognized association of the host country, but not all wished to do so, preferring to keep their 'independence'.

Other people fled to western Europe from their homelands to escape the new oppressive regimes. When they did so they brought their national Scouting with them and created their national associations 'in exile', some of which were recognized by World Scouting. It was not an ideal solution, and these groups posed problems of their own, especially in relation to the host national associations. In addition, they were contrary to World Scout Conference resolutions on the subject of national Movements on foreign soil. But, like it or not, it provided a means by which Scouting from some oppressed countries could survive.

Democracy re-emerges

And survive Scouting did. The appointment of Mikhail Gorbachev in 1985 as head of state of the Soviet Union heralded the introduction of liberal reforms in the countries behind the Iron Curtain and the eventual collapse of communism. One by one democratic elections were held or independence restored, and within a matter of months the world had changed dramatically.

As each country reappeared from its long winter, Scouting too was re-established or emerged again from out of the shadows. The first was Hungary in 1988. Everywhere it seemed there were men and women remembering their days as Scouts or Guides some 40 years earlier. More surprisingly, out of attics and from underneath floorboards came the Scout uniforms, badges and flags that people had kept hidden all those years, often at great personal risk.

Catching up

The revival of Scouting in these countries has not been without its problems. Many of those in exile were too old to return home, and their children and grandchildren had become integrated into new countries, but the parents wanted to preserve some element of their homeland through their membership of such things as an exile association, even though the very reason for that exile association had ceased to exist.

On the other hand, World Scouting has emerged much stronger as a result, not just in terms of membership numbers but also in terms of its global coverage – it is now truly a world Movement. It has provided new opportunities for contacts and friendships to be made with more established associations and made the concept of the worldwide Scouting family the reality that Baden-Powell wished it to be.

Left: Indonesian Scouts at the Asia-Pacific Region celebrations in 1994.

The development of Scouting worldwide

The most remarkable and significant aspect of Scouting's first century is the development of the Movement around the world. Baden-Powell's favourite image of the little acorn growing into the great oak tree symbolizes this perfectly, but even he would have been startled by the concept of 28 million young members around the world after a full century of Scouting.

A worldwide Movement

World affairs are reflected in the list on page 124, which shows the spread of Scouting. The dates map the ebb and flow of international relations, at war and in peace. For instance, only four countries took up Scouting during the Second World War (Algeria, Burundi, Rwanda and Burkina Faso), and in some of the countries directly involved in the conflict Scouting was banned in favour of compulsory political youth groups. In these countries Scouting was forced underground, with Scouts becoming key members of resistance movements, risking their lives to continue. The Second World War was proved to be a ground for Scouting principles. Because the Movement stood for peace and (at that time) brotherhood, it became a bond for those resisting and trying to survive tyranny. Scouting was no longer a 'lifestyle option' but a matter of moral and physical survival.

Despite their early original foundation dates, some national organizations have only recently joined and been recognized by the World Organization of the Scout Movement (WOSM), and others have restored Scouting (some more than once) following government bans on membership. Many nations have changed their names and their borders since 1907. The dates given in the table relate to the foundation of Scouting in these nations as they are now known.

Scouting and religion

In some countries the development of Scouting relates as much to their religious affiliations as to an independent decision to join the worldwide Movement. Sub-groupings within Scouting, such as the International Catholic Conference of Scouting, make it easier and more likely that sympathetic countries will join in. The internal politics, culture and political allegiances of a country are at least as important as their physical geography in this context.

One of the most influential factors in the formation of many of the earliest National Scout Organizations (NSOs) was the presence of Baden-Powell himself. His overseas tours, particularly those in 1909 and 1912, were the inspiration needed to get fledgling Movements off the ground.

Scouting around the world

People in many countries and under many different kinds of political regime have given their lives for Scouting and to Scouting. People have gone – and still go – to extraordinary lengths of personal endurance and self-

sacrifice to sustain a Movement in which they believe wholeheartedly. Entire books have been written about the development of Scouting in each one of the 216 different countries now involved, and it isn't possible to do justice to their stories in the confines of one chapter of one book. The best we can do is give a flavour of Scouting in some of the first countries to take it up, showing the course that it ran and the effect it has had on national identity. This section is only a very, very small part of a great world story – one that is far from over.

A full list of countries that are members of WOSM and the numbers of Scouts and Guides in those countries in 2005 is given on pages 186–187.

Above: Is it a hat, or is it a flag? Young participants at a Swiss Guide and Scout event.

Left: Participants enjoying the Central American Scout Jamboree in Panama, 2001.

Below left: A Scout from the United Arab Emirates, Arab Region.

⚜ Countries without Scouting (as at 2005)

Andorra
China, People's Republic of
Cuba
Korea, Democratic People's Republic of Korea (North Korea)
Laos, People's Democratic Republic of
Myanmar (Burma)

⚜ The spread of Scouting

This list is a compilation based on the official foundation date currently recognized by WOSM and the foundation dates claimed by the NSOs themselves, based on their own records. Foundation dates are disputed for many reasons: Scouting developed over long periods in some areas before it was officially founded, or else it took place in some communities and not in others. Changes to national borders and the disbanding and refounding of Scouting in some countries mean that Scouting may have taken place earlier in some areas than is recognized by the current official foundation date. This list is therefore approximate.

DATE OF FOUNDATION	COUNTRY
1907	Britain
1908	Australia, Canada, Ireland, Malta, New Zealand, South Africa
1909	Belgium, Chile, Denmark, Guyana, India, Russian Federation, Sierra Leone, Zimbabwe
1910	Armenia, Brazil, Finland, Greece, Jamaica, Kenya, the Netherlands, Singapore, United States of America (Boy Scouts of America)
1911	Belize, Bulgaria, Czech Republic, France, Germany, Hong Kong, Malaysia, Norway, Slovakia, Sweden, Thailand, Trinidad and Tobago
1912	Argentina, Barbados, China (Scouts of China), Estonia, Ghana, Hungary, Iceland, Indonesia, Italy, Lebanon, Mauritius, Palestinian Authority, Spain, Sri Lanka, Switzerland
1913	Bahamas, Cyprus, Japan, Portugal, Slovakia, Venezuela
1914	Fiji, Luxembourg, Romania
1915	Bolivia, Costa Rica, Croatia, Nigeria, Serbia and Montenegro, Slovenia
1916	Peru
1917	Colombia, Latvia, Namibia
1918	Lithuania
1919	Poland
1920	Ecuador, Israel, Mexico, Togo
1921	Gambia, Macedonia, Madagascar
1922	Korea, Liberia
1923	Philippines, Turkey
1924	Congo (Democratic Republic of), Grenada, Panama, St Vincent and the Grenadines, Surinam
1925	Uganda
1926	Dominican Republic, Papua New Guinea
1928	Albania, Guatemala, Swaziland
1929	Tanzania
1930	Senegal, Zambia
1931	Liechtenstein
1932	Benin, Haiti
1933	Brunei, Morocco
1934	Tunisia
1935	St Lucia, Sudan
1936	Botswana, Gabon, Lesotho
1937	Cameroon, Côte d'Ivoire, Nicaragua
1938	El Salvador
1939	Algeria
1940	Burundi, Rwanda
1943	Burkina Faso
1946	Mauritania, Uruguay
1947	Niger, Pakistan
1948	Oman
1950	Ethiopia
1952	Honduras, Kuwait, Nepal
1953	Bahrain
1954	Jordan, Libya, Yemen
1956	Qatar
1960	Chad, Mozambique, Paraguay
1961	Saudi Arabia
1963	Maldives
1972	Bangladesh, United Arab Emirates
1973	San Marino
1975	Comoros
1990	Monaco
1991	Bhutan, Moldova, Tajikistan
1992	Mongolia
1993	Kiribati
1994	Georgia
1997	Azerbaijan
1998	Angola
1999	Bosnia and Herzegovina
2002	Cape Verde, Seychelles
2005	Guinea

The first 15 years

The first 15 years of Scouting were by far the most 'expansionist' in its history. Of the 216 countries now listed by WOSM, 70 started their Scouting in the first decade after 1907.

The increasing number of nations joining the Movement in this period forced 'Imperial Headquarters' to consolidate the fledgling Scout Movement into the Boy Scouts' Association in 1912, under a royal charter, in order to coordinate Scouting in Britain and give guidance abroad. While Baden-Powell was reluctant to overmanage Scouting and constrict it with committees and policies, it was essential to be able to identify what Scouting was, and what it was not, no matter where it was practised.

In the earliest years Scouting was principally taken up in British colonies and territories, spreading further and faster once Baden-Powell and others began to travel, spreading the word and personal examples along with it.

The International Bureau

As early as 1911 B-P was writing about the creation of a 'foreign department' in the leaders' magazine, *Headquarters Gazette*. From 1920 the International Bureau (later the World Scout Bureau, based in London until 1959) took on responsibility for the administration of the Movement worldwide. By the time he died in 1941, Baden-Powell had seen the Movement spread to 113 countries.

The celebration of a decade of Scouting in 1917 had to be postponed because of the First World War. This was not a time to be celebrating when so many former Scouts were giving their lives on different sides of the conflict. Lists of the fallen appeared in each edition of *Headquarters Gazette*. Only after the war, when international relationships were being rebuilt, could any work towards the development of a 'foreign department' bear fruit and the idea of an international jamboree involving Scouts from overseas become possible. The 1920 Jamboree at London's Olympia was a watershed for Scouting as an international Movement. By then, 72 countries had a Scout Movement.

The International Conference

From this first truly international jamboree, and from the meetings between different contingent leaders that took place there, came the concept of the International Conference, to be held every other year (now every three years), with the interim work being conducted by an International Committee. An International Bureau was to act as the secretariat. The titles have changed, but this work still goes on (as we will see in the final chapter of this book), and international jamborees are still catalysts for change and development.

Below: Mad antics at EuroJam, held in Essex, England, in 2005.

Australia

New Zealand

The growing family

The influence of Scouting, and of Baden-Powell's personal charisma, spread rapidly in the first decade. What follows is a brief outline of the ways and the places in which Scouting first developed, and how it survived to the present day. It is impossible to overestimate the degree to which Scouting worldwide was affected by the two world wars. Scouting was something for which people have lived (having experienced travel and international friendships) and for which people have died, resolved to continue despite the risks. War made the Movement absolutely determined to focus on world peace and fellowship thereafter.

It is sadly not possible to show all the emblems of all the National Scout Organizations of every country discussed – some countries have four or more NSOs. The World Organization of the Scout Movement can provide a comprehensive list of emblems on request. Emblems appear here grouped together above their country's name.

Australia and New Zealand (1908)

The children of these two Commonwealth countries were keen on Scouting from the moment *Scouting for Boys* appeared in 1908. Baden-Powell and his wife, Olave, travelled to Australia and New Zealand in 1912, and the visit encouraged enormous interest in and commitment to the new Movement. Because Australia and New Zealand were allies with Britain in two world wars, there was a great deal of shared history and fellowship between many senior volunteers in the early years of the Movements. Australian and New Zealand prisoners of war joined other former Scouts in keeping Scouting alive in prison camps during the Second World War.

At first, the Australian state branches reported separately to the 'Imperial Headquarters' of the Boy Scout Association in London, but they collectively became the Scout Association of Australia in 1971. Australia and New Zealand became members of WOSM in 1953, and they are founder members of the Asia-Pacific Scout Region.

Never backwards in coming forward, Scouting in Australia and New Zealand has initiated many innovations – since taken up by other countries, including Britain. They were among the first nations to allow women to vote, and girls were admitted into New Zealand's Venturer section (the most senior Scout section) in 1979, into the Scout section in 1987 and into Cub Scouts and Kea Scouts (the most junior section, which is named after a cheeky and intelligent New Zealand bird) in 1989.

Both nations have worked hard to ensure the integration of their different cultures in all aspects of their Scouting. The youngest sections use Maori (in New Zealand) or Aboriginal (in Australia) names and terms, games, skills and crafts to reinforce nationhood alongside personal development.

Australia hosted the 31st World Scout Conference and the 16th World Scout Jamboree in 1988, which was attended by 15,000 Scouts from 94 countries. New Zealand hosts its 18th jamboree in December 2007, and both nations will be well represented by contingents at the 2007 centenary celebrations in Britain. Their characteristic up-beat, 'have-a-go' attitude is famous the world over and epitomizes the essence of Scouting.

Australian Scout

❧ Nature project

Following flooding and a landslide in Nepal, Venturer Scouts, Rovers and Leaders from Australia have been travelling out to Nepal in July and December each year, to undertake four weeks' work at a time with Nepalese Scouts on the reforestation and stabilization of an area of 'washaway' near Pokhara. Work involves preparing the ground, building, fencing, planting trees and safeguarding their survival. This is an ongoing project, preventing future damage and building friendships and partnerships with the Scouts of Nepal.

South Africa

South African Scout

South Africa (1908)

South African Scouts claim, with some justification, that they were the first real Scouts. Baden-Powell's experiences in South Africa with the Mafeking (now Mafikeng) Cadets and the South African Constabulary and his knowledge of African scouting methods formed the basis for the original Scout programme. The Wood Badge, based on Chief Dinizulu's necklace, is still the highest award in leadership training.

Scouting as we know it started in Cape Town, Johannesburg and Natal, only months after the Brownsea Island camp, and by 1909 many groups were registered at 'Imperial Headquarters' in London. Racial segregation was standard throughout South African society, but Scouting was popular in black, white, mixed race and Asian communities, and each of the four segregated communities had its own recognized Branch of Scouting (see page 97).

The Afrikaner government created the Voortrekkers and other organizations designed to rival Scouting and indoctrinate young people with a specific political agenda. Although Scouting was never actually banned by the government, when they were confronted by the possibility of expulsion from WOSM in the 1970s, the four Branches decided to come together to form a single organization. This was an exceptionally brave decision, because mixed-race gatherings were illegal at that time.

The leaders of the modern Movement bear the scars of that period. The patron of the South African Scout Association is former President Nelson Mandela, who was imprisoned on Robben Island for his stand against apartheid. Nkwenkwe Nkomo, imprisoned for eight years for his role in the Black People's Convention, was Chief Scout for ten years and is now one of the 12 members of the World Scout Committee. These days South African Scouting is not only multi-racial but includes girls on equal terms to boys.

Scouting's earliest history is no longer what marks South African Scouting out for special commendation, however. The stand that Scouts and their leaders made against apartheid in the 20th century and the action that they are now taking to deal with the HIV/AIDS pandemic make them worthy examples of the best of Scouting in some of the worst of circumstances. The South African Scout Association is an active member of the Africa Scout Region.

SCOUTS CANADA

Canada

Canadian Scout

Canada (1908)

Scouts Canada and the Association des Scouts du Canada (ASC) are the two Canadian Scout Associations now recognized jointly by WOSM as the National Scout Organization of Canada. There are at least eight others, with different histories and representing different cultural or religious backgrounds. Significant numbers of refugees (particularly from Poland and the Ukraine) have settled in Canada in the past century, and their communities now have Scouting groups with distinct identities.

In 1910 Baden-Powell contacted Earl Grey, the governor general, to ask him to set up Scouting in Canada, and since then the governor general has also been the Chief Scout of Canada. The governor general is currently (2005) Adrienne Clarkson, so Canada has a female Chief Scout.

Scouts Canada is administered by a general council. The Canadian General Council was a branch of the British Association from 1914 until 1946, when it became an independent member of the Boy Scout World Conference. The name Scouts Canada has been in use since 1976, and Scouting is now open to girls at all levels. The eighth and fifteenth World Scout Jamborees were held in Canada.

Scouts Canada prides itself on its partnership and sponsorship arrangements with many different faith organizations and compatible charities, working with them to gain support for Scouting in the community. Covering some of the most northerly inhabited territory in the world, Scouts Canada is working on inclusive outreach programmes for populations in the Yukon, the Northwest Territories and Nunavut. This involves sponsorship and partnership with companies able to transport personnel and equipment to extreme environments and with Scout volunteers who can speak and write English or French and Inuktitut.

Malta

Chile

Sierra Leone

Guyana

Malta (1908)

The island of Malta, too, has a claim to being one of the early influences on Scouting. We know that Baden-Powell was in Malta in the early 1890s as assistant military secretary to his uncle General Sir Henry Smyth, governor of Malta. Malta became the first overseas branch of the Boy Scouts Association and remained as such until 1966, when the Scout Association of Malta became an independent member of WOSM.

Malta gained its independence 1964, becoming a republic within the British Commonwealth in 1974. The three inhabited islands (Malta, Gozo and Comino) in the archipelago have a total population of approximately 360,000. Nowadays, boys and girls are both welcomed in Scouting and there are more than 2,500 young members of the Movement.

Maltese Scouts were notable for their bravery in the defence of their country from aerial bombardment by Italian forces during the Second World War, earning special praise from Baden-Powell himself, who always regarded Malta with special affection. The Maltese Scouts were collectively honoured with Scouting's highest award, the Bronze Cross for Gallantry (granted 'for special heroism or action in the face of extraordinary risk'), the specific citation reading 'in recognition of their courage and devotion to duty in the face of continuous enemy action in the war for freedom'. Their determined spirit is evidenced by the rebuilding of their association's headquarters on the exact site of the original building in Valletta, which was destroyed by bombing in 1942.

Chilean Scout

Chile (1909)

When Baden-Powell spoke directly to the public about Scouting in Santiago in 1909 the Chilean Movement was born. Chile was the only Latin American country to send delegates to the jamboree at Olympia in 1920, and in 1999 the 19th World Scout Jamboree was held at Picarquin, 75 kilometres (46 miles) from Santiago, one of Chile's top campsites and Scouting centres.

The Asociaciòn de Guias y Scouts de Chile now combines Guiding and Scouting under one association, integrating former brother and sister associations in one Movement.

Sierra Leone (1909)

From 1896 until 1961 Sierra Leone was a British protectorate. The country had been the base for the British suppression of the African slave trade since 1787. The population, centred on Freetown, was made up of colonial British subjects, the descendants of freed African and Jamaican slaves brought there by the British and local tribespeople. By 1855 there were 50,000 former slaves in Freetown.

Sierra Leoneans fought with the Allies in the First and Second World Wars. However, the conditions in which they were forced to live and work at home were appalling, particularly those involved in the mining industry. In 1951 Sierra Leone became a self-governing democratic country, and in 1961 it became independent within the Commonwealth. However, from 1967 until 2002 it endured a long period of violent unrest – political coups, anarchy and times of harsh military rule – which culminated in the arrival of an international peace-keeping force of more than 17,000 soldiers. Since 2002, however, the democratically elected president, Dr Ahmad Tejan Kabbah, has maintained a situation of peace and prosperity unparalleled in recent decades.

In the early years Scouting was taken up by white British colonials, but the Sierra Leone Scouts Association is now fully integrated. It was recognized by WOSM in 1964, before the outbreak of conflict, and by 2005 there were more than 7,000 Scouts in Sierra Leone.

Guyana (1909)

Formerly a British colony (when it was known as British Guiana), Guyana's first Troop met in Queen's College compound and from there it spread throughout the country. Once Guyana had gained its independence and become a republic in 1970, the new president automatically became Chief Scout, and that tradition remains, with each new president becoming Chief Scout on their election. As in many other countries, Scouting is associated with the community provision of local churches and schools. Guyana took its turn as the host for the fourth Caribbean jamboree in 1969, but before and since it has sent delegates to international jamborees all over the world.

Zimbabwe

India

Zimbabwean Scouts

Zimbabwe (1909)

Scouting's continued existence in Zimbabwe shows the power of optimism and faith over extreme adversity. The history of the area is complex and blood-soaked, and the history of Scouting here is no less convoluted.

In 1888 the Ndebele (one of the ethnic groups in the area) granted Cecil Rhodes, who was a friend of Kipling and Baden-Powell, the right to mine for diamonds, but the white settlement of Rhodesia that followed was the cause of unrest until 1897. Scouting started in white Rhodesia in 1909, and it continued when Southern Rhodesia became an independent British colony in 1923. African boys had also taken up Scouting and organized themselves under the title of Pathfinders.

By 1950, despite political upheaval and racial segregation in other areas, the two organizations came together, and in spite of the violent troubles of the intervening period and the exodus of people from rural areas, on independence in 1980 Zimbabwe had a single national organization, the Boy Scouts' Association of Zimbabwe, which was recognized by WOSM.

Now Scouting in Zimbabwe is fighting to survive again, taking a moral stand against injustice and prejudice. It draws great strength from its membership of the Africa Scout Region.

India (1909)

The growth and survival of Scouting in India is a fascinating story. While the country was under British rule, Indian boys were not at first officially admitted into the Boy Scouts' Association at 'Imperial Headquarters'. The government was concerned that Scout training could be seen as encouraging young Indians to learn skills that might lead to anti-British insurrections. With

determined characters such as the social reformer Mrs Annie Besant, who was an early supporter of Indian self-government, leading Branches of Scouting, this was not an unjustifiable concern on their part. Mrs Besant, who later became president of the Indian Home Rule League and of the Indian National Congress, was, in fact, admired by Baden-Powell and by many supporters of Indian Scouting.

The best way to get over this temporary hurdle was for supporters of Scouting in India to create local groups and get on with Scouting without official recognition. The first Scout Troop for Indian boys was formed in 1908 under the guidance of a Scottish missionary, but it was disbanded in 1910. Three Troops for Anglo-Indian boys were started in 1909. A large number of separate associations developed, including the Indian Boy Scouts Association, the Boy Scouts of India and the Boy Scouts of Bengal, and by 1911 there were at least nine different associations.

Eventually, Baden-Powell himself was invited to India in 1921 (see page 72), and the situation was partially resolved by the formation of the Boy Scouts in India Association, which was based in New Delhi. Baden-Powell wrote *Scouting for Boys in India* especially for the Indian Scouts in 1923, complete with new drawings, quotations from Annie Besant's books on Indian life and from Kipling's *Kim*, and specifically Indian references and parables from the holy books of India's main religions.

Independence and partition came in 1947, and in 1951 first all the Scout associations and then the Guides of India came together as one group, the Bharat (Indian) Scout and Guides. Today, Scouting is a fundamental part of everyday life in India. Families across the country embrace the opportunities it provides for young people and respect its traditional values.

Belgium

Belgian Scout

Belgium (1909–13)

Scouting in Belgium started as early as 1909, but the first Scouts were British and Anglo-Belgian boys gathered together by Harold Parfitt, the organist at the Anglican church in Brussels. They were seen practising 'Scoutcraft' in a park by a Belgian boy, the son of Dr Antoine Depage, the king's surgeon. While she was on holiday in Britain, the boy's mother bought a copy of *Scouting for Boys* and gave it to her husband. Dr Depage was very impressed and set up the Boy Scouts de Belgique (BSB), appointing Harold Parfitt as Chief Scout. Scouting then spread in Belgian colonies overseas. Incidentally, Dr Depage and Harold Parfitt were also instrumental in starting Scouting in Turkey, where they were both posted in the First World War, and Dr Depage was in charge of the Balkan ambulance service.

Catholic Scouting in Belgium has a connected but different history. In 1910 Abbé Petit met a BSB Scout patrol and was impressed by their conduct. He was already running a welfare centre and decided to start a Catholic Movement in addition to his welfare work. The Catholic Troops were initially attached to colleges.

However, the invasion of Belgium by the Nazis in the First World War forced Scouting underground, and a number of factions developed while it operated in secret. The Open (or neutral) Scouts had been created, and they merged after the war with the BSB, but there is now also a Belgian association called the Federation for Open Scouting. Following a 1932 training course at Gilwell Park, which was attended by the heads of several of the different Belgian associations, the Belgian Interfederal Bureau was created, forging links between the associations.

During the Second World War Belgian Scouting was again forced underground, although it continued in refugee camps and prisoner of war camps, in the armed forces and among refugee children sent to Britain.

The WOSM now recognizes four Belgian national organizations, reflecting the different needs of the French- and Flemish-speaking populations and the Protestant and Catholic faiths. Describing themselves as 'head in the air, feet on the ground', they work hard to ensure that their activities are youth-led and relevant to modern young people.

Denmark

Armenia

Denmark (1909–10)

The precise start date for Scouting in Denmark is debated, as it is in many countries, especially where more than one association exists. Det Danske Spejderkorps (DDS) was officially founded in 1910, but it was in 1909 that a schoolboy called Ove Holm (one of the Danish Movement's greatest proponents and founding members) asked his headmaster, Dr Hartvig-Møller, to start Scouting. The boys of the school had just heard a rousing speech by a professor of education who had seen Scouting in Britain, and they wanted to be part of it all.

Hartvig-Møller became Scoutmaster of one of the two troops formed in Copenhagen (København). Carl Lembke, a cavalry officer and the Scoutmaster of the second Copenhagen Troop, translated *Scouting for Boys* into Danish, and it was published as quickly as possible. Baden-Powell made a personal visit to the country in 1911, and the second World Scout Jamboree was held in Denmark (at Ermelunden near Copenhagen) in 1924. One of only three official jamboree organizers, Ove Holm was organizing secretary and administrator. He later became Chief Scout of the DDS.

The WOSM currently recognizes five Danish national organizations under the Danish Scout Council. Kristeligt Forening for Unge Mænd – Spejderne i Danmark (KFUM), which is also known as the Young Men's Christian Association (YMCA) Scouts, shared an official 1910 start with the DDS, and they came together initially but parted company in 1916 and have remained separate since. Scouting in Greenland and the Faroe Islands also comes under the Danish Scout Council's banner, as does the Danish Baptist Scout and Guide Association.

Guiding and Scouting merged under the DDS name in 1973, so the DDS is entirely mixed. Denmark is in the vanguard of countries promoting sexual equality, and the DDS operates a 'two out of three rule' – that is, no more than two out of three members of any committee at national level can be of the same sex. All national appointments are held jointly, each title-holder having a counterpart of the opposite sex.

Russian Federation (1909) and Armenia (1910)

Russian Scouting began in 1909, but following the revolution in 1917 when the tsar was overthrown and during the period of instability between 1917 and 1920, Scouting was in limbo. Oleg Pantuhoff, the father of Russian Scouting, fled to Turkey, but once he was safe, he instigated the foundation of the council of Russian Scouts, which coordinated exiled Russian Scout groups. Scouting was suppressed following the creation of the Soviet Union in 1922. Russian exiles and emigrants continued to practise Scouting in the countries where they settled, and Russian Scouting in Exile was recognized as a specific group from 1928 until the end of the Second World War. When the Soviet Union ceased to exist in 1989, Russian Scouting returned to its home territory, and there are several different Russian associations. The WOSM now recognizes the Russian Association of Scouts/Pathfinders as the national organization of Russia. There are 18 'new' eastern European associations, ten of which are now recognized by WOSM, representing territories that were formerly part of the Soviet Union. Those Russians who remained abroad continue to practise 'Russian Scouting' in their adoptive homes.

By 1910 Scouting was firmly embedded in Armenian society, where it as supported by the Armenian Church. Trapped and torn between allegiance to their neighbours Russia and Turkey (which fought on opposing sides in the First World War), Armenians became exiles all over the world and took their Scouting with them, particularly to the Middle East and France. Armenian Scouting at home is now being fuelled by the success and encouragement of the exiled Armenian Scout Movement, which is still based in different countries around the world. The modern Armenian Scout Movement is officially known as Hayastani Azgayin Scautakan Sharjum Kazmakerputiun (HASK).

Scouting has an important job to do in Russia and Armenia. It has a vital part to play in improving life for Russian children, in practical and psychological terms, and Scouting worldwide is working hard alongside Russian Scouts to ameliorate the conditions in which thousands of Russian children live. Working with WOSM, Network Russia is a British Scout fellowship which organizes exchanges and visits to encourage involvement with Russian Scouting. Part of their recent work has been to help renovate an orphanage at Kolumna, outside Moscow.

Russian Scout

United States of America

United States of America (1910)

The Boy Scouts of America (BSA) is one of the largest Scouting organizations in the world, with over 6 million members. But it began in the most inauspicious circumstances – with a chance meeting in the street in the London fog.

In the winter of 1909 a publisher from Chicago named William Boyce was on a business trip to London. He got lost in a thick fog, and a young boy appeared and offered to show Boyce the way to his business address. When he arrived Boyce was so grateful that he offered the boy some money as a gift. This was politely refused with the comment that 'Scouts don't accept tips.'

Boyce was surprised, not only by the refusal but also by this new idea of 'Scouts'. He made further enquiries and was led to Scout headquarters, where he managed to meet Baden-Powell himself.

William Boyce's experience was a high spot in his life. He employed up to 30,000 boys and had experience of organizing them as a sales force for his weekly newspapers, but he had never met a boy who had made such a lasting impression on him. When he returned to the United States some days later he took with him copies of *Scouting for Boys* as well as some uniforms and badges, and he was instrumental in starting the Boy Scouts of America, which was incorporated on 8 February 1910. He involved others, such as Ernest

Thompson Seton (see page 26) and Daniel Beard, both of whom had already established youth organizations themselves and were gifted writers and backwoodsmen.

As the first national Scout commissioner, Beard merged his own boys' organization, the Sons of Daniel Boone, into the Scouts and helped to design the original American Scout uniform. Seton had his own youth organization, the Woodcraft Indians, and he became the first Chief Scout of the Boy Scouts of America, writing many books on scoutcraft.

In 1911 James West became the first Chief Scout executive of the Boy Scouts of America, and although he was physically handicapped he led American Scouting until his retirement in 1943.

The identity of the boy whose good turn led to the formation of the Boy Scouts of America remains unknown to this day. When their highest award for good service, the Silver Buffalo, was created in 1926, the first was awarded to Baden-Powell. The second was awarded to this unknown Scout, although, of course, no one knew who he was. Instead, a large bronze bust of a buffalo was given to the UK Scout Association in memory of the 'unknown Scout'. On 4 July 1926 at Gilwell Park the buffalo was presented to Baden-Powell by the American ambassador in London, in the presence of the Prince of Wales (later King Edward VIII). This bronze continues to be an attraction to the many American Scouts who visit Gilwell Park each year.

American Scout

Finland

Jamaica

Brazil

Kenya

Brazilian Scout

Kenyan Scouts

Finland (1910)

Scouting and Guiding started simultaneously in Finland. They operated in parallel until they came together in 1972 to form Suomen Partiolaiset (or the Guides and Scouts of Finland), a single mixed national organization. Finnish Scouting has a strong focus on peace, working on the principle that educating the youngest generation about other cultures can only benefit the world in the future. Finland is always well represented at world jamborees.

Jamaica (1910)

Jamaican Scouting was founded by an Anglican clergyman, the Rev. Joseph Graham, who started with one Troop in Brown's Town, St Ann's Bay, having been sent a copy of the first edition of *Scouting for Boys* by a friend. When former Scout leader Harry Mills came out from Britain in 1911 to work on the railways, he started the second Troop, which was established in Kingston.

In 1912 Baden-Powell himself visited Jamaica. He was on his way to the USA on the SS *Arcadian*, and it was on this voyage that B-P met the woman who was to become his wife. Olave St Clair Soames was travelling to Jamaica with her father for a three-month stay. Once in Jamaica, Baden-Powell encouraged the existing members and promoted the Movement.

In 1913 the Jamaica branch of the Boy Scout Association was registered, and in 1920 the Boy Scout Association of Jamaica was recognized. There have been contingents from Jamaica at every World Scout Jamboree since the first in 1920, and in 1952 Jamaica hosted the first Caribbean jamboree.

Brazil (1910)

Baden-Powell visited Brazil in 1909, and the União dos Escoteiros do Brasil (UEB; Brazil Scouts Association) was founded the following year. UEB is an active member of the International Catholic Conference of Scouting (ICCS). Young members of the UEB are actively involved in many health and social education programmes within their communities, giving Scouting a very high public profile in the country.

Kenya (1910)

Baden-Powell knew Kenya before Scouting was founded, but he returned to that country for a visit in 1935, going back for the final time in 1938 and spending his last years there.

The first Nairobi Troop was formed at St John's Church, Pumwani, in 1910. and fundraising for victims of the First World War was the first recorded Good Turn by the 40 Scouts and Cubs then in Kenya. Three Kenyan boys represented the country at the jamboree in London in 1924, and 20 went to Arrowe Park for the Coming of Age Jamboree in 1929.

At first, Scouting developed mainly among white and Asian Kenyans, and Troops were racially segregated. The first black African Troop, the 1st Kikuyu Troop, was formed in 1927. The Kenya Boy Scouts Association was formed in 1933, integrating all the Scouts under one title.

Kenyan Scouting is now divided into four age sections, each of which has a Kiswahili name to distinguish the nation's Scouting style – Sungura, Chipukizi, Mwamba and Jasiri Scouts now represent Kenyan Scouting wherever they travel around the world. Kenyan Scouting is at the forefront of the fight against drug use and HIV/AIDS in the country, and it has a very high public profile nationally as a result.

The Netherlands

Singapore

The Netherlands (1910)

Scouting and Guiding have been strong in the Netherlands since they began in 1910. There were originally two Scout and two Guide associations, reflecting the Catholic and Protestant traditions, but in 1973 they merged to become Scouting Nederland, which is coordinated by professional staff at the National Service Centre at Leusden. It is one of the most progressive Scouting organizations in the world, and Dutch Scouts are welcomed at every World Scout Jamboree for their open good humour and enthusiasm. The significant part Scouting played in the Netherlands during the Second World War is described on pages 107–108.

Singapore (1910)

Singaporean Scouting began under the wing of the YMCA, with which it shared a headquarters. From 1867 Singapore had been a British Crown Colony, and Scouting was taken up initially by white colonial boys. In 1915, during the violent mutiny of sepoys, Scouts undertook many different roles, maintaining the infrastructure and communications systems of the community and acting as telegraph operators and messengers.

By 1919 the first Malay-speaking Troops were starting, and Scouting had spread to the whole Malay peninsula by 1920. It needed central organization, so a chief commissioner was appointed for this overseas branch of the Boy Scout Association. He became responsible for the British Crown Colony of the Straits Settlements (Singapore, Penang and Malacca) and the Federated Malay States. Singaporean schools began to offer Scouting as an extracurricular activity.

In 1934 Baden-Powell visited to encourage membership and commitment. Singapore Scouts were affected as profoundly as the rest of the population during the Second World War by the occupation of the Japanese and aerial bombardment by Allied forces. Scouts served as auxiliary air-raid wardens and first-aiders, among other roles. Scouting was carried out underground, and it survived the war. Singapore gained its independence in 1965 and the Singapore Scout Association was recognized by WOSM in 1966.

Dutch Scout (top)
and Singaporean Scout

Hong Kong

Hong Kong (1911)

Once a small British naval base during the Opium Wars with China, Hong Kong was ceded to Britain by China under a treaty in 1842. In 1912 China became a republic, and thousands of refugees flooded into Hong Kong, swelling the population still further. Britain retained sovereignty until it reverted to China, by mutual agreement, in 1997.

Scouting actually arrived in Hong Kong in 1909, with the arrival of *Scouting for Boys* from Britain, but the Movement itself took a little longer to take root. The first recognizable Scout Troops were set up in 1911, mainly by British army officers who were extending their range of training to include younger boys. The 1st Hong Kong Group (St Joseph's College) was founded in late 1913 and registered in 1914. The Hong Kong Branch of the Boy Scouts Association was registered and recognized in 1915.

Most leaders were called to active service during the First World War, which brought the full development of a Hong Kong Movement to a standstill. Many of the soldiers returned, however, and focused on Scouting with renewed enthusiasm. Lieutenant Colonel F. J. Bowen was one such. He had been one of the founders of the first Troop and was in a position to re-form what remained of the Hong Kong Movement. The Boy Scouts Association, Hong Kong Branch, held its first rally in January 1921.

From 1937 China was at war with Japan, while the people of Hong Kong were preparing to support the Allies against Nazism. A second wave of Chinese refugees arrived in Hong Kong, and Scouts were drafted into service to help the overstretched social services. Scouts were acting as air-raid patrols, dispatch riders and auxiliary paramedics, and leaders were either on active service (again) or acting as reserves for the fire brigade, police force, volunteer defence forces or air-raid patrols.

In 1941 Britain was forced to surrender Hong Kong to the Japanese, and the Japanese remained as an occupying force until their own surrender in 1945. Britain reclaimed Hong Kong and Scouting resumed. In 1996, on their 85th anniversary, Hong Kong Scouts raised more than 1 million dollars to enable poorer Scouts to visit other countries for jamborees. Since 1997 Hong Kong has been a Special Administrative Region of the People's Republic of China, but Scouting continues to expand. It is their aim that every school in Hong Kong will have a Scout Troop.

Hong Kong Scouts

⚜ School project

The Development of School-based Scout Groups Project set out to establish Scout Groups in all schools in Hong Kong, so that all young people could enjoy the benefits of Scouting. This was in line with The Scout Association of Hong Kong's vision to involve young people throughout their formative years in a non-formal educational process. In December 2001, 5,800 Scouts gathered at the 90th Anniversary of Hong Kong Scouting Jamboree. The theme, in the best tradition of Scouting, was 'Do My Best'.

Germany

Malaysia

German Scout

German Scouting was resuscitated and did a great deal to raise people's morale in the difficult post-war period. The inclusion of German Scouts in international jamborees has done a great deal for European integration since the end of the war, and the famous circular black tents are a welcome sight wherever they are pitched.

The WOSM now recognizes three member groups of the Union of German Scout Associations as national organizations of unified Germany. The Bund der Pfadfinderinnen und Pfadfinder is a mixed organization, within which young people can be part of a single-sex or a mixed group of people their own age. One important aspect of their work involves partnership projects in Poland and Kazakhstan. The Catholic association for boys, Deutsche Pfadfinderschaft Sankt Georg, survives, and the third organization is Verband Christlicher Pfadfinderinnen und Pfadfinder (VCP), which combines Christian Scouting and Guiding in one association.

Germany (1911)

Dr Alexander Lion translated *Scouting for Boys* into German and co-founded the Deutscher Pfadfinder Bund (DPB) in 1911. Although the DPB survived the First World War, its members were excluded by the British Boy Scouts Association from the first World Scout Jamboree at London in 1920. London had suffered so much from aerial bombing and so many British troops had been killed in the fighting that the organizers balked at the prospect of German Scout Troops appearing in public in London. They could not guarantee their safety.

German Scout leaders were called to a meeting at which most of them signed the Naumburger Entschluss, a protest document that effectively excluded their association from international Scouting. Those who didn't agree broke away and formed many different associations, most of which hoped to be recognized by international Scouting. The Deutscher Pfadfinderschaft Sankt Georg became a collective of all the previously existing Catholic Scout groups. The total suppression of Scouting in 1933 brought an end to the existence of about 40 different associations.

German refugees from Nazism took German Scouting to their new homes. Fleeing Austrian Scouts did the same, as did Scouts from all the countries that were annexed and occupied by the Nazis. After the war

Malaysia (1911)

As is the case in many countries with modern independent Scout Movements, Scouting in Malaysia was initially an imported aspect of British colonial society that was adopted and enhanced by the people of the country and now supports their independent identity. Malaysia has been invaded and occupied many times, being spread over a beautiful and fertile collection of islands on ancient trading routes between Europe, India, the Middle East and China. As a result, the culture of modern Malaysia is enhanced by a unique combination of Chinese, Indian, Islamic and European (mostly Portuguese, British and Dutch) influences. Islam is the religion of about 60 per cent of the population.

The island known to the British as Borneo is now divided among Malaysia, Indonesia and Brunei, and Malaysia has sovereignty over the northern states of Sabah and Sarawak (formerly British North Borneo). Scouting began in Sabah in 1913, but it started in Kuala Lumpur, now the capital of Malaysia, in 1911. Kuala Lumpur, which is on the Malay peninsula, was formerly the capital of the British protectorate Malay States, and Scouting spread from there. In 1963 newly independent Malaya was joined by Sarawak, Sabah and Singapore to become Malaysia, but Singapore (see page 135) became a republic in its own right in 1965.

Persekutuan Pengakap Malaysia (Scout Association of Malaysia) exemplifies the modern Malaysian spirit of integration and harmony. After serious rioting in 1969, which resulted from racial and religious tensions, Malaysia was under emergency government until 1971, when new policies regarding the tolerance of ethnic difference came into effect. Malaysians have a great deal of experience of integrating multiple cultures under one identity, and Scouting has been an important aspect of this history.

Sweden

Swedish Scout

Sweden (1911)

It is said that in 1909 a copy of *Scouting for Boys* fell off a shelf on to the head of a Swedish army reservist and physical education teacher, Captain Ebbe Lieberath, who went on to translate it into Swedish and start the first Troop in Gothenburg. He became the first Chief Scout of the Sveriges Scoutförbund (Swedish Boy Scouts). Another tradition states that Scouting was started in 1908 by one Emil Winqvist. The YMCA adopted Scouting methods, too, and YMCA Scouts were formed in 1911. Guiding and Scouting had merged in all associations by 1961, and WOSM now recognizes five national organizations in Sweden, all of which combine Scouting with Guiding under single associations.

The Frälsningsarmens Scoutförbund, the Salvation Army Guide and Scout Association, was founded in 1916. KFUK-KFUMs Scoutförbund, the Swedish YWCA-YMCA Guide and Scout Association, was founded in

1911. Nykterhetsrörelsens Scoutförbund, the Swedish Temperance Guide and Scout Association, was founded in 1927. SMU-Scout, the Guide and Scout Organization of the Swedish Covenant of Youth, was founded in 1931. Finally, Svenska Scoutförbundet, the Swedish Guide and Scout Association, was formed from the separate Scout and Guide associations.

Since Scouting began in Sweden, its royal family have been enthusiastic and active supporters of the Movement. The present king, Carl XVI Gustaf, is not only Chief Scout of Sweden but also honorary president of the World Scout Foundation. Besides his many official duties in Sweden and on behalf of world Scouting, he led campfire songs at the 20th World Scout Jamboree in Thailand in 2003, performing a 'rocket' stunt and sleeping in a tent alongside his country's contingent. His commitment and enthusiasm were noted with admiration by Scouts from all over the world.

Belize

Norway

Belize (1911)

Now an independent member of the Commonwealth, this neighbour of Mexico and Guatemala was known as British Honduras between 1862 and 1973. It is one of the smallest countries in Central America. Scouting began here as one of the many overseas branches of the Boy Scout Association. Independence came in 1981, and in 1987 the World Scout Committee recognized the Scout Association of Belize as a member organization. In 1988 the Scout Association of Belize was certified as a member organization of the Inter-American Conference.

The modern culture of Belize is extremely complex and colourful. Languages and traditions derive from those of both its first peoples (the Maya, Olmec, Toltec, Aztec and Inca civilizations) and its immigrants over the last five centuries. Belize was conquered and invaded by Spain in 1542 and again in 1567 – the people kept rebelling – and the Spanish rulers left in 1642. The Spanish had been bringing slaves from Africa to their colonies since 1501, so there were a great many in Belize. In the 1650s Belize was annexed by the British, and thousands more African slaves were brought in during the following century. When Britain began moves to stop the slave trade in 1787, Belize became a base for British naval anti-slavery patrols, and thousands of freed slaves settled in the country. Slavery was officially abolished in Europe in 1838, but it continued in the USA until 1863.

As a result of the influence of the traditions of Africa and the Caribbean, the culture of Belize is now more Caribbean in flavour than Central American, but all the cultures play a part in its unique identity. Scouting unites these traditions to create a national Movement for all the young people of the country.

Norway (1911)

Norwegian Scouting takes place through several organizations, overseen by the Speidernes Fellesorganizasjon. Norges Speiderforbund (Norwegian Guide and Scout Association) and KFUK-KFUM Speiderne I Norge (YWCA-YMCA Guides and Scouts of Norway) are recognized by WOSM as the national organizations of Norway. The Norwegian Boy Scouts Association (Norsk Speidergutt-Forbund, which was founded in 1911, merged with Norwegian Guides in 1978 to form Norges Speiderforbund.

In 1909 a Captain Grøttum attempted to start a form of Scouting under the title of Norske Gutters Speiderkorps, but it foundered, despite initial popularity, when Baden-Powell came to Norway in 1911. Following *Scouting for Boys* more closely, the 1st Kristiania (Oslo) Troop had also started, under Christian Dons, in 1910, with a second Troop based at Frogner School operating under the same sort of principles. These two came together to form Norsk Speidergutt-Forbund. When B-P arrived he met Captain Grøttum and Christian Dons to sort out the muddle. Ultimately, the structure and organization of Norsk Speidergutt-Forbund proved more stable, and it survived to join with Guiding to form a single Movement in 1978.

Norwegian Scouting is still well known for its focus on outdoor living and survival skills, something that stood them in good stead when Norway was invaded by the Nazis in 1939, only the day after Denmark had fallen (see pages 108–109).

Norwegian Scout

France

French Scouts

France (1911)

There are many Scouting organizations in France, five of which are now recognized by WOSM as national organizations. Catholic, Protestant, Jewish and Muslim Scout associations are recognized separately, and although other organizations, whose aims are principally paramilitary or cadet-style training, are accepted by the French government, they are not recognized by the Federation of French Scouts or by WOSM.

Eclaireurs et Eclaireuses de France (EEF) is a joint Scouting and Guiding association that was founded in 1911. Eclaireurs et Eclaireuses Unionistes de France (EEUF) is a mainly Protestant Scouting and Guiding association, also founded 1911. Scouts de France is a Catholic co-educational association, which was founded in 1920.

Eclaireurs et Eclaireuses Israelites de France (EEIF) is a Jewish co-educational association, founded in 1923, and Scouts Musulmans de France (SMdF) is the Muslim association, founded in 1990.

The stories of the heroism and team-spiritedness shown by Scouts in France during the Second World War, when Scouting became the living spirit of freedom (see page 107), have left the Movement with a wealth of examples of what Scouting has meant in reality for so many.

The sixth World Scout Jamboree was held at Moisson in 1947, and Scouts from all over the world had an opportunity to show fellowship with a country that had twice in the space of 40 years experienced bloodshed and occupation by enemy forces.

Czech Republic

Slovakia

Bulgaria

China

Czech Republic and Slovakia (1911–12)

Czechoslovakia was a founding member of WOSM, and Scouting flourished in the country from its foundation in 1911 until 1948. Professor Antonín Svojsik translated and adapted *Scouting for Boys* for boys who had already taken up Scouting by themselves. Like Baden-Powell, he tried leading Scouting activities himself at an experimental camp in 1911. In 1912, following another successful camp, the organizers decided on the programme and first structure of the organization that was to become Junák – Czesky Skaut.

Junák has been dissolved three times in its history. In 1940 the Nazis forced Scouting underground, although it immediately re-emerged in Prague and by 1946 had 120,000 members. Scouting could not be killed off; it became a symbol of Czech and Slovak independence of spirit. During the Second World War, when Scouting had to go underground to survive, a Scout 'orchestra' moved around the streets, playing old Czech tunes on a strange assortment of instruments to cheer the oppressed people. They were never suspected by the Nazis because they looked just like the other boys. In fact, Scouts were also passing food and messages for the resistance movement and hiding fellow Scouts and resistance members in the mountains to keep them safe from the Gestapo. Even the youngest Scouts did something to help, and many died. Fifteen Scouts, aged between 12 and 16, were betrayed to the Gestapo, shot and thrown into a common grave.

In 1948 the communist regime took over from the Nazis and dissolved Scouting again, replacing it with a communist movement that borrowed a great deal from its non-political ancestor. Junák bravely resurfaced, for just two years between 1968 and 1970, and then it was banned by order of the Federal Ministry of the Interior.

When the Berlin Wall fell in 1989 and the Soviet Union collapsed, Junák resurfaced triumphantly in 1990. When the Czech Republic and Slovakia were formed in 1992 from the former Czechoslovakia, there were two new Movements to match. Slovensky Skauting belongs to the Republic of Slovakia and the Czech Republic has Junák – Svaz Skautu a Skautek. Since 1996 Junák has been a member of WOSM and now has more than 70,000 male and female members. Slovensky Skauting, which was recognized by WOSM in 1997, has more than 4,000 members.

Bulgaria (1911–13)

Despite its early foundation dates, Bulgarian Scouting came to an abrupt end during the Second World War. Scouting had 60,000 members at that point, but the Movement was suppressed under post-war communist rule. When the Berlin Wall fell in 1989, Scouting was reborn. The new national Movement, Organizatsia na Bulgarskite Skauty, was recognized by WOSM in 1999. The annual national camp has been restored, and visiting contingents from other countries have done a great deal to encourage and restore Bulgarian Scouting. There are now over 2,000 members and the numbers are rising again.

China (1912)

Scouts of China is an association recognized by WOSM under the General Association of the Scouts of China, but it is based in Taipei, Taiwan, and this has been the case since 1937. There is now no recognized Scout Movement in the People's Republic of China itself.

Baden-Powell visited China and Japan on his grand tour of new Movements in 1912 and was very impressed by the enthusiasm and proactivity he found there. The first Troop was set up in Wuchang in 1912 by the Rev. Yen Chia-lin, and the General Association of Scouts of China was founded in 1934.

Baden-Powell continued to be proud of the 15,000 Chinese Scouts and Guides who were members before war broke out with the Japanese in 1937. The city of Shanghai set up an organization called the Scouts War Service, and all its members were active as auxiliary first-aiders or military guides and civilian wardens. Thirteen of them were killed.

After China fell to the Japanese, the Shanghai area was turned into a vast internment camp, in which Scouts tried to continue to operate, managing to do so as long as they didn't wear uniform openly. Scouts interned here came from all over the world, but they had Scouting in common, and this saved many lives. They set up successful Scout farms, raising livestock and improving people's meagre diets, and ran a newspaper to keep everybody in touch and morale high. When bombs fell on the camps, Scouts were among the first to offer practical help and support, despite being exhausted and malnourished themselves. Wolf Cub Packs were deployed fetching food for the sick and elderly and keeping babies occupied and clean. This story was repeated in many internment camps across China. When the Weisien and Chefoo camps in northern China were liberated, out walked seven Rover Scouts, 50 Scouts and 46 Cubs.

From 1949 Scouting in communist China took a military turn, and as a consequence, in 1950, Scouts of China pulled out to its present base in Taiwan. Scouts of China is an enthusiastic and active member of the Asia-Pacific Scout Region.

Indonesia

Estonia

Indonesian Scout

Indonesia (1912)

There are some 206 million people in the Indonesian archipelago, and a large proportion of them are Scouts. Scouting started under the influence of the Dutch Pathfinder Scouts, but since independence in 1949 Indonesian Scouting has grown enormously and is now one of the largest single associations in the world. The Gerakan Pramuka (Scout Association) was founded in 1961 from various independent (religiously or politically affiliated) groups.

Estonia (1912)

Estonia is one of the many countries where Scouting started early and was then halted by Soviet occupation and communist rule. The first Estonian Troops date from 1912, and the Estonian Scout Association, which was founded in 1919, was a founder member of what became WOSM.

Estonia was occupied by Germany during the First World War, and many Scouts fought and died in the war of liberation in 1919, including Anton Öunapuu, one of the first Estonian Scout leaders.

Estonia was under communist rule from 1940 until 1989, and Scouting was suppressed, but as soon as the country regained its independence Scouting resurfaced. The Eesti Skautide Ühing has sent delegates to many international jamborees since 1989, and Scouting is a growing Movement once again, open to males and females of all religions.

Italy

Italian Scout

Italy (1912)

The two national organizations of Italy that are recognized by WOSM are members of the Italian Scout Federation. AGESCI (Associazione Guide e Scouts Cattolici Italiani) and CNGEI (Corpo Nazionale Giovani Esploratrici ed Esploratori Italiani) both take girls and boys, but they are differentiated by their religious standpoints. AGESCI was formed from separate Scouting and Guiding associations in 1974.

Italian Scouting first got under way in Rome, where it was seen initially as a form of personal training and was sponsored by the Lazio Track and Field Society. Giovanni Esploratori Italiani was founded formally in 1913. Guiding commenced shortly afterwards, in 1914. Scouting had a very positive effect on national morale, particularly among the boys taking part, and the government soon adopted Scouting as a 'national institution'. The head of state (initially the king) became its chief patron, and government officials took other posts within the organizations to reinforce its place in the national social structure.

State involvement became a double-edged sword, however, when Scouting failed to conform to the demands of a fascist state under Benito Mussolini. Italy was forced to pull out of the Scout Movement in 1927, when Mussolini gained complete control. Baden-Powell visited him to try to make a difference, but Mussolini's Balilla Movement had appropriated several aspects of Scouting, making it impossible for Scouting to survive.

B-P also had an audience with the pope in an effort to try to save Catholic Scouting at least, but although Scouting continued in the Vatican City, it was forced underground across the rest of Italy. Many Scouts joined the partisans, helping Allied soldiers to escape through the Alps to neutral Switzerland.

When the Allies relieved Rome and carried on northwards, Scouting sprang back to life in their wake. By 1944 Italian Scouting was back within the International Bureau, and two years later there were 65,000 Scouts in Italy. As originally, the head of state is the Movement's chief patron.

Iceland

Japan

Japanese Scout

Iceland (1912)

Based in Reykjavik, the modern Bandalag islenskra skata (BIS; Icelandic Boy and Girl Scout Association) started life in 1911 under Ingvar Ölafsson, who had witnessed Scouting in Denmark. The first Troops, collectively known as Skátafélag Reykjavikur, opened in 1912. The YMCA also took to Scouting and formed a Reykjavik Scout group in 1913, adding a Guide section in 1922. The Guides and Scouts merged in 1944 to create BIS as we now know it. Most Scouts are still based in Reykjavik, which is by far the most densely populated place in Iceland, but there are Troops serving the more rural areas.

Icelandic Scouting has its own special flavour, as is only natural in such a remarkable place. With volcanoes, geysers, thermally heated water and very few trees, camping here is different from anywhere else in the world. As the custodians of this unique area, Icelandic Scouts are encouraged to take a serious interest in their natural environment, and they have published a guidebook for teachers, helping other young people to take an active interest in their surroundings.

Japan (1913)

Although *Scouting for Boys* was translated into Japanese in 1910, nationally coordinated Scouting took some time to get organized. There were groups of Troops in different places following *Scouting for Boys*

more or less closely, but there were other Movements for boys based on warrior training principles from older traditions within Japan, so Scouting had considerable competition. Baden-Powell visited Japan in 1912 and met a British leader with a troop of non-Japanese boys, but he had also already been introduced to General Maresuke Nogi in London and had enthused to him about the new Movement.

The Boy Scouts of Japan were founded in 1922 by Count Yoshinori Futara and Viscount Miciharu Mishima. Devastating earthquakes provided the new Scouts with a great deal of practical work (as they have also done in recent years), which raised their national profile. Twenty-five Japanese Scouts attended the 1924 World Scout Jamboree in Denmark. They were led by Rear Admiral Count Tsuneha Sano, who also attended a course in Scout leadership at Gilwell Park and who went on to lead the first Japanese national training course.

After this auspicious beginning, and with good relations between so many Japanese Scouts and fellow Scouts round the world, it was particularly upsetting to the Movement that Scouting was dissolved by the Japanese government in 1941, only a few days after Baden-Powell's death. After the Second World War Japanese Scouting was re-registered with the World Bureau, and Viscount Miciharu Mishima, one of the Japanese Movement's founders and by then an elderly man, attended the 1951 International Conference in Salzburg to represent his nation, bringing the story full circle.

Just the beginning…

These stories from the very beginning of Scouting represent only a small proportion of the total picture, but if these vignettes of the early years have done their job, they will have made readers want to find out more about the whole story and bring it right up to date. The early years of Scouting in the period up to and including the Second World War serve to highlight the fact that the Movement became first a bond and then a reason to live for many thousands of people all over the world at a time when they might otherwise have given up all hope.

Baden-Powell's ideal – 'Scouts do their best' – was accepted as the ultimate challenge by even the youngest Scouts in the most appalling circumstances, even in times and situations that Baden-Powell himself could not have imagined. That Scouting survives and flourishes today is due in no small part to them.

Above: The colours of Scouting blowing in the wind – the Movement seems to spring back even in countries where it has been suppressed for decades.

Right: Many countries use this World Membership Badge as their emblem – the arrowhead symbol is recognized worldwide.

Now and
the future

A century of success is a huge tribute to all those involved, from the beginning to the present day. However, even such a rich and fascinating history is something that needs to be acknowledged and then set to one side to a certain extent, because the aim of the Movement itself is to focus on now and the future – the world that faces and will face young people today and tomorrow.

Adopting a worldview

One of the most remarkable aspects of modern Scouting is its global appeal, and it is this that sets it apart from other youth movements in history. The global scope of Scouting is also one of its most attractive aspects as far as young people are concerned.

A principal role of modern Scouting is to encourage young people to take a worldview, not just of themselves but also of their responsibilities as individuals and as members of their society. When they join thousands of other youngsters – whether at a well-attended event or simply by belonging to the family of Scouting – they are encouraged to focus on the similarities and the commonality of their experiences. The differences of opinion and cultural obstacles that frequently prevent adults from communicating with each other are often broken down by contingents of Scouts camping together at international events.

Sometimes it seems as if Scouting has always existed. With 28 million Scouts worldwide, the movement's 'established' image is both a source of pride and a challenge to those now active in the Movement.

A global appeal

Left: Adventure comes in many forms! Scouting encourages young people to increase their skills in their chosen area, whatever that may be.

Just like their predecessors, thousands of young people still owe to Scouting their first experiences of sleeping outdoors, travelling away from home or going abroad. Adventures that would otherwise have been beyond an individual child's budget or self-confidence lie at the core of the modern Movement. And this is true of all national Scout associations around the world.

In August 2007 young representatives of all 216 Scouting nations plan to take part in Scouting's Sunrise on Brownsea Island, where it all started, to see in a new century of Scouting together.

Getting it together

An international World Scout Jamboree, no matter where it is held, is an awe-inspiring sight. It is a real testament to the international vision and appeal of Scouting. But even the largest jamboree can include only a tiny proportion of the young people who belong to the greatest fellowship of youth and future hope on earth.

World Scout Jamborees still take place every four years, and the competition to play host to a World Scout Jamboree is every bit as fraught as an Olympic bid. International jamborees attract participants from almost every nation on earth in the spirit of fellowship, rather than rivalry or competition, although a certain amount of attention is paid to the presentation of each national contingent's base camp and identifying neckerchief.

Between international World Scout Jamborees, many international camps are held, with participants coming from both neighbouring countries and further afield. These camps often have exotic or challenging names or acronyms to give them a distinct identity for the young people who are participating.

Every year two special mini-jamborees focus on international communications between fellow Scouts – and no one has to leave home! JOTI (Jamboree on the Internet) and JOTA (Jamboree on the Air) allow Scouts to talk to each other via the internet and radio, live all round the world.

Summer camps

The traditional summer camp is still a feature of Scouting. Many summer camps now have a specific theme to bind the bases and wide games together, such as Space Camp, Pirate Camp and Knight Venture Camp. These camps provide a mixture of traditional Scout programmes – adventurous activities, practical skills, campfires and fellowship – and novelty. They are an opportunity for Scouts to extend their experience into new areas specific to the theme, such as archery, falconry, rope climbing and astronomy. The main point is still to encourage young people to work together, to experience independence from their families in an outdoor environment and to challenge their habits and assumptions about life and about themselves.

The summer camp is still one of the main attractions of Scouting as far as young people are concerned. Beaver Scouts invited to attend a Cub Scout campfire still sit, round-eyed with excitement, on log benches, watching the Cubs and trying to join in with the songs, hoping that next year they might be able to stay at camp. Nothing is likely to replace the magic of a Scout campfire, anywhere else in the world, for the foreseeable future.

Above: Young Swiss participants enjoying an international experience with their contingent.

Left: It's all about trust – testing a bridge made by fellow Scouts.

Left: Cultivating friendships and environmental awareness through Scouting.

Top right: Litter-picking is a small but worthwhile 'good deed' for the whole community, and it teaches the Scouts about the damage that litter can do to wildlife.

Middle right: Wearing his friendship badge with pride, this young African Scout is an unwitting ambassador to his peers.

Bottom right: Bangladeshi Scouts enjoying access to new technologies at the 20th World Scout Jamboree in Thailand, 2003.

Spanning the globe

Modern Scouts really do have the whole world in their hands – there are only six countries where Scouting does not presently exist. However, because it spans so many cultures, the Scout Movement has to have a single identifiable governing body for all the recognized national organizations to refer to.

World Organization of the Scout Movement

The World Organization of the Scout Movement (WOSM) is based in Geneva, Switzerland. A non-governmental organization, it is governed by the World Conference, which meets every three years, with delegates attending from every country with a recognized Scouting organization.

The World Committee, which is made up of elected senior volunteers, is WOSM's executive body. Its role is to implement the resolutions passed by the World Scout Conference. In the three years between conferences, the 14 members of the committee meet twice annually in Geneva. They act as independent advisers and executives to the Movement, rather than as representatives of the countries from which they come. Twelve of the Committee are elected for six-year terms, but the secretary general and the treasurer are members by virtue of their official positions. The chairmen of the regional Scout committees join them at committee meetings.

The secretariat of WOSM and Scouting worldwide is the World Scout Bureau, which serves the Movement on a practical level from its base in Geneva and through all the regional offices. The World Scout Bureau itself dates back to the early years of Scouting. Founded in London in 1920 to handle the necessary business of a globally expanding movement, the offices moved to Ottawa in Canada in 1959 before transferring to Geneva in 1968. Since then Geneva has become the hub of global Scouting administration.

World Scout Foundation

Since 1978 the funding for WOSM, the World Committee and the World Bureau has come principally from the World Scout Foundation. A board of senior volunteers governs the foundation, and Carl XVI Gustaf, king of Sweden, is currently (2005) honorary president. The role of the foundation is to invest capital donations received from governments, corporations and foundations, legacies from individuals and gifts from members of the Scout Movement so that foundation assets can continue to grow sufficiently to support the work of the Movement around the world.

Regional matters

To make sure that Scouting is as relevant as possible to young people's real lives and local cultures, Scouting has to be 'managed' on a regional basis, and there are six Scout regions:
- Africa Region, managed from Nairobi;
- Arab Region, managed from Cairo;
- Asia-Pacific Region, managed from Manila;
- Eurasia Region, managed from Yalta-Gurzuf and Moscow;
- European Region, managed from Geneva and Brussels;
- Interamerican Region, managed from Santiago, Chile.

The regions are self-governing to the extent that each national organization within each Scout region has its own identity and programme, a version of the Scout Promise relevant to the established main religions and government of the area and a recognized uniform. The World Bureau is responsible for maintaining relations with each NSO and for developing Scouting in that country, particularly if it is new there.

The degree to which Scouting is integrated into a national way of life depends to a considerable extent on the style of that country's government at the time and the length of time that Scouting has been established there. Scouting is a new concept in some nations, whereas others have had a recognized NSO for almost as long as Britain and the USA. Some nations have disbanded or banned Scouting in the past, only to restore it with a change of regime. Some countries, such as Thailand, have incorporated Scouting into their compulsory education system. Kings and heads of government are sometimes active participants as well as being enthusiastic patrons of the movement.

The WOSM, the World Committee and the World Scout Bureau are in place to ensure that what takes place under the name of Scouting in any of the regions and NSOs is recognizable as Scouting to the Scout Movement

⚜ Making a SCENE

Environmental conservation is only one of the areas of special interest to WOSM and the U Fund, but anything undertaken in this area has a far-reaching impact.

Scout Centres of Excellence for Nature and Environment (SCENEs) are gradually being developed all over the world, designated as such by NSOs under a single charter. They are open to all visitors, Scout and non-Scout alike. The SCENE project aims to increase the network of special sites further, so that young people can learn from first-hand experience about the natural world and what it takes to care for it.

The WOSM describes SCENEs as sites designed 'to strengthen the three fundamental roles of nature and environment in Scouting: education through nature and the environment; learning about nature and the environment; action for nature and the environment'. There are currently SCENEs in Australia, Austria, Denmark, Iceland, South Africa, Switzerland and the USA.

as a whole, and it is empowered to suspend an NSO from membership if necessary. Military training units, political youth groups, child labour forces and other unsuitable youth groups may not operate under the Scout flag. It should be possible to recognize the spirit of Scouting anywhere in the world, irrespective of the race or creed of the uniform's wearer.

The U Fund

The Scout Universal Fund was set up 'to help Scouts to help others', thereby extending the meaning and impact of the Scout Promise far beyond home shores. The fund is administered by WOSM, but the money comes from NSOs, Scout groups and individuals. Unless the donor specifies how the money should be spent, the fund is allocated by a group within the World Scout Committee on the basis of need.

The basic needs of developing countries are the focus of much of the U Fund's spending. Working together with the NSO of the affected area, the U Fund supports initiatives on:
• health and sanitation;
• housing and shelter;
• environmental conservation;
• food and nourishment;
• literacy and skills training.
All these are essential areas in which Scouting has been instrumental in improving local provision.

Above: Community relations are improved between generations through outreach programmes.

Peer pressure

Scouting exists to enable young people to be the best they can be, no matter the circumstances in which they find themselves. It is fundamentally about the empowerment of young people.

There are areas, however, in which it is hard for children to survive, let alone come to fulfil themselves as individuals, and in these places Scouting has a multiple role. Scouting can be a surrogate community when the village or the home has been destroyed. Scouting may also provide the only structure in lives that are otherwise chaotic or supply the core philosophy supporting individuals who have been victims of abuse or neglect.

Research carried out by European Guidelines for Youth AIDS Peer Education has shown that young people respond best to examples set by their peers, and providing supportive, enthusiastic and knowledgeable peers is something Scouting does well. This is proving to be of vital importance to life-saving and life-enhancing programmes in some of the most challenging areas in the world.

Peace in their time

Scouting has been bringing nations together for almost a century, a fact the movement will be celebrating in 2007. The proof of that – and the culmination of a century of effort – is 'Gifts for Peace'.

All NSOs have pledged to undertake national projects involving every single member of Scouting in their country in some way between 2005 and 2007. The individual Gifts for Peace will be presented to national leaders – presidents, prime ministers, parliaments and so on – on 1 August 2007 to encourage them to continue the efforts thereafter. Collectively, all the Gifts for Peace will be displayed at the centenary 21st World Scout Jamboree in July 2007.

The scope is enormous, and most projects are ongoing efforts that will continue far beyond 2007. There are three main working areas to guide participants: managing conflict without violence, challenging prejudice and encouraging solidarity.

Examples of projects under way are extremely diverse, reflecting the current situation and the history of each area. Ranging from anger management and anti-bullying projects to bridging sectarian and religious divides, ending local gang warfare, preventing disease and housing street-children, all the Gifts for Peace projects focus on young people and their place in the creation of a better society.

It is the scope of Gifts for Peace – the fact that any Scout anywhere in the world could say, in 2007, what they did towards their nation's Gift for Peace – that makes this different from any other project already being undertaken.

Above: Experience of teamwork is always worthwhile, even if it's only about writing a shopping list!

Left: For more than a decade, Scouting programmes have been encouraging children into education and offering peer-group support.

Fighting epidemics and endemic disease isn't solely the business of medical teams, especially when some conditions are preventable through education and changed habits. Making sure that young people have the information and the tools to make a difference is often the key to changing adult behaviours – the child is master of the adult in many situations, especially where new technology is concerned. Children can also effectively side-step adult hierarchies and go to the core of the problem in a way that adults might fear to emulate. It is also the case that peer-education and example are far more effective than conventional top-down education when it comes to influencing people to make lifestyle changes.

Practical support

To make sense of the modern Movement as a whole, it is necessary to give specific examples of the ways in which Scouting makes its presence felt across the globe. Each example, no matter the scale of its impact, tells a wider story about the role of Scouting today.

Ever since the First World War the 'trained uniformed volunteer' aspect of Scouting has propelled Scouts to the domestic front line in cases of public need and national emergency. As Scouting expands wider and wider and increasingly into the developing world, the areas of need

In areas ravaged by disease, political instability, war, drought, floods, earthquakes and famine there are many opportunities to demonstrate fellowship and common humanity and to provide practical support. Sometimes that is both the best and the least that anybody can do.

Below: Local community projects can become part of a disaster relief programme if events overwhelm your environment.

Helping hands

Above: Scouts forms part of a chain of international helpers on a 20th World Scout Jamboree community project in Thailand.

expand exponentially. 'Being prepared' refers to the need for psychological strength, as well as practical support, in places where the basic necessities for human survival are in short supply.

Collaboration and empowerment

The Africa Scout Region has harnessed its collective strength and pulled together to take on huge projects affecting the futures of the nations it covers. It has worked alongside other youth organizations, with support from WOSM and non-African NSOs, charities and non-governmental organizations. The organizational abilities of the national groups within the Africa Scout Region and of other youth organizations in these areas have produced communication structures from which the whole continent has benefited.

The needs and resources of the NSOs within the Africa Region vary widely, but the commitment is the same no matter where they are found. Collaboration between the Africa and the Arab Scout Regions has been particularly fruitful, with African delegates attending the Arab Youth Gathering (sponsored by Unesco), an environmental seminar and the Arab-Africa Jamboree, which was organized by the Libyan Scout Association.

HIV/AIDS

The population of Africa is disproportionately affected by the HIV/AIDS pandemic. In some areas as many as one in four people has HIV/AIDS, but the average across Sub-Saharan Africa is still one in seven.

A paper put together by the six largest global youth organizations suggests that there were 8.5 million children between 15 and 25 years of age living with AIDS in Africa in 2003.

The devastation over successive generations is incalculable, but Scouts and other youth groups in the region are dealing with the 'here and now', hoping that future generations will reap the rewards. The 'Big 6' global youth organizations are the World Organization of the Scout Movement (WOSM), the World Alliance of YMCAs, World YWCA, the World Association of Girl Guides and Girl Scouts, the International Federation of Red Cross and Red Crescent Societies and the International Award Association. Of the 100 million young people worldwide represented by these six groups, 20 million live in Africa.

Under the 'Empowering Africa's Young People' initiative and following the Pan-African Youth Forum on HIV/AIDS, which was hosted by the Senegalese

government in Dakar in March 2004, the Scouts of the Africa Region have come together 'to empower young people through holistic approaches to prevention, care, access to treatment and support'. Delegates from many other NSOs were also present at the Forum.

The goal is still to reduce the transmission of HIV/AIDS among 10- to 25-year-olds in Sub-Saharan Africa through peer-education in order to 'build the capacity of volunteer-based, grassroots, youth organizations to design and implement more effective youth-focused HIV/AIDS prevention programmes'. The statistics are already showing significant signs of improvement in Uganda alone, thanks to these efforts.

In addition to skills-based peer-education and advocacy against stigma, the Scouts of the Africa Region are giving young people the skills-training to earn an income – something that is absolutely necessary when many 'families' have a child under 16 as their most senior surviving member.

Ambassadors for information

Information is a primary tool in disease eradication, and
Scouts are often the best people to deliver it where it's
needed. They are young and enthusiastic, but in their
uniforms they also stand together as a collective force for
good that is recognized by their own communities.

The eradication of polio and leprosy is another goal
that Scouting has taken to heart, in Africa and the Asia-
Pacific Regions particularly. Unicef and the Angolan
Scouts have worked together to screen more than
500,000 children for polio.

Working in partnership with the World Health
Organization (WHO) and AHM Leprosy Relief, all National
Scout Organizations whose nations are affected by
leprosy have pledged to work to eradicate the disease
entirely and to remove the stigmatization of those who
have the disease. More than a million Indian children
have already been screened for leprosy by combined
groups of Scouts and Guides.

Brazilian Scouts are at the forefront of a campaign to
rid Brazil of schistosomiasis, a water-borne disease carried
by snails. More than 90 per cent of the population of one
village, Serra Pelada, were infected in the mid-1980s, but
in one weekend alone the Rover Scouts of the Espirito
Santo region made one-to-one contact with 42 per cent
of the population of Serra Pelada, through street
exhibitions, leaflets and fliers, and by knocking on doors.

Street Scouting

The plight of street-children (whose numbers are
growing, largely because of the HIV/AIDS pandemic) is
certainly a side-effect of disease and deprivation, but it is
a huge issue in itself. The Sunrise Project is one of the
more remarkable schemes to grow from Scouting. One
would not necessarily expect the most senior Scout
volunteers to apply themselves so very personally, but the
Chief Commissioner of the Ugandan Scouts Association
and Senior Manager in the Uganda Social Services

Commission has set an example to her fellow Scouters worldwide. Victoria Namusisi Nalongo and her volunteer team took over a failed working-farm project and opened it to 20 street-children. Run on the Scout principles of 'Duty to God' (no matter what your religion), 'Duty to Others' and 'Duty to Self', the centre is expanding to take on more children and build new accommodation.

Holding Scout Membership documents protects the children from harassment when they are outside in the street and gets them access to free government health care. The children's 'family choir' raises money for the Sunrise Project, and the wider community respects them for the first time in their lives. The action of one senior Scout volunteer is now an example to every other leader.

Similarly effective efforts on behalf of street-children are being undertaken by NSOs and local groups in Egypt, Chile, Brazil and many other countries. Some of these projects are being done with specific support from other NSOs or from organizations such as Unicef, and some try to deal with other issues in tandem, such as child labour or health screening.

Egyptian Scouts are involved in long-term projects, supported by Unicef, to improve the situation for street-children and for working children. Thousands of Egyptian street-children have now had access to social care, health care, literacy classes, vocational training, sport and improved working conditions as a result of these efforts.

More than 35,000 Chilean street-children have been given health screening and information by Chilean Scouts in recent years.

In Brazil 20 million children under 16 years of age live on the streets. In partnership with Scouts de France, the UEB (União dos Escoteiros do Brasil) has undertaken pilot projects in the city of Fortaleza, which can now be applied by other Scout groups. These include Weigh-in Days to check infant weights, peer-education programmes (on water and dental hygiene, dengue and sexually transmitted diseases) and setting up Scout groups in areas where there have never been any. As a result, there are now four permanent education centres in Fortaleza alone, and thousands of city children have been reached by Scouting.

A force for good – disaster relief

The ability and willingness of Scouts worldwide to act on their Promise and lend a hand have been tested and proved many, many times since 1907. Some of the most challenging situations arise in the aftermath of natural disasters, when structures and infrastructures prove to be equally fragile.

In the days following the Asian tsunami in December 2004, local Scouts immediately mobilized themselves to coordinate relief efforts in the affected areas. With schools and family structures destroyed, there was a great risk that surviving children would fall into destitution, begging, addiction and violence. Focusing on the needs of the young, at least five official projects were set up in Sri Lanka and Tanzania, using existing Scout leaders and training others. Scouts offered skills training, built camps of tents and temporary shelters, and ran recreational projects to keep children off the streets.

The Tanzania Scout Association set up Emergency and Disaster Preparedness management training to ensure that, in the event of another such disaster, a significant number of adults would 'be prepared'. Fifty Scouts were trained for three months, and each of them then went on to train eight more, in different areas along the coast of the Indian Ocean, so that more than 400 people can now train others in specialist management skills.

The World Scout Bureau Tsunami Scout Aid Fund, set up days after the disaster and receiving money donated by NSOs all over the world, directed funds to these (and other) projects in affected provinces. Staff of the World Scout Bureau donated a day's salary each to the fund, encouraging others to do the same. Local Scout groups, NSOs and many individuals took enormous pride in the money raised to help with these projects. The following examples, selected from hundreds available, show modern Scouting in action.

By the end of February 2005, UK Scouting had raised £68,468 and a further £70,160 followed in the next two months. Mexican Scouts collected more than 1 million cans for recycling, creating the largest Scout emblem ever seen, and they presented the fund with $29,871. Hong Kong Scouts raised $160,000 by April 2005. Brunei Scouts shipped 13 container-loads of clothing to Indonesia. The king of Sweden went in person to Thailand, taking $40,000 as a gift from the Scouts of Sweden, the Swedish members of the Baden-Powell World Fellowship and the World Scout Foundation. Thailand's Baden-Powell Fellows then matched this amount. The offers of money and help by Scouts from around world to those affected by the tsunami were unqualified in generosity and spontaneity.

European outlook

The European Scout Region, which includes countries that are not currently members of the European Union, such as Norway and Albania, focuses a great deal of its funds and awareness-raising efforts on encouraging its young people to take part in life as world citizens.

In some areas, such as eastern Europe and Ireland, a great deal of time and patience have been spent building bridges between communities that were at war with each other until very recently. It is always noticeable that children are prepared to go to greater lengths than their elders in this respect, and Scouting creates a forum for cross-border and cross-cultural activities.

Huge efforts are being made to integrate Scouts living in places such as Bosnia and Herzegovina, Croatia, Hungary, Latvia, Serbia and Montenegro, Macedonia and other eastern European countries. In countries like these, which were only recently in conflict, Scouting needs a great deal of support and attention from the entire region if young people are to be ambassadors for future peace and cultural integration.

Working for peace
Scouts from relatively prosperous and stable economies share a common dream for peace with those who have seen violence and disease and disaster. One of the most common expressions of fellow-feeling is giving – time, money, clothing, equipment, first aid – and every year thousands of Scouts take action on behalf of those less fortunate than themselves by fundraising, raising

awareness of issues locally and getting themselves as work forces to areas where help is needed.

More than 10,000 young people from the different associations in the Irish Republic and Northern Ireland have been brought together on many occasions, supported by the British Council and Cooperation Ireland. In 2004 the separate Protestant and Catholic Scout Associations of the Republic of Ireland came together to become Scouting Ireland. As their Gift for Peace, the UK Scout Association of Northern Ireland and Scouting Ireland, supported by the European Union programme for Peace and Reconciliation and the International Fund for Ireland, are working together to set up cross-border Scout citizenship projects for all the Scout sections.

Left: A Hungarian Scout parades the flag of World Membership.

Right: Projects such as the Essex Experience are working hard to enhance the lives of urban youngsters and socially deprived children.

Below: Looking forward to a joint future – Scouting Ireland's 'Gifts for Peace' project is setting an example for other organizations.

Self-esteem and self-harm – changing behaviours

The developed world has its fair share of problems, and children are often the first to display the signs of a wider social malaise or deprivation. Deprivation takes many forms – bullying, vandalism, self-harm, absenteeism from school, under-age drinking, smoking and drug abuse can all be symptomatic of a privileged society with not enough time for its own children. The children of the wealthiest societies can be the most attention-deprived of all.

Movements run by adult volunteers – people who spend their spare time on other people's children – can be a solution, or at least part of a solution. Young people are often incredulous that any adult would spend time with them 'for free'.

Many very valuable projects are being run by Scout groups in Britain, on the continent of Europe and in Australia, New Zealand and the US that reach out to local youngsters and get them involved with practical community projects, as well as with more traditional 'uniformed Scouting'.

One of the most notable and successful is the Essex Experience in Britain, which was set up to involve young people on the margins of their peer groups – people who are in danger of becoming excluded, not just from their peers but from society as a whole.

A national role

One face of British Scouting becomes very visible to the public on national and ceremonial occasions. For historical and practical reasons, Scouts in Britain have taken part in a large number of nationally (and internationally) significant events, ranging from an annual presence at the Service of Remembrance at the Cenotaph to duties at the funerals of Diana, Princess of Wales, and Queen Elizabeth, the Queen Mother.

British Scouts have been seen on television around the world, crisply uniformed, calmly organized and representing, on that day and at that moment, the nation's youth. It is not necessarily the most representative aspect of the movement as far as its active members are concerned, but it is nevertheless an important component of the public image of Scouting nationwide.

It is an enormous responsibility for every Scout involved, and for Scouting in Britain as a whole. Those

Left: In black mourning neckerchiefs, these proud Scouts stand in front of the Palace of Westminster, where the Queen Mother was lying in state.

Right: Scouts on duty in the marquee in April 2002. The books of condolence remained available to the public into the early hours of the morning until the funeral.

Scouts who have actually been involved in any of these occasions have always taken a great deal of pride in their extremely visible roles. For the individual, it is a responsibility that takes some getting used to, and it requires a degree of self-discipline, being a very different experience from going on a night hike, travelling to an international jamboree or undertaking local leadership duties. The pressures can be both psychological and physical, but the reward for each individual is a lasting sense of pride, national identity and fellowship.

Operation Marquee was the most striking example in recent history of all these factors. It was instigated following the role of Scouts in the aftermath of the death of Diana, Princess of Wales, when the demonstration of public grief required the mobilization of all police, support services and voluntary organizations to handle the crowds, the queues to sign books of condolence and the arrangement and dispatch of masses of flowers and gifts. The presence of uniformed young people, quietly and inofficiously guiding people, taking flowers and handling grieving individuals, led to a formal invitation to the Scout Association to be involved in preparations for similar occasions.

When the death of Queen Elizabeth, the Queen Mother, was announced in April 2002, Operation Marquee swung smoothly into action, and Scouts began to arrive for the first briefings and shifts. Surprised and exhilarated and not at all sure what to expect, they soon absorbed the atmosphere and the enormity of the situation in which they were intimately involved.

Their main duties involved standing guard over the books of condolence, and 60 Scouts worked in rotation, in three shifts of 20 Venture Scouts and Queen's Scouts. They monitored public movements, encouraging and looking after the people standing in the immense queue that tailed away as far as the eye could see. They also ensured that the books were safe overnight. Watches continued into the early hours of the morning on the days leading up to the funeral, for as long as the people queued to sign them.

When the Queen became anxious that those who were still queuing would not all have the opportunity to file past the catafalque in Westminster Hall before it was moved for the funeral, a rotating watch of Scouts was detailed to stand either side of the coffin to keep the mourners moving but without causing offence. Following the funeral, the entire contingent lined the road to pay their respects as the cortège drove slowly past Baden-Powell House.

The Queen requested to be able to thank the Scouts personally, on her birthday and at the annual Queen's Scout parade and service at Windsor Castle later that April, and when she allowed them the honour of wearing royal purple scarves as a special contingent in exchange for their black mourning neckerchiefs, the reaction was one of enormous personal pride and jubilant fellowship.

As Charles Paddon of 1st Alborough Hatch said:

Operation Marquee could be described as the opportunity of a lifetime ... However, one of the best things that came from carrying out this State Duty was the friendship that we had as a team of people ... it helped to make the Windsor Parade one of the most enjoyable days that I have had for a long time.

Representing Scouting

Thousands and thousands of Scouts experience this sort of pride in their actions every year, usually without the world's press in attendance, and it is just as important to the individual and as significant to the whole movement, but to have taken part in this event in British history, and to have excelled at the task, is something that no one will ever forget.

In Britain it is now quite common for five or more generations of one family to have been involved in Scouting, but young people are increasingly inclined to follow trends set by peers or those slightly older than themselves rather than consciously following in their great-grandfather's footsteps. Making sure that the movement is attractive to individuals and their wider peer group is the challenge for the many adults now working in Scouting.

If young people worldwide are becoming increasingly brand-conscious, and recent studies have shown that they are, Scouting must be an identifiable and attractive brand, locally and worldwide. Britain is the 'original' home of Scouting, and Scouting's centenary is the British centenary too. However, Scouting in Britain is far from being backward-facing or isolationist. Some of the most influential innovations affecting the whole movement worldwide derive from British practice and vision.

G APP was funded for its first three years by the British Department for Education and Employment, but since 2000 the national Scout Association has taken on the full role in association with the World Association of Girl Guides and Girl Scouts (WAGGGS). GAPPsters, as they are known, take part in all major British and international Scouting events, spreading the message to new audiences.

Girls allowed

One area where Scouting has a particular mission is in the recognition of female equality. Focusing on females within the movement, it is hoped that there will be positive effects on our wider society.

Scouting is a microcosm of wider society – girls have equal status 'in law', but perceived inequalities and a male-dominated history can affect the ability of women to take full advantage of this. The Scouting Movement is keen to ensure that it is effectively co-educational rather than nominally so.

The 1999 World Scout Conference agreed the Movement's policy on girls and boys, women and men in Scouting. In partnership with the European Scout Region (and financed by the fund for European Scouting), WOSM's Educational Methods Group launched a research project on Gender and Education in Scouting in 2001. The project was conducted by Professor Harriet Bjerrum

The Global Awareness Partnership Project was set up in 1997 by the British Scout Association jointly with the National Federation of Young Farmers Clubs as a peer-education programme. Its aim was to promote awareness of world issues – such as fair trade, healthy living and environmental conservation – and global citizenship to young people.

Below: Scouting in Canada embraces all the cultures represented within the nation, including those of the most northerly territories.

Mind the GAPP

Nielsen, from the Centre for Women's Studies and Gender Research at the University of Oslo. She worked with Scout leaders from four different European countries who acted as her research assistants.

Professor Nielsen concluded that Scout leaders must take some responsibility for the stereotyping and behaviour of Scouts of both sexes in their care, and that self-analysis for adult leaders is a necessary first step before the behaviours and attitudes of the Scouts themselves can be challenged. Creating an atmosphere where glamorous high-status tasks and mundane house-keeping tasks are allocated evenly and a wide variety of physical and cerebral activities are on offer is essential to foster the individual talents within mixed-gender groups.

Equality for women and men is currently a strategic priority for WOSM, affecting every recognized Scout organization. The Big 7 organizations, including WOSM, are also focusing on the vital role of women's education in developing countries. The chief executive officers of the five largest non-formal education organizations have produced recommendations for a national youth policy on the availability of non-formal education to all, regardless of gender.

Brand, image and reality

It is frequently assumed that Scouting is a static organization, not an adventurous movement. Scouting

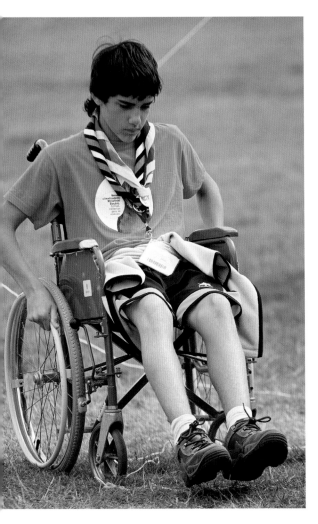

works hard to promote an accurate image, but it is fighting against old stereotypes of Scouting, and habits are notoriously hard to break.

In Britain Scouting has been promoting global citizenship, teamwork, outdoor exercise, self-esteem and ethnic diversity for a century – long before government initiatives in these areas. Some of the oldest Scout groups in Britain are Jewish, and there is an increasing number of Muslim, Sikh and other faith-based Scout groups within the national Association, reflecting the demographics of the local population. At least half the Beaver Scouts – those aged six to eight – in Britain are girls, and by 2007 all Scout groups and sections will be co-educational. There is also a policy of inclusion and support for members with physical or learning difficulties.

Nor is Scouting just an activity for the privileged few, which is a charge levelled occasionally. It has never been that. Even the most cursory glance through the previous pages, which demonstrate the extraordinary actions taken by Scouts worldwide on behalf of their communities over the last century, should disabuse readers of that misconception.

Risk and responsibility

The Scout Movement worldwide is still for people who want to do, make and be something – it's for adventure-seekers. In an acutely risk-averse environment, the concept of adventure has challenging implications, particularly for parents. However, it is possible to stretch yourself in many ways, and risk revising your self-perception or your worldview, without experiencing physical danger.

The focus within Scouting is on positive action and worldwide comradeship, from the youngest Beaver Scout taking pride in recycling cans to an Explorer Scout travelling overseas to help build a school. The adventure comes through actively taking part and seeing the results of your actions. The promise of adventure is an attractive proposition for people of any age.

Above: No mountain too high, not even if it's a mountain of dishes – even menial chores can be fun if you do them together.

Left: Open access to all, no matter what – leaders must equip themselves with a wide range of coping skills to ensure that Scouting remains open to everybody.

Left: Every year, Scouting renews itself yet again with new faces and fresh challenges.

Visualizing the future

As home of the oldest national Scout organization, Britain still has a role as an innovator in a Movement that was founded to focus on the future.

In 2002 a ten-year Strategic Vision was drawn up to take Scouting in Britain through to 2012. The 2007 centenary year is pivotal for the Strategic Vision, giving a focal point for the development of structures and facilities. Working on potential scenarios and observing social trends towards a more fragmented, '24/7' society, which is less dependent on traditional nuclear-family structures and with more technically and socially sophisticated young people, the Strategic Vision focused on the positive actions that should be taken to ensure that Scouting survived and remained relevant.

Changing perceptions

One of the most important aspects of the Strategic Vision has been the focus on changing the public perception of Scouting. Rather than Scouting being regarded as a lifestyle choice (such as a hobby club or one of the many youth groups available), it is hoped that it will be seen as an essential element in community life. Instead of maintaining hundreds of thousands of small groups, the aim should be to create fewer but larger groups. This will establish group pools of resources, both human and financial, which will offer relevant local Scouting based in centres of excellence, after-school clubs, young offenders' units, hospitals or 'other centres of community provision'.

A community-wide message is always best communicated locally and through working examples. The Strategic Vision promoted greater accessibility and support for Scouts with disabilities. It also stipulated that every Scout group should be co-educational by 2007, to ensure that nobody would be excluded from Scouting at any level.

This move caused considerable heartache for a few leaders, especially those who had run boys-only sections for more than a decade. However, continuing single-sex Scouting was not an option for a Movement determined to promote equality of accessibility. Girls and women have had roles in Scouting from the outset, from the

enthusiastic but unregistered Girl Scout groups of a century ago to fully warranted leaders, but it is time to ensure absolute parity for the next Scouting century. The UK Scout Association could hardly remain a signatory to Big 7 initiatives on the treatment of girls and women in society yet continue to exclude girls from Scouting.

Everyday Scouting

The Scout Association, historically known as 'Headquarters' by Scout leaders throughout Britain, exists to support, monitor and review the programme on offer to Scouts throughout the country. It insures Scout buildings, offers fact sheets on all aspects of handling 'other people's children', provides a telephone information centre, legal representation and fundraising advice, produces publications (including an award-winning members' magazine), training and other leader resources, and supports national and international events. The Scout Association also acts as guardian of the 'Scouting brand', handling press coverage and enquiries, generating media interest in Scouting and marketing Scouting in new areas.

Grassroots Scouting – the weekly meetings, summer camps, fundraising, sleepovers and leaders' meetings – continues as it has done for a century, not unchanged but with renewed confidence in itself. It hasn't just survived for a century – it has thrived and stayed relevant for a century.

Graduates of Scouting are often prepared to stand up and be counted, as leaders and as spokespeople for the Movement, and some of them are well-known adults who can act as ambassadors in public, including David Beckham, Richard Branson, Chief Scout Peter Duncan and many others. However, it is local Scouts operating in their own communities who make the everyday difference to the world around them and to the image of Scouting as a whole.

Scouts' honour

A great deal of thought went into the original Scout Promise, and it has been revised only very slightly in a century. Changes usually reflect differences in religion and national politics or the degree to which Scouting is established as part of state provision.

The exact meaning and personal implication of every phrase of the Promise is the subject of intense discussion locally and nationally, reflecting the social and political mood of the time. However, when it was once suggested in Britain that the first phrase, 'On my honour', might be changed, angry Scouts wrote to their national magazine, furious that adults were implying that their generation had no sense of honour.

In a general climate of moral relativism, for a young person to be able to stand up and say, with any degree of conviction and in front of their peers, that he or she promises, on their honour, to do their duty to anything is unusual, awe-inspiring and encouraging. The fact that 28 million young people worldwide can do just that should give us immense hope for the future.

Above: Nothing will ever replace the fun and camaraderie of a Scout Camp.

Right: Getting to grips with the Founder. Young visitors to Gilwell still want to hear about the man and the amazing story of Scouting.

Appendices

UK Scouting: A chronology 1907–2006

1907
August Experimental camp on Brownsea Island, Poole.

1908
January Part 1 of *Scouting for Boys* is published (15 January).
April First issue of boys' magazine *The Scout* is published.
August First 'national' Scout camp is held at Humshaugh.

1909
May Headquarters opens at 116 Victoria Street, London.
July First edition of adults' magazine *Headquarters Gazette* is published.
August Camp on training ship *Mercury*, Bucklers Hard, near Southampton, leads to the formation of the Sea Scouts.
September Rally at Crystal Palace, London, is attended by 11,000 Scouts; Scoutmasters' conference takes place.
October Rally in Glasgow, Scotland, is attended by 6,000 Scouts. King Edward VII agrees to the introduction of the King's Scout Award (after 1952 this is known as the Queen's Scout Award).
December Council and Executive Committee are formed, with Baden-Powell as Chairman and Maj.-Gen. Sir Herbert Plumer as Vice-Chairman.

1910
January Girl Guides Association is inaugurated. F. W. Pixley is appointed as first Treasurer of The Boy Scouts Association.
March Some 14 new proficiency badges are added. Silver Wolf is introduced, to be awarded to any King's Scout who has gained 24 proficiency badges; it later becomes the highest good service award for adults.
April Letter of appeal for financial help for the central administration of the Movement is sent out above the signature of the Chief Scout.
June Sir Herbert Plumer suggests the formation of Senior Patrols; those experimenting are asked to report their successes and failures.
September First annual census: 100,298 Scouts, 7,688 Scouters.
October Sea Scout branch is formally formed.
November It is ruled that Troop property belongs to the Troop Committee.

1911
January H. G. Elwes is appointed Editor of *Headquarters Gazette* First annual meeting of the Headquarters Advisory Committee.
March First edition of Scouting's rule book, *Policy, Organization and Rules* is approved.
June Scouts are on duty at the coronation of King George V.
July Connaught Banner is inaugurated as an annual rifle shooting competition (by November it has become the Connaught Shield). Windsor rally is held; 26,000 Scouts are reviewed by King George V.

November School farm for Scouts starts at Buckhurst Place, Sussex.
December Tenth Scout Law is added to the previous nine published from the outset in *Scouting for Boys*.

1912
January It is decided to have a General Manager and two Secretaries; J. A. Kyle cannot accept this and resigns as Secretary. Col. Ulick de Burgh, Deputy Chief Commissioner, is placed in charge of Headquarters Office as Managing Director (an honorary appointment) and A. G. Wade becomes Joint Assistant Secretary with E. Cameron; later in the year they are appointed Joint Secretaries. Royal Charter of Incorporation is granted by King George V.
June Silver Wolf will now be awarded to King's Scouts of at least two years' service who gain 12 proficiency badges.
August Nine people drown off Leysdown, Kent, as a result of a sudden squall, which capsizes an ex-naval cutter taking 23 Scouts of the 2nd Walworth Troop to camp.
November For the first time a contingent of Sea Scouts (with a Service Whaler) appear in the Lord Mayor's Show.

1913
May Duke of Connaught is appointed first President of The Boy Scouts Association.
June Invitation is received from Danish Scouts for a party of 50 Scouts to be present at a camp to be held in Denmark.
July Birmingham Exhibition and rally are attended by 18,000 Scouts.
September Endowment fund is launched; the target is £250,000 but the fund is closed at £88,500 in December 1914.
October Wreck of the sailing ketch *The Mirror* when a steamer crashes into the ship, cutting her almost in half; an Assistant Scoutmaster and three Scouts are drowned and 11 are saved (the ketch had been presented to the Association by the *Daily Mirror* newspaper in 1912).
November Scouts' Friendly Society is formed (at the time 'every lad on attaining the age of 18 has by law to subscribe to an Approved Society of this kind,' wrote B-P. 'so he may as well belong to the Scouts' Friendly Society as to any other').

1914
January First announcement of experimental scheme for Wolf Cubs or Young Scouts.
April Conference is held at Manchester; one innovation is the 'Scout's Own', a non-denominational act of worship.
May Sir William Smith, founder of the Boys Brigade, dies. First National Good Turn - Scouts' Day of Work is organized for Sir Arthur Pearson's Fund for the National Institute for the Blind.
June Inspection on Horse Guards Parade of London Scouts by Queen Alexandra.
August Outbreak of First World War; War Service is introduced.

1915

March General Purposes Committee is formed at headquarters.
September British Scout Hut is established at Étaples, France, for the benefit of British troops.
October The price of a Scout hat increases to 2s 6d (12p).

1916

February Conference of 500 Patrol Leaders is held at Manchester; the Chief Scout is present throughout (smaller conferences have been held in preceding years but this is the most elaborate to date).
May Jack Cornwell dies from wounds received while serving on HMS *Chester* in the Battle of Jutland; for his courage and constancy under danger he is posthumously awarded the Victoria Cross.
June First conference 'for all officers interested in Cub work' is held at Scout headquarters.
July Introduction of Senior Patrol Leader, who must be a First Class Scout and wear a third white stripe. It is decided that, if the war ends before then, there should be a jamboree in 1918 to celebrate the 10th anniversary. Roland Philipps is 'killed in action'.
September Vera Barclay is appointed Wolf Cub Secretary. The heroism of Jack Cornwell is commemorated by the introduction of the Cornwell Scout Badge to be awarded for exceptional courage; a Cornwell Memorial Fund is established to give help to Cornwell Scouts.
December *The Wolf Cub's Handbook* is published. Roland House, a Scout hostel in Stepney, east London, is left to Scouting by Roland Philipps and opened by the Chief Scout. Wolf Cub display at the Caxton Hall, London.

1917

March Scouts acting as regular instructors to Wolf Cub Packs are entitled to wear a badge showing a wolf's head in green on a khaki background over the left shirt pocket. First Commissioners' Conference is held at Matlock Bath, Derbyshire.
June Senior Scout Section is introduced. New Headquarters building at 25 Buckingham Palace Road, London, is made possible by the generous help of Dr J. J. Acworth and is opened by the President, the Duke of Connaught; B-P presents the duke with a Gold Wolf. On the same day news is received of the death of E. S. Carlos, the artist whose picture *The Pathfinder* is already well known.
September Commissioners' conference is held at Dunblane, Scotland.
October C. Dymoke Green is appointed Assistant Secretary. Medal of Merit, a gallantry award, is changed to one for specially good work on behalf of the Movement.

1918

January Col. U. de Burgh resigns as Deputy Chief Commissioner to enable him to concentrate on the development of Senior Scouts.
February Hubert Martin is appointed International Commissioner.

April D. Francis Morgan is seconded from the War Office to become Assistant Secretary.

June Wolf Cub Conference is held at Denison House, London.

July C. Dymoke Green is appointed General Secretary.

August The name of the Senior Scout Section is changed to Rover Scouts.

September The first Chief Scout's Commissioners (P. W. Everett, H. G. Elwes, A. Gaddum, J. M. Sladen, A. J. Tassell and Maj. F. M. Crum) are appointed by B-P.

December S.O.S. Fund to help allied Scouts of invaded countries is set up by B-P and administered by the International Commissioner, Hubert Martin.

1919

January It is decided that a World Scout jamboree will be held in 1920. William de Bois Maclaren purchases Gilwell Park for use as a Scout campsite and adult training centre. The question is posed: 'Is it desirable and, if so, feasible, that the Council of the Association should be made elective and representative?'.

April Capt. Francis Gidney is appointed first Camp Chief at Gilwell.

July TS *Northampton* is transferred to the Association thanks to the generosity of Lord Northampton to serve as a Headquarters for Sea Scouting (see September 1921). Gilwell Park is opened for the training of adults and for camping.

September First training course for Scout Leaders is held at Gilwell Park.

November Commissioners' Conference is held at Minehead, Somerset.

1920

January It is decided that 'Scout Officers' (Scouters) should no longer wear Boy Scout proficiency badges.

May Commissioners' Conference is held at Gilwell Park; B-P visits and camps there.

July An appeal is launched for £10,000 for Roland House; to save the hostel P. B. Nevill had himself taken a lease on the property with all the financial responsibility. King George V receives overseas Scouts. First World Scout Jamboree (30 July to 8 August) is held at Olympia, London, with Scouts camping in Richmond Park. Baden-Powell is acclaimed Chief Scout of the World (7 August).

December Youlbury Campsite, Oxford, is given to Scouting by Sir Arthur Evans.

1921

January Lt-General Sir Edmond Elles resigns as Chief Commissioner. Lord Hampton is appointed Deputy Chief Commissioner.

July F. W. Pixley resigns as Treasurer; Col. A. D. Acland is appointed Acting Treasurer. Sir Ernest Shackleton chooses Patrol Leader Marr and Patrol Leader Mooney to go in *The Quest* on his expedition to the Antarctic.

September First Gilwell Reunion; at the Scouts' Own an Arab reads from the Qur'an and a Hindu recites the Scout Law. TS *Northampton* is given up because, in B-P's view, it is 'too expensive a luxury and one impossible to continue'.

October B-P introduces the Ipse test (*ipse* is a Bantu word for 'whither') and the test was to be an initiation ceremony for Scouters and Commissioners; it was never taken up enthusiastically and was allowed to fade out. Open Conference is held at the Hotel Metropole, Leeds, and attended by 250 Scouters.

1922

January Lord Hampton is appointed Chief Commissioner; Col. A. D. Acland is appointed Treasurer of the Association.

June *Rovering to Success*, a handbook for Rover Scouts, is published.

September Posse of Welcome for the Prince of Wales at Alexandra Palace, London, is attended by 20,000 Wolf Cubs, 43,000 Scouts and 2,000 Rover Scouts.

1923

January *Headquarters Gazette* changes its name to *The Scouter*; Ernest Young becomes Joint Editor.

March Open Conference is held at Queen's College, Cambridge.

July The woggle is introduced for holding the scarf.

October Capt. Francis Gidney resigns as Gilwell's Camp Chief.

November John Skinner 'Belge' Wilson is appointed Gilwell's Camp Chief.

December The circulation of *The Scouter* reaches 14,000.

1924

January Headquarters Equipment Department opens the first branch shop at 34–35 Wormwood Street, London (near Liverpool Street Station). The Gilwell scarf is restricted to those who have completed all three parts of the Wood Badge.

July King George V reviews overseas Scouts at Buckingham Palace. Festival service for overseas Scouts is held at Westminster Abbey.

August Imperial Jamboree is held at Wembley; 34 parts of the empire are represented. Second World Scout Jamboree held later in Denmark.

September Special tests for disabled Scouts are introduced.

1925

April Open Conference is held at the Grand Hotel, Bristol.

September The first training course for public schoolmasters is held.

December The Wood Badge is adopted for Leaders in both Scout and Cub sections. First Scout Musical Festival is held at the Royal College of Music, London.

1926

January Scout Headquarters draws attention to the growing custom of wearing silk shoulder knots and shoulder knots over 15 cm (6 in) long, braid down the seams of shorts, brass buttons and other metal adornments, all of which were contrary to the rules.

March Ernest Young is appointed Editor of *The Scouter* (he has been Joint Editor with H. G. Elwes since 1923).

April First National Rover Moot is held at the Royal Albert Hall, London, and attended by 7,000 Rover Scouts.

July Presentation at Gilwell Park of the Bronze Buffalo by the Boy Scouts of America to the UK Association to commemorate the unknown Scout whose good turn inspired the beginning of Scouting in the USA; the presentation is made by the US ambassador to Baden-Powell and the Prince of Wales.

August Baden-Powell suggests that Sir Alfred Pickford should succeed him as Chief Scout in the event of his death.

September Disabled Scouts branch is introduced.

October Sir Montagu Burrows is appointed Commissioner for Disabled Scouts.

November National Wolf Cub Palaver is held in London; the Duke of York (later King George VI) receives the Silver Wolf.

1927
January The first performance of the Roland House pantomime, written and produced by E. Stuart Monroe with music by Harman Howland.
April Open Conference is held in Bournemouth, Dorset, and attended by over 600 Scouters.
May Suggestion for an Air Scout branch is rejected.
June Special courses for Commissioners are authorized.
November The Chartered Association [Boy Scouts Association] Protection Order is issued, giving legal protection to the name of the Association and certain titles and badges. Thanks to the generostiy of Mrs Colebrook, Rosemary Home opens as a Scout convalescent home; J. R. Stanley is appointed Warden.

1928
January The concept of the Scout Group is introduced (previously Wolf Cub Packs and Scout Troops had been registered separately); Packs and Troops are now linked together under a Group Scoutmaster. Title of Commissioner for Disabled Scouts is changed to Commissioner for Special Tests.
April Stanley Ince succeeds Claude Fisher as the Warden of Roland House. Open Conference is held at York.
May Second National Rover Moot is held at Yorks Wood, Birmingham.
July 21st birthday reunion of the original Brownsea boys at Baden-Powell's home at Pax Hill, Bentley, Hampshire.
October P. D. Power is appointed first Headquarters Commissioner for Scouts (previously there had been separate departments for Cubs and Rovers but, surprisingly, not for Scouts).

1929
January Prince George (later the Duke of Kent) is appointed Commodore of Sea Scouts. George [Jim] Dymoke Green is appointed Editor of *The Scouter*.
July Festival service is held in Westminster Abbey, London. International Friendship Fund for the promotion of international friendship is created through a donation from Mortimer Schiff.
August Third World Scout Jamboree held at Arrowe Park, Birkenhead.
December Deep Sea Scouts branch is formed and is open to all Scouts who chose the sea as their profession.

1930
April Open Conference is held at Birmingham University; there is a record attendance of 1,000 Scouters and Commissioners. On doctor's advice, P. B. Nevill resigns as Headquarter Commissioner for Rover Scouts; he is succeeded by Lt. Col. Granville Walton, who hands over his duties as Overseas Commissioner to his assistant, Harold Legat.
May George [Jim] Dymoke Green, son of the General Secretary and, since January 1929, Editor of *The Scouter* dies aged 28; in 1931 a lynch gate is erected in his memory on the south side of Gilwell's training ground.
June Percy Everett is knighted for his services to the Scout and Guide Movements.
August Third national Rover Scout Moot is held at Auchengillan, Glasgow's Scout campsite.

1931

January A. M. 'Tiny' Chamberlain is appointed first Travelling Commissioner.

April Camping standards are published and the camping standards certificate is issued. Open Conference is held in Brighton, Sussex, and is attended by 750 Scouters and Commissioners.

December Lord Somers is appointed a Chief Scout's Commissioner.

1932

January Annual meeting of the Council at which Lord Somers is elected a member and Sir James Leigh-Wood is elected Treasurer (in succession to Col. A. D. Acland).

May A new award for good services, to rank between the Silver Wolf and the Medal of Merit, is introduced; at first called the Silver Medal, it is soon changed to the Silver Acorn. B-P welcomes the idea but thinks the new award should be worn around the neck as an order in the same way as the Silver Wolf, but it is agreed that it should be a medal worn on the breast (some 20 years later it was decided the Silver Acorn should be worn around the neck as an order).

October–November The first Gang Show is produced by a 'Holborn Rover' (who is later revealed to be Ralph Reader).

1933

January A completely revised edition of *Policy, Organization and Rules* is published.

August In an effort to attract non-Scout readers, the name of *The Scout* magazine is changed to *Every Boy's Weekly, The Scout*; the content, especially the fiction, becomes more colourful, and Scouting is relegated to second place. The move is unpopular with the Movement, and the circulation drops steadily (see July 1935). Cruise on the SS *Calgaric* for Scouters and Guiders. Fourth World Scout Jamboree held in Hungary.

September Open Conference is held in the Assembly Hall, Edinburgh.

1934

March First issue of the Rover Scout magazine, *The Rover World*, is published; for some years the London Rover Scouts have published a magazine, *The London Rover*, but it was decided to change its form to widen its appeal.

March–April Adriatic cruise for Scouters and Guiders.

April First parade of King's Scouts at Windsor Castle, reviewed by King George V, is followed by the first National Scout Service in St George's Chapel.

July Boy Scouts Association Trust Corporation is set up to act as the sole and permanent trustee of certain forms of Scout property; it was incorporated under the Companies Act 1929 and licensed by the Lord Chancellor as a trust corporation.

1935

April–May First train 'cruise' organized by *The Scout*; a special train is chartered and becomes home for a week for 100 Scouts with stops made for sightseeing (there were five subsequent such 'cruises').

May Quetta earthquake; 1,000 Rover Scouts render conspicuous service.

July The boys' magazine (see August 1933) reverts to its former title, *The Scout*, and Haydn Dimmock (Editor 1919–54) is given carte-blanche to develop it along Scout lines.

September Open Conference is held at Manchester Grammar School and attended by 1,200 Scouters and Commissioners.

October Lord Somers is appointed Acting Chief Scout.

November A new design for the Thanks Badge is approved to replace the old swastika design (the swastika has been adopted by the German Nazi party as its logo, but the original design had been chosen in 1909 because for over 2,000 years the swastika had been an internationally recognized sign of good luck; several incidents were reported of people wearing the old badge being assaulted when abroad).

1936

January Special Tests Branch becomes the Handicapped Scouts Branch. The Cub and Scout Sections are invited to give their opinions about the introduction of a Leaping Wolf badge, which would be worn by a Wolf Cub who attains a certain proficiency when he became a Scout; the Scout Section showed little interest in the idea so it was not pursued.

April King Edward VIII speaks to the King's Scouts after the annual parade at Windsor and the National Scout Service, the only occasion that the King's/Queen's Scouts have actually been addressed by the sovereign. First production of *Boy Scout* in the Royal Albert Hall, London.

June Lord Somers is appointed Deputy Chief Scout.

August Great Tower Scout Campsite is opened by Baden-Powell.

October National Commissioners' Conference is held in Norwich; it is the first Commissioners' Conference for 15 years.

1937

February Lord Somers is accepted throughout the empire as Deputy Chief Scout.

April Broadstone Warren Scout Campsite, Sussex, is opened. The *Gang Show* film is premiered. A parade of King's Scouts at Windsor Castle is reviewed by King George VI accompanied by three queens: Queen Elizabeth (later Queen Elizabeth, the Queen Mother], Queen Mary (the king's mother) and Queen Ena of Spain; also present are Princess Elizabeth and Princess Margaret; it was the only Parade and National Scout Service ever attended by Baden-Powell.

May Phasels Wood Scout Campsite, Hertfordshire, is opened. Coronation of King George VI. Scout-Guide Thanksgiving service, Westminster Abbey, London.

August Fifth World Scout Jamboree held in Holland.

October RRS *Discovery* is transferred from the Colonial Office to the Association for use as a training ship.

November Royal Command Performance of the Gang Show.

1938

February The fourth Scout Law is amended to read: 'A Scout is a friend to all and a brother to every other Scout, no matter to what country, class or creed the other may belong'.

April A museum is opened at Scout Headquarters, known as B-P's room, where various mementoes of the Founder and the honours he has received are displayed along with other historical records. The Boy Scout Fund is launched at the Mansion House, London, because the Movement is in need of money and anxious about its future; an influential committee was established under the chairmanship of Lord Somers, and by the time the fund was closed, more that £263,000 had been contributed. Second production of *Boy Scout* attracts nearly 25,000 people and raises £1,300 for the Boy Scout Fund.

May Chalfont Heights Scout Campsite, Middlesex, is opened.
July First international Wolf Cub Leaders' Conference held at Gilwell Park.
August Cruise on SS *Orduna* for Scouters and Guiders.
September Charles Dymoke Green retires as General Secretary after 21 years; he had first joined the staff in February 1917 as Organizing Secretary, and after Headquarters moved to Buckingham Palace Road he was appointed General Secretary. He is succeeded by P .E. Berryman.
November *The Rover World* ceases publication and becomes a supplement in *The Scouter*.

1939

February National Service Badge is introduced for Scouts, Rover Scouts, Old Scouts and Scouters.
May Frylands Wood Scout Campsite, Surrey, becomes a Headquarters site.
June Walton Firs Scout Campsite, Surrey, is opened. First Scout Soapbox Derby is held at Brooklands.
September Germany invades Poland. Some Headquarters departments are evacuated to Gilwell Park. The Deputy Chief Scout writes to Commissioners outlining Headquarters policy in the event of war. RRS *Discovery* becomes the Headquarters of the Sea Scout section of the River Emergency Service of the Port of London Authority. Scheme for collecting wastepaper is launched.
November The Admiralty asks Scouts and Rover Scouts to volunteer for training as convey signallers.
December The Association's General Secretary, P. E. Berryman, is recalled to the Royal Air Force; A. W. 'Fred' Hurll is appointed Acting General Secretary.

1940

March Lord Somers is appointed Red Cross Regional Commissioner for the Middle East; Lord Hampton, Sir Percy Everett and Sir Alfred Pickford are appointed to act for him during his absence. The *Forces Bulletin* is introduced; it is a short monthly newsletter on matters of general Scout interest for members of the movement serving in the forces. War Distressed Scouts Fund is launched.
May Rosemary Home is closed because it is sited in an area that might quickly become dangerous. Tolmers Scout Campsite, Hertfordshire, is opened.
August *The Scout*, which has a circulation of 20,000, is transferred from Pearsons to the Boy Scouts Association; since the first issue in 1908 the weekly had been published by Pearsons but the company has decided it cannot continue; on taking it over, Headquarters reduces the price from 3 pence to 2 pence.
September C. Beresford Webb, Editor of *The Scouter* and Publicity Secretary, is called up for military service; E. E. Reynolds is appointed Acting Editor of *The Scouter* and F. Hayden Dimmock becomes Acting Publicity Secretary. Roland House is bombed and extensively damaged (it will be damaged by incendiary bombs and land-mines in 1941 too).
November Gilwell Park is requisitioned by the army.

1941

January Robert Baden-Powell dies at Paxtu, Nyeri, Kenya. Memorial service for Baden-Powell is held at Westminster Abbey, London. Lord Somers is elected Chief Scout of the United Kingdom and Dependent Territories. Air Scout Branch is formed.
March The election of Lord Somers as Chief Scout of the British Empire is announced.

April Chief Scout proposes to set up a commission to consider post-war developments. All important exhibits in B-P's room are removed for safety to Eastnor Castle, the home of Lord Somers.
August Stanley Ince, Warden of Roland House and only adult to have been awarded the Cornwell Scout Badge, dies.
September Bradley Wood Scout Campsite, Yorkshire, acquired.
October Sir Percy Everett is appointed Deputy Chief Scout for Britain.
November P. E. Berryman, the General Secretary, resigns because he has decided to remain in the Royal Air Force after the war; A.W. Hurll is appointed to succeed him.
December The Admiralty recognizes the Association as a body entitled to recommend applicants for entry into the Royal Navy under the Y Scheme, by which Scouts aged 17 and over can volunteer; those accepted become members of the Navy but are placed in an unpaid reserve until called up for National Service. Although the Y Scheme no longer exists, Admiralty recognition continues.

1942

January Duke of Connaught, President of the Association, dies; J. F. Colquhoun is appointed Deputy Chief Commissioner.
February The first Field Commissioner is appointed.
March The Duke of Gloucester is appointed President of the Association by King George VI.
April B-P Memorial Fund launched.
June Sir James Leigh-Wood retires as Treasurer of the Association after 13 years and is appointed a Vice-President; Evelyn Bunbury is appointed as Treasurer in his place.
July The report of the Chief Scout's Post-War Commission is published in *The Scouter* for comment. King George VI visits Scout Headquarters. First national Air Scout camp is held at Avington Park, Itchen Abbas, Hampshire.
August The Duke of Kent, Commodore of Sea Scouts, dies. The generosity of the Manor Charitable Trust makes possible the opening of Wych Warren, the house adjoining Broadstone Warren Scout Campsite, Sussex, as a convalescent home.
September Lady Olave Baden-Powell, the World Chief Guide returns to Britain and takes up residence in a grace and favour apartment at Hampton Court.
December National Air Scout exhibition is held at Dorland Hall, Regent Street, London.

1943

May Senior Scout scheme is published for comment in *The Scouter*.
July J. S. Wilson resigns as Gilwell's Camp Chief and is succeeded by R. F. (John) Thurman.

1944

January Revised tests for Tenderfoot, Second Class and First Class badges are published and will come into effect from March 1944; the tests were published nine months previously for criticism and were amended in the light of comments received. Lady Baden-Powell is elected a Vice-President of the Association at the Annual General Meeting.
February Lord Hampton resigns as Chief Commissioner and is appointed by the Chief Scout as one of his Chief Scout's Commissioners; Brig. W. E. Clark is appointed Acting Chief Commissioner.
March First party of Scout International Relief Service workers go to Greece. The Post-War Commission had recommended that the

reconstitution of the Council and Committee of the Council be considered; the Committee agrees that a scheme be drawn up and put to the Movement for comment.
April Sea Scout exhibition is held in the Scottish Drill Hall, Buckingham Gate, London.
May Work day on behalf of the Scout International Relief Service raises £33,000.
July Lord Somers dies. Memorial service for Lord Somers is held in St George's Chapel, Windsor Castle.
August E. E. Reynolds resigns as Editor of *The Scouter* and is succeeded by Rex Hazlewood.
September Scout International Relief Service Team leaves for Normandy.
November Rosemary Home is to close and be sold.
December Gilwell Park is returned to the Movement.

1945

February Lord Rowallan is elected Chief Scout of the United Kingdom and Dependent Territories. The first post-war Conference of County Commissioners and County Secretaries is held.
March Portrait of Lord Somers by Oswald Birley is unveiled by Lord Rowallan in the library at Scout Headquarters.
April Permission is given by the Board of Admiralty for recognized Sea Scout units in Britain to wear a special burgee, triangular in shape on a blue background with the Scout badge in gold surmounted by the Admiralty Crown. Lord Rowallan visits Belgium. Lord Rowallan is elected Chief Scout of the British Commonwealth and Empire.
May Gilwell Park reopens; during the course of this year alone over 12,000 Scouts camp there.
July Lady Somers is appointed a Vice-President of the Association. The Civil Defence Badge is discontinued (but could continue to be worn). Scouts begin to help dismantle indoor steel air-raid shelters
September The Post-War Commission report, *The Way Ahead*, is published. Youlbury Scout Campsite, Oxfordshire, is transferred to the Association. Headquarters decides to publish Scout books and literature itself; until now all have been published by independent publishers.
October Linking-up journey by the International Commissioner, Glad Bincham, and the General Secretary with Scouts in Belgium, France, Holland and Luxembourg. Tovil Scout Campsite, Kent, is leased to the Association.

1946

March Preliminary Training (training prior to the Wood Badge) is introduced; the Gilwell woggle (a two-strand Turk's head in leather) may be worn by those who pass the course. Somers House at 46 Brandon Street, Walworth, is opened as a Scout Centre for south-east London in memory of the former Chief Scout (it closed August 1953).
April The first Medals for Meritorious Conduct are awarded to Robert Schaffner (Luxembourg) and Eric Scott for their undaunted courage and unbreakable spirits in concentration camps. St George's Day National Scout Service and Parade of King's Scouts resumes at Windsor after a break of six years.
July The Earl of Athlone is appointed a Vice-President of the Association; previously he had been Chief Scout of South Africa and Canada.
August An organization for British Scouts in Germany is established.
August–September Lord Rowallan undertakes coast-to-coast tour of Canada accompanied by the General Secretary.

October Senior Scout Section officially starts. Revised scheme for Proficiency Badges comes into force. New plan for Rovers is introduced.

1947

January The cover price of *The Scouter* is increased from 3 pence to 6 pence, the first price rise since its inception as *Headquarters Gazette* in 1909. Rear Admiral Viscount Mountbatten of Burma is appointed Commodore of Sea Scouts.

January–March Lord Rowallan, accompanied by F. H. J. Dahl, visits Gambia, Sierra Leone, Gold Coast and Nigeria; the West African Jamboree is believed to be the largest single gathering of the different peoples of West Africa that has been held so far.

April Memorial stone to Baden-Powell is unveiled in Westminster Abbey by the Duke of Gloucester; a later tradition for staff to place flowers on the stone on the anniversary of Baden-Powell's birthday leads to the creation of the annual Scout and Guide Founder's Day/Thinking Day service in the abbey. First reception for the presentation of the newly instituted royal certificates to King's Scouts.

July One-third of the original manuscript of *Scouting for Boys* is found and given to the Association (the missing two-thirds have never been discovered). Brig. W. E. Clark is appointed Chief Commissioner. King George VI reviews Commonwealth Scouts at Buckingham Palace.

September 21st Gilwell Reunion.

October Long Service Decoration is introduced for 15 years' efficient service. Sir Alfred Pickford ('Pickie') dies; he had held many positions in Scouting, including Training Commissioner, Publicity Commissioner, Development Commissioner, Overseas Commissioner, a Chief Scout's Commissioner and President of Middlesex Scouts; he made his name as Overseas Commissioner and attended the Paris conference in 1922 as a British delegate and was there elected one of the original members of International Committee (later the World Scout Committee).

November Conference at Gilwell Park discusses the future of Old Scouts.

1948

January E. Dennis Smith is appointed Headquarters Commissioner for Wolf Cubs, the first ex-Cub to hold the appointment.

April The structure of Headquarters is reorganized and the full-time staff post of Chief Executive Commissioner is introduced; A. W. Hurll is appointed to the role.

May Lord Rowallan visits the USA to attend the Annual Meeting of the Boy Scouts of America.

May-June The first post-war production of *Boy Scout* takes place at the Royal Albert Hall, London (it was staged again in 1949, 1951, 1953, 1955 and 1959).

June The B-P Guild of Old Scouts is inaugurated at the Royal Albert Hall; the Guild later becomes an autonomous body independent of, but closely allied to, the Association. The Salvation Army is recognized as a sponsoring authority, which means the merging of Salvation Army Scouts into the Movement. A plaque is unveiled by Sir Percy Everett, Deputy Chief Scout, on the wall of the old windmill on Wimbledon Common marking the 40th anniversary of *Scouting for Boys*; it was in the Mill House adjoining the windmill that B-P wrote parts of the book. Kingsdown Scout Campsite, Kent, is acquired through the good offices of P. B. Nevill.

July First weekend rally for university Scout and Guide Clubs and Rover Scout Crews is held at Youlbury.

October First National Conference is held at Filey, Yorkshire; it differs from the pre-1939 Open Conferences in that every county is given a quota of places and expected to fill them with a cross-section of Scouters and administrators; it is so successful that these became biennial events.

December Brynbach Scout Campsite, Wales, is transferred to Scout Headquarters.

December–April Lord Rowallan visits Australia and New Zealand.

1949

March Brig. W. E. Clark resigns as Chief Commissioner; the positions of Chief and Deputy Chief Commissioner are abolished and some duties transferred to the Deputy Chief Scout.

April First Bob-a-Job Week. Production by Headquarters staff and friends of *We'll Live Forever*, a new musical play by Ralph Reader. First post-war Commissioners' dinner.

May The beret is introduced as alternative headgear for Senior Scouts, Rover Scouts and Scouters.

June Headquarters assumes responsibility for the payment of all premiums for Scoutmasters' indemnity insurance. First liaison Chaplains' Conference is held at Headquarters and attended by 60 clergy and ministers of the Church of England, the Church in Wales, the Roman Catholic Church, the Free Churches and the Salvation Army. Wych Warren convalescent home closes; the introduction of the National Health Service makes Wych Warren an anachronism.

1950

January–March Lord Rowallan visits the Union of South Africa, Northern and Southern Rhodesia and Nyasaland.

March Report on the use and recruitment of manpower is published.

August Loss of the 1st Mortlake's boat, *Wangle III*, in the English Channel with all 10 Sea Scout members of her crew; a public enquiry the following year made recommendations about future voyages of this kind but did not consider it imprudent to undertake or permit such cruises.

September Revival of the Soapbox Derby (last held in 1939).

September–October Second National Conference is held at Filey, Yorkshire; it includes the first performance of Ralph Reader's story of a Scoutmaster, *Great Oaks*.

October–December Lord Rowallan visits Kenya, Zanzibar, Tanganyika and Uganda.

October Air Scout Troops fulfilling certain conditions are granted official recognition by the Air Ministry and allowed to wear a badge of an albatross in gold above a roundel on a background of RAF blue. Inaugural meeting of the B-P Guild of Old Scouts as an autonomous body is held at Church House, Westminster.

November Scouts are forbidden to hitch-hike except in emergencies.

December The London Gang Show is revived for the first time since the war to great acclaim.

1951

January The price of *The Scouter* is increased to 9 pence.

February The price of *The Scout* is increased to 3 pence. King George VI dies and is succeeded by Queen Elizabeth II, who later agrees to become patron of the Association in succession to her father. General Sir Rob Lockhart is appointed Deputy Chief Scout.

July The posts of General Secretary and Assistant Secretary are abolished; the post of Administrative Secretary is introduced, and C. C. Goodhind is appointed to this role.

1952

January–April Lord Rowallan tours the Caribbean, visiting Antigua, Bahamas, Barbados, Bermuda, British Guiana, British Honduras, Dominica, Grenada, Jamaica, St Lucia, St Kitts, St Vincent and Trinidad.

February Perry Wood Scout Campsite, Surrey, is left, together with an endowment, to the Association by the Rev. F. W. Baggalley. Sir Percy Everett, Deputy Chief Scout, dies.

April A Bar to the Silver Acorn is instituted. Senior Scouts, Scouts over 15, Rover Scouts and Scouters are permitted to wear berets on formal as well as informal occasions. Fourth annual Bob-a-Job week; the Movement is asked to earn an extra 'bob' (now 5p) per head to help Headquarters finances. Queen Elizabeth II reviews the national parade of Queen's Scouts at Windsor Castle and takes the salute for the first time.

August Two Scouts drown in the Lynmouth flood disaster in Devon.

September Third National Conference is held at Skegness, Lincolnshire. Brynbach Scout Campsite closed as it had proved too costly to maintain in comparison with the limited use its position made possible.

1953

June Coronation of Queen Elizabeth II; Scouts assist the crowds camped out overnight and sell programmes. Honorary Freedom of the Borough of Chingford is given to Gilwell in commemoration of the coronation and to strengthen the long and close association between the borough and Gilwell. Lord Rowallan announces that the queen has accepted the Gold Wolf that had previously been worn by the Duke of Connaught.

July S. J. L. Egerton is appointed the Association's Treasurer in place of Evelyn Bunbury.

November–December The 21st birthday performance of the Gang Show is attended by Princess Margaret.

1954

March Debate in the House of Lords on the Scout Movement and communism, in which Viscount Stansgate proposed the motion: 'That in the opinion of this House the imposition of political and religious tests by the Boy Scout Movement is foreign to its Charter and purpose and repugnant to our national tradition and liberty of conscience.' Lord Rowallan convinced the House that the motion was misconceived, and one peer who heard the debate noted that 'in my 50 years' experience of public life, I have never heard a case so torn to shreds and tatters that it ceased to exist as was the speech of the mover of the most noble Lord, Lord Rowallan'. Not one of the speakers who followed supported Lord Stansgate and the motion was withdrawn.

May–June Lord Rowallan visits the Canal Zone (Egypt), Cyprus, Gibraltar, Malta, Greece and Italy.

June First of a new type of Queen's Scout receptions is held, with over 1,100 camped at Gilwell Park. F. Hayden Dimmock resigns as Editor of *The Scout* after more than 36 years; he dies less than a year later. Rex Hazlewood takes over as Editor of *The Scout* in addition to his duties as General Editor and Editor of *The Scouter*.

July Lord Rowallan visits Scandinavia.

September Fourth National Conference is held at Filey, Yorkshire. Boy Scouts are allowed to wear berets.

September–October Lord Rowallan visits Borneo, Brunei, Ceylon, Hong Kong, Malaya, Sarawak and Singapore.

October A special committee is established to consider a report on the declining numbers of Scouts.

November The cover price of *The Scout* is increased to 6 pence.

December Queen Elizabeth II attends a performance of the Gang Show at the Golder's Green Hippodrome, London.

1955

April The King George VI Memorial Foundation makes grants totalling £50,000 to the Movement.

July At the AGM the Association's Council approves a scheme for the reconstitution of the Council and its Committee to make the governing body of the Association more representative; the proposals are passed to the Privy Council for approval. RRS *Discovery* is handed over to the Admiralty as an additional training ship for use by the Royal Naval Volunteer Reserve; the cost of upkeep had become too great for the Association. First gliding course for Scouts at Lasham airfield, Hampshire. First Cub Day at Gilwell is attended by 5,000 Wolf Cubs.

December–February Lord Rowallan visits Australia for the Pan-Pacific Jamboree and Papua New Guinea, Fiji, Tonga and the Solomon Islands.

1956

January Fortieth birthday year for Wolf Cubs.

February International Scout Club is formed.

March Training courses for Patrol Leaders are introduced.

April New rules for Rover Scouts are published; the upper age limit confirms that Rover Scouting is the fourth training Section of the Movement.

June Publication of *Scouts of Tomorrow*, the report into declining numbers. 1,800 Cubmasters camp at Gilwell for a week. Wolf Cub Good Turn Week. A new musical play by Ralph Reader, *Voyage of the Venturer*, is performed by London Scouts and Guides in the Royal Albert Hall.

September The first National Commissioners' Conference for over 20 years is held at Skegness, Lincolnshire, and is attended by 1,000 people.

1957

January A new Lord Somers House is opened in Ilford, Essex, as a home for 14 men who will work in Scouting in their spare time and as a headquarters for Scouting in that area.

February Public appeal launched for the Baden-Powell Memorial Fund at the Mansion House by the Lord Mayor of London in the presence of the Duke of Gloucester. Centenary of the birth of Robert Baden-Powell; thanksgiving service in Westminster Abbey; local Scout and Guides also hold thanksgiving services for B-P's life; thanksgiving service from B-P's old school, Charterhouse, is televised.

February–March Performances of *Great Oaks* at the Golder's Green Hippodrome, London.

March Freedom of the City of Edinburgh is conferred on Lord Rowallan.

April Peter Baden-Powell (B-P's son) is appointed a Chief Scout's Commissioner.

May National Camp for Troop Leaders and Patrol Leaders is held at Gilwell Park. Lord Rowallan is appointed a Knight of the Thistle.

June Longridge Scout Boating Centre at Marlow, Buckinghamshire, is opened by Sir Cecil Harcourt to help fill fill the gap left by RRS *Discovery*. Good Turn Week.

July Lord Maclay, president of the Boys' Brigade, and the Earl of Scarbrough are appointed Vice-Presidents of the Association. A railway engine is named *Rowallan*.

August Jubilee jamboree postage stamps are issued. The Gang Show is staged at the Birmingham Hippodrome. Golden jubilee, Indaba and Moot held at Sutton Coldfield, Birmingham.

November The Gang Show features in the Royal Variety Performance at the London Palladium.

November–December Silver jubilee production of the Gang Show takes place at the Golder's Green Hippodrome, London.

December A special committee is appointed to review the training of Scouters and its organization in all aspects; the subsequent report (appearing in 1959) recommends among other things that before a Scouter receives a warrant he should undergo pre-warrant training in the spirit, basic skills and methods of Scouting.

1958

April European 'Duty to God' Conference is held at Gilwell Park.

June E. G. Neate is appointed Chief Training Commissioner to coordinate the activities of the training sections and branches of the Movement and adult leader training. National Chaplains' Conference is held at Gilwell Park.

July Lord Burnham and Sir Godfrey Thomas are appointed Vice-Presidents of the Association.

July–August Third regional Agoon camp for handicapped Scouts at Gilwell Park is visited by Princess Alexandra.

August Obelisk to commemorate the 1957 Jamboree, Indaba and Moot is unveiled in Sutton Park, Sutton Coldfield. Fortieth birthday Rover Moot is held at Auchengillan, Scotland.

September National Conference is held at Skegness, Lincolnshire

September–October Lord Rowallan visits Canada.

November Sir Harold Gillett becomes Lord Mayor of London; he had been a member of the Council and the Committee of the Council as well as of the Finance Sub-Committee and Chairman of the Baden-Powell House Committee. Previously he had been a District Commissioner. Decision taken to proceed with the building of Baden-Powell House.

1959

January Sir Charles Maclean is appointed Deputy Chief Scout.

February The Association announces it will join the Duke of Edinburgh's Award Scheme, having excused itself from the experimental stage from 1956 on the grounds of pressure of work due to the 1957 jubilee celebrations and badge test revisions in 1958.

April 'Service of Youth' Conference at Oxford is arranged by the Association to discuss common problems with local education authorities. County Commissioners and Secretaries' Conference is held at Church House, Westminster.

May Headquarters Overseas Department becomes the Commonwealth Department. Lord Rowallan attends the Central African Jamboree, Ruwa Park, near Salisbury, Southern Rhodesia.

June Supplemental charter, restructuring the Council, is approved. First meeting of the new Council. Sir Charles Maclean is appointed Chief Scout designate. Lord Rowallan is appointed a Vice-President of the Association.

August Commonwealth Conference, New Delhi; it is announced that, at the request of the Commonwealth Associations, Sir Charles Maclean will succeed Lord Rowallan as Commonwealth Chief Scout.

September Fortieth anniversary Gilwell reunion, during which Lord Rowallan formally hands over as Chief Scout to Sir Charles Maclean.

1960

January The Association becomes a participating member of the Duke of Edinburgh's Award Scheme.

August National Sea Scout jubilee camp.

1961

July Baden-Powell House in South Kensington, London, is opened by Queen Elizabeth II as the Movement's living monument to the Founder; the statue of Baden-Powell, sculpted by Don Potter and situated outside the house, is unveiled by the Duke of Gloucester.

October Soapbox Derby is renamed as National Scoutcar Races.

November Long trousers are introduced as alternative wear for Senior Scout Troops and Rover Scout Crews.

1962

June Twenty-first birthday celebrations of the Air Scouts.

August First exchange visit of Scouts with the USA.

September National Scoutcar Races are held at Blackpool.

November Thirtieth anniversary of the Gang Show is attended by Queen Elizabeth II.

1963

July Chief Scout's reception for Queen's Scouts is held at the Tower of London. National Scoutcar Races are held at Brighton.

1964

January First meeting of the Chief Scout's Advance Party, a working group established by the Chief Scout to review and make recommendations about every facet of Scouting.

April Twenty-fifth National Scout Service and Parade of Queen's Scouts, Windsor.

July National Scoutcar Races are held at Skegness, Lincolnshire.

October British Scouts visit Japan for the first time.

November The London Gang Show takes part in its third Royal Variety Performance.

1965

May First national Scout band championships.

1966

January Golden jubilee celebrations for the Wolf Cub section begin.

February Scout and Guide Founder's day service at Westminster Abbey as part of the abbey's 900th anniversary celebrations.

June Publication of the Chief Scout's Advance Party Report leads to important changes to Scouting.

September *The Scout* magazine ceases publication.

October Introduction of the revised wording of the Scout Law and Promise.

1967

May The Boy Scouts Association is renamed The Scout Association.

June The Equipment Department moves to Lancing, West Sussex.

August National Patrol Leaders' camp is held on Brownsea Island; a memorial stone to the 1907 camp, carved by Don Potter, is unveiled.

October New uniform is introduced. Senior Scouts and Rover Scouts are phased out in favour of Venture Scouts. Implementation of the new training scheme and age ranges for Cub Scouts, Scouts and Venture Scouts. The Programme and Training sub-committee is formed with various National Boards for the sections, leader training and activities reporting to it. The Duke of Edinburgh visits Baden-Powell House.

1968

January Prince Andrew joins the 1st Marylebone Cub Scout Pack; for the duration of his membership the Pack meets at Buckingham Palace.

March Three national Scout activity centres announced: Lasham, Hampshire, for air; Longridge, Buckinghamshire, for water and boating; and Whernside, Yorkshire, for caving. First Fleur-de-Lys ball is held.

April The Duke of Edinburgh, accompanied by Cub Scout Prince Andrew, takes the salute at the parade of Queen's Scouts, Windsor.

May First national Scout and Guide Folk Fest held at Baden-Powell House, London.

June First national Scout and Venture Scout kart championship. First national Scout cycle-cross meeting.

August Rex Hazlewood retires as General Editor and is succeeded by Ron Jeffries.

1969

April Minimum standards relating to Group strength and progress in training are introduced.

May National Family Camp held at Gilwell Park.

1970

March Bob-a-Job Week is renamed Scout Job Week in anticipation of currency decimalization.

April Queen's Guides join the annual parade of Queen's Scouts at Windsor Castle for the first time to mark the Guide Movement's diamond jubilee year.

October A. W. Hurll retires and Ken Stevens is appointed his successor as Chief Executive Commissioner.

1971

January A new World Scout Membership Badge is introduced for British Scouts; the World Scout Conference decides that the same badge be worn by Scouts in many countries. *The Scouter* is renamed *Scouting* to broaden its readership to include all adults in the Movement.

February The premiere of a new Scout film, *These are Scouts*, is attended by Lady Olave Baden-Powell, the World Chief Guide.

April The B-P Guild rejoins The Scout Association.

June Lord Maclean announces his retirement as Chief Scout with effect from September.

December Scouts and Guides fill the Royal Albert Hall for Folk Fest 5 folk music concert.

1972

April The Duke of Kent reviews 500 Venture Scouts who have gained the Queen's Scout Award in a new-style ceremony at Windsor Castle.

July At a meeting of the Council of the Association held at St James's Palace, London, Sir William Gladstone is appointed Chief Scout of the United Kingdom and Overseas Branches.

October The queen and Duke of Edinburgh attend the 40th anniversary year production of Ralph Reader's Gang Show.

1973

September European Scout Public Relations Officers' Conference at Baden-Powell House is attended by 30 different countries.

1974

April The queen, accompanied by the Duke of Edinburgh, takes the salute from 650 Queen's Scouts at the annual Queen's Scouts Parade at Windsor Castle.

June The Duke of Gloucester, the Association's President from 1942 to 1972, dies aged 74.

August A working party is established to consider how to maintain and improve adult support for Scouting.

October The final London Gang Show is staged at the Gaumont State Theatre, Kilburn, London, as Ralph Reader retires from writing and producing. Operation Lifeboat, a weekend fundraising event in aid of the Royal National Lifeboat Institution, is held.

December Headquarters moves from 25 Buckingham Palace Road into temporary accommodation at Baden-Powell House while a purpose-built office extension to the hostel is built.

1975

January A new corporate identity symbol 'Scouts' is launched incorporating the Scout badge in place of the letter 'o'.

February The Duke of Kent is appointed President of the Association by the queen.

May Scouts present £91,363 to the Royal National Lifeboat Institution for a new lifeboat to be named *The Scout* (see July 1977).

September The Association's new president, the Duke of Kent, visits Baden-Powell House for the first time.

1976

January Cub Scouts' diamond jubilee celebrations begin; the year's activities include a National Cub Scout Leaders' camp at Gilwell Park.

March New adult support decisions are announced; the B-P Guild becomes the Scout Fellowship.

July Olave, Lady Baden-Powell visits the Association's new Headquarters in the office block extension to Baden-Powell House.

September Girls are formally allowed to become Venture Scouts after a number of experimental schemes had been permitted and a joint section with the Guides considered. Fiftieth Gilwell reunion is attended for the last time by Olave, Lady Baden-Powell, who makes a final speech after the Scout's Own.

November The queen formally opens the new Scout Headquarters at Baden-Powell House.

December Joint Scout and Guide badge is launched to support the queen's silver jubilee appeal.

1977

June Olave, Lady Baden-Powell, the World Chief Guide, dies aged 88; her ashes are later taken for burial next to B-P in Nyeri.

July The queen names the new RNLI lifeboat *The Scout* at Hartlepool where the boat is stationed.

September New training programme for Cub Scouts is launched.

November Lord Rowallan dies.

1978

June £134,000 is donated by Scouts and Guides to the queen's silver jubilee appeal.

July Scouts take part in the Royal Tournament at Earl's Court, London, for the first time with Midlands Massed Scout Bands and Field Gun display by 4th Seven Kings Sea Scouts.

November Scouts assist the elderly to retune radios to new wavelengths at the request of the BBC.

1979

January Cub Scout section launches 'Cub Country' to aid community projects in Nepal during the International Year of the Child; the project eventually raises £165,000.

May Scouts cook a 3 km (2 mile) sausage, the world's longest, at the Great Children's Tea Party in Hyde Park, London.

July Sir William Gladstone is elected chairman of the World Scout Committee.

August Gilwell Park celebrates its 60th anniversary. Earl Mountbatten of Burma, Commodore of Sea Scouts, is murdered by the IRA.

December Ron Jeffries resigns as General Editor and Editor of *Scouting*.

1980

March The National Air Activities Centre at Lasham, Hampshire, closes due to rising costs.

September Sir William Gladstone announces his intention of standing down as Chief Scout once a successor had been found.

1981

January Alan Gordon becomes General Editor and Editor of *Scouting*.

February New memorial stone to Lord and Lady Baden-Powell is unveiled at Westminster Abbey.

March Because of the rising number of people without a job a special 'Scouting and Unemployment' scheme introduced.

July 500 Venture Scouts act as torchbearers at the royal fireworks in Hyde Park, London, as part of the wedding celebrations of the Prince and Princess of Wales while Scouts line the wedding route to St Paul's Cathedral.

September Maj.-Gen. Michael J. H. Walsh is appointed Chief Scout designate.

1982

January Speaker's reception for 75 famous former Scouts and present-day Scout representatives at the House of Commons launches 'The Year of the Scout', marking the Movement's 75th birthday.

February Sir William Gladstone retires and Maj.-Gen. Michael Walsh succeeds as Chief Scout.

March Scouts feature on commemorative postage stamps issued by the Post Office as part of a special youth movement issue.

May Ralph Reader dies. 250,000 Cub Scouts take part in National Cub Scout Tea-Making Fortnight. The queen visits the Association's new Hawkhirst Adventure Camp, Cumbria, to inaugurate the Kielder Water Scheme.

July Lord Maclean, now the queen's Lord Chamberlain, attends Baden-Powell House's 21st anniversary reception.

August 1,500 Scouts from many countries take part in Extoree '82 at Gilwell Park, an international camp for handicapped and able-bodied.

Seventy-fifth Anniversary camp held on Brownsea Island for 92 UK Scouts plus 56 from overseas.

October After schemes in Canada and Northern Ireland, Beavers are introduced as an informal provision for 6- to 8-year-old boys in Britain.

1984

April Cardinal Basil Hume preaches at the National Scout Service in St George's Chapel after the Duke of Kent has reviewed 1,200 Queen's Scouts.

September A drop in the number of young people in the population affects UK Scout membership. New Scout Section training programme and progress award scheme are announced. The White House, Gilwell Park, is closed because of the dangerous condition of the building.

1985

January Venture Scout relay team carries a friendship torch from Baden-Powell House to Southampton to kindle a friendship flame during Mafeking centenary celebrations in South Africa.

February Premiere of the news *Scouts* film in London.

April New Scout Section training programme is launched.

July–August 200 Venture Scouts take part in clean water projects in Sri Lanka.

1986

January Cub Scout Rainbow Year 70th birthday celebrations.

March 1,300 UK Venture Scouts take part in Viking Venture, Denmark.

April Beavers become full Members of the Association and are renamed Beaver Scouts.

May Woodland Scout Camp opens at part of the National Garden Festival, Stoke-on-Trent.

July The Duke of Kent opens a new-look 'B-P story' exhibition at Baden-Powell House to mark the hostel's 25th birthday.

1987

March Scottish Headquarters moves from Edinburgh to new offices at its campsite at Fordell Firs.

June 500 Venture Scouts assist with the organization of the St John Ambulance centenary party in Hyde Park, London; at the same event 250 Scouts from Greater London North East enter the record books by cooking a 14.5 km (9 mile) sausage and setting a new world record.

October Ken Stevens retires as Chief Executive Commissioner and is succeeded by Col. Tony Black.

December For the first time the UK contingent to the 16th World Scout Jamboree in Australia includes Ranger Guides.

1988

January Venture Scout Section begins a year of celebrations for its 21st birthday. Sherpa '88 appeal is launched in aid of the Sherpa people.

February The Duke of Kent visits Gilwell Park.

April Maj.-Gen. Michael Walsh announces his retirement as Chief Scout as soon as a successor can be appointed.

October W. Garth Morrison, Chief Commissioner of Scotland, takes over as Chief Scout. Venture Scouts celebrate their 21st birthday with 'Everest' climbs in major cities throughout Britain; an event in Leicester Square, London, is attended by Sir Edmund Hillary and members of his original 1953 Everest team.

1989

March London Venture brings together 1,500 Swedish Senior Scouts and 3,500 British Venture Scouts for an international weekend camping at Crystal Palace; King Carl XVI Gustaf of Sweden leads the overseas visitors; the highlight of the weekend is a musical celebration at the Royal Albert Hall.

April The first commercial sponsorship of a Scout proficiency badge occurs when the Scout athlete badge is sponsored for three years by Matchstick sportswear.

June The result of a uniform consultation leads to the abolition of headgear for all sections.

July 10,000 young people from over 40 countries attend the Discovery '89 camps at five sites in the United Kingdom.

October A new amateur radio station at Gilwell Park is opened.

December The Scout Leadership Training Programme receives an official commendation from the Department of Employment.

1990

January 'Scouts go for a Million' campaign is launched; it eventually raises £141,998 for Barnardo's.

February The decision is made in principle for The Scout Association to become full co-educational and to allow girls to join the Beaver, Cub and Scout sections for the first time.

March Launch of the Promise Appeal to raise £10 million for Scouting with a reception at 10 Downing Street.

June 'Green Charter' competition is launched to raise awareness in environmental projects.

1991

January Cub Scouts begin celebrations to mark the 75th birthday of the section. Fiftieth anniversary of Air Scouting.

February A new training programme for Cub Scouts is launched.

July The Association's Royal Charter is amended formally to allow girls to be invested into the younger sections of the Movement. 170 children from the Chernobyl area of the Soviet Union arrive in Britain for a holiday hosted by British Scouts and Guides.

November 2,000 Cub Scouts take part in a Grand Howl and thanksgiving service in Central Hall, Westminster, to celebrate the 75th birthday of Cub Scouting.

1992

February The Promise Appeal becomes the first national appeal in aid of the Association since 1938; 1992 is designated 'Promise Year'.

October National Woggle Day raises funds for the Promise Appeal.

December Group Scout Leader/Commissioner training scheme wins a National Training Award from the Department of Employment. The Promise Appeal closes having raised about £2.5 million.

1993

September £2 million redevelopment programme begins at Gilwell to expand the training facilities and to restore the White House.

November Amendments are made to the Cub and Scout Law to made them gender free.

1994

January Col. Brian Evans-Lombe, the last surviving member of the original camp on Brownsea Island dies, aged 100.

July European Venture takes 6,000 UK Venture Scouts to Europe.

September Gilwell Reunion celebrates 75 years of Gilwell Park.

November White House restoration is finished.

1995

June The queen visits Gilwell Park to reopen the White House and the refurbished training centre.

July 3,000-strong British contingent of Scouts and Guides gather at Crystal Palace before leaving together for the 18th World Scout Jamboree in the Netherlands.

October 700 Scouts stage *In the Spotlight*, a fast-moving showcase of musical and creative ability at the Royal Albert Hall, London.

1996

May During the Chief Scout's Picnic weekend at Gilwell Park, Garth Morisson stands down as Chief Scout and is succeeded by George Purdy, Chief Commissioner of Northern Ireland.

July The Committee of the Council confirms that the long-term vision is of a fully co-educational Scout Movement in Britain. Derek Twine succeeds Col. Tony Black as Chief Executive.

September Cub Scouts start 80 days of special events, including a nationwide challenge to travel round the world in 80 days to commemorate 80 years of Cub Scouting.

October The Association's website is launched. Baden-Powell House closes for £2 million refurbishment scheme. IPP/Ulanov/Local Support Services.

1997

February The Scout Association equal opportunities policy is announced.

June The Duke of Kent re-opens the renovated Baden-Powell House International Scout Hostel and Conference Centre.

September Scouts assist in clearing away floral tributes outside the royal palaces in London left following the death of Diana, Princess of Wales.

1998

February 'Voice for Young People' policy introduced to put young people under the age of 25 on all national committees. A National Child Protection Coordinator is appointed to promote the Association's Child Protection Policy and its implementation. After several years of planning a decision is taken by The Scout Association to make a bid at the World Scout Conference in 1999 to host the centennial World Scout Jamboree in Britain in 2007.

April Kosovo clothing appeal coordinated by the Association has overwhelming results.

May World Scout Foundation reception held at the Natural History Museum, London, is attended by the Queen, the king of Sweden, the Duke of Edinburgh, the Duke of Kent and King Constantine of Greece.

1999

April Scout Information Centre opens at Gilwell Park.

July Britain is chosen to host the 2007 Jamboree by the World Scout Conference meeting in Durban, South Africa.

September Youth representatives are elected to the Committee of Council as full trustees of the Association for the first time. Programme Review consultation begins, the first comprehensive review of the whole training programme since 1966.

October Financial difficulties face the Association; the report, *The National Cost of Supporting Scouting*, results in some job losses, Field Commissioners become Field Development Officers and the Programme and Development sub-committee replaces the Programme and Training sub-committee and the supporting National Teams (formerly National Boards) are abolished. The decision is taken to co-locate all Headquarters departments at Gilwell.

2000

May After months of research, consultation and planning the Programme Review report is received by the Committee of the Council. Gilwell House foundation stone is laid and building work commences on a new £2.25 million Headquarters building.
July A major uniform consultation exercise is undertaken.
December Headquarters closes at the extension to Baden-Powell House and the office building is sold.

2001

January Headquarters co-location to Gilwell House is completed.
February New logo is launched. New uniform is launched during London fashion week.
April The Duke of Kent opens Gilwell House.

2002

February New training programme is launched. Age ranges are revised. Explorer Scouts and the Scout Network are introduced.
April Queen's Scouts assist at the lying-in-state of Queen Elizabeth, the Queen Mother.
June 120 Scouts take part in the queen's golden jubilee parade.

2003

May Branchet Lodge, a new accommodation building, is opened at Gilwell.
September New adult training scheme is launched at the University of Warwick.
December Venture Scouting closes. National campsites strategy agreed to improve quality of Headquarters site.

2004

July Peter Duncan is elected to succeed George Purdy as Chief Scout.
September During the Gilwell Reunion George Purdy retires as Chief Scout and formally hands over to Peter Duncan.
October The first of the new-look, A5-size, bi-monthly *Scouting* magazine is sent free to all adults in Scouting.

2005

July–August The United Kingdom hosts EuroJam, a jamboree for the European region, at Hylands Park, Chelmsford.

2006

April Lord Baden-Powell, grandson of the Founder, reviews the Queen's Scouts Parade at Windsor.
September National Conference held at University of Warwick to launch 2007 celebrations and plans.

Scouting around the world (numbers in 2005)

COUNTRY	SCOUTING MEMBERSHIP	COUNTRY	SCOUTING MEMBERSHIP
Albania	1,730	Germany	123,937
Algeria	11,120	Ghana	2,311
Angola	13,777	Greece	18,992
Argentina	44,981	Grenada	1,665
Armenia	2,256	Guatemala	11,395
Australia	98.084	Guyana	294
Austria	13,785	Haiti	9,859
Azerbaijan	1,414	Honduras	5,174
Bahamas	729	Hong Kong	74,147
Bahrain	1,820	Hungary	11,243
Bangladesh	908.435	Iceland	1,526
Barbados	3,032	India	2,138,015
Belgium	88,271	Indonesia	8,909,435
Belize	1,211	Ireland	36,783
Benin	19,605	Israel	21,920
Bhutan	6,716	Italy	100,675
Bolivia	7,521	Jamaica	6,272
Bosnia and Herzegovina	1,514	Japan	220,223
Botswana	4,660	Jordan	15,538
Brazil	66,375	Kenya	151,722
Brunei Darussalam	2,772	Kiribati	1,333
Bulgaria	1,832	Korea, Republic of	252,157
Burkina Faso	10,165	Kuwait	6,061
Burundi	6,661	Latvia	1,179
Cape Verde	1,500	Lebanon	14,334
Cameroon	6,535	Lesotho	371
Canada	212,259	Liberia	2,418
Chad	8,132	Libyan Arab Jamahiriya	13,698
Chile	33,812	Liechtenstein	752
China, Scouts of	69,452	Lithuania	1,500
Colombia	12,808	Luxembourg	5,418
Comoros	2,200	Macedonia, former Yugoslav Republic of	1,988
Congo, Democratic Republic of	62,842	Madagascar	9,473
Costa Rica	9,752	Malaysia	96,893
Côte-d'Ivoire	6,436	Maldives	4,518
Croatia	4.068	Malta	2,531
Cyprus	4,478	Mauritania	3,790
Czech Republic	26,435	Mauritius	3,076
Denmark	47,475	Mexico	39,327
Dominica	1,100	Moldova, Republic of	1,540
Dominican Republic	8,702	Monaco	49
Ecuador	4,132	Mongolia	8,655
Egypt	74,598	Morocco	12,304
El Salvador	3,970	Mozambique	16,675
Estonia	1,167	Namibia	1,816
Ethiopia	1,000	Nepal	12,341
Fiji	2,821	Netherlands	57,484
Finland	26,885	New Zealand	23,537
France	102,405	Nicaragua	2,056
Gabon	3,835	Niger	4,352
Gambia	15,632	Nigeria	46,701
Georgia	1,092	Norway	19,929

COUNTRY	SCOUTING MEMBERSHIP
Oman	10,654
Pakistan	526,403
Palestinian Authority	20,275
Panama	2,263
Papua New Guinea	2,811
Paraguay	1,000
Peru	12,677
Philippines	1,956,131
Poland	85,822
Portugal	70,863
Qatar	3,244
Romania	4,930
Russian Federation	14,000
Rwanda	18,884
San Marino	159
Saudi Arabia	19,267
Senegal	26,373
Seychelles	unknown
Sierra Leone	7,902
Singapore	11,163
Slovakia	4,118
Slovenia	6,357
South Africa	13,118
Spain	74,561
Sri Lanka	21,653
Saint Lucia	393
Saint Vincent and The Grenadines	541
Serbia and Montenegro	30,493
Sudan	13,550
Suriname	2,601
Swaziland	4,994
Sweden	60,122
Switzerland	52,349
Tajikistan	1,504
Tanzania, United Republic of	102,739
Thailand	1,305,027
Togo	8,890
Trinidad & Tobago	4,655
Tunisia	28,483
Turkey	8,174
Uganda	77,894
United Arab Emirates	5,824
United Kingdom	498,888
United States	6,239,435
Uruguay	3,965
Venezuela	14,513
Yemen	6,481
Zambia	7,427
Zimbabwe	1,612

See page 124 for dates of foundation.

Index

Page numbers in *italic* refer to illustrations

Selected bibliography

Hilary St. George Saunders, *The Left Handshake: The Boy Scout Movement during the War 1939-1945* (London: Collins, 1949)

John S. Wilson, *Scouting Round the World* (London: Blandford Press, 1959)

Piet J. Kroonenberg, *The Undaunted: Keeping the Scouting Spirit Alive; The Survival and Revival of Scouting in Central and Eastern Europe* (Geneva, Switzwerland: Oriole International Publications, 1998)

The 1916 edition of *'The Boy Scout Association's Headquarters Gazette'*; the 1945 edition of *Scouting for Boys in India*.

Acknowledgements

Picture acknowledgements
The artwork on page 21 top is © of **Octopus Publishing Group Limited**/Brindeau Mexter.

All photographs have been reproduced by courtesy of **The Scout Association**, apart from the following: **Alamy**/Andrew Holt 168-169. **Corbis U.K. Limited** 54-55; /Bettmann 106, 120. (c) **Disney Enterprises, Inc. Used by permission from Disney Enterprises, Inc.** 114 top. **Getty Images** 27, 93, 94; /W. & D. Downey 25 right; /Pierre Jahan 107; /Museum of the City of New York/Byron Collection 26; /Walter Sanders 121; /Djibril Sy 158 top. **Octopus Publishing Group Limited**/Andy Komorowski 12 bottom, 13 top, 13 bottom, 14-15 top, 14 bottom, 19 bottom, 21 centre, 21 bottom, 22 bottom, 23 bottom right, 24 top, 31 bottom, 37 top, 38, 39, 41 bottom left, 41 bottom right, 45 bottom, 47 top, 47 centre, 52 centre, 52 bottom, 57 left, 59 top, 63 top, 67, 72 top, 76 bottom, 79 bottom, 82-83, 89 bottom, 91 bottom, 100, 101 bottom, 113 top, 114 centre. **Painet Inc.**/Sally Weigand 136. **World Scout Foundation**/Yoshi Shimizu 161 bottom. **World Organisation of the Scout Movement (WOSM)** 144, 145 bottom; /Jean-Luc Bertrand 164,/SEN2003 156 bottom left; /Jesus Inostroza 123 bottom, 126, 129, 130, 135 top, 142; Jesus Inostroza/PAN2001 123 centre, 152, 187 top right, 187 bottom centre; Jesus Inostroza/THA 2003 131, 151 bottom, 155, 156 top, 179 bottom, 181 top, 187 top centre, 187 centre, 187 bottom right; /Andrés Morales 127, 134 left, 137, 138, 160; /Victor Ortega 133, 139, 143; /Victor Ortega/GVA 2004 171 top; /Victor Ortega/TWA 2003 173 centre; /S. Pijollet-Hall/KEN 134 right, 153 bottom left; /Jean Pierre Pouteau 128, 151 centre, 165 top right, 183; /Franklin Shu 135; /Swiss Guide and Scout Movement 123 top, 153 top right; /World Scouting 132, 150, 151 top, 154, 177 bottom; /World Scouting/INA 1994 122; /World Scouting/INA 2003 158 bottom, 181 bottom.

Author acknowledgements
Thank you to everyone who contributed to this book in any way, particularly to Paul Moynihan, Anna Sargent, Pat Styles, Hilary Galloway and Chris James at The Scout Association and Victor Ortega and Richard Amalvy at the World Organization of the Scout Movement who provided invaluable picture research and support.

Join the adventure
The Scout Association provides adventurous activities and personal development opportunities for 400,000 young people aged 6–25. Internationally, there are over 28 million young people enjoying the benefits of Scouting across 216 countries.

To find out about opportunities for young people and adult volunteers in the UK, please visit www.scouts.org.uk For information about World Scouting please see www.scout.org

Executive Editor **Trevor Davies**
Managing Editor **Clare Churly**
Editor **Alice Bowden**
Design Manager **Tokiko Morishima**
Designer **'OME Design**
Photographer **Andy Komorowski**
Senior Production Controller **Ian Paton**